John Kam~~~~~~~~~~~~~~~~~~~~~~~~~~~~~decade before becoming ~~~~~~~~~~~~~~~~~~~~~~~~olitical writers, commentators and pundits. As Editor of the *New Statesman*, he took the magazine to thirty-year circulation highs and won a series of awards. He is now Chief Executive of Index on Censorship, one of the world's leading free expression organisations. His three previous books include the acclaimed *Blair's Wars*, a devastating survey of the former Prime Minister's foreign policy. He is married to BBC journalist Lucy Ash and lives in London.

Further Praise for *Freedom for Sale*:

'I was impressed by how *Freedom for Sale* identified the attractions of sovereign autocracies which deliver prosperity and individual self-expression while dispensing with public freedoms. The bargain accepted by increasing numbers of people around the world is reminiscent of the deal Mephistopheles put before Faust' Michael Burleigh, *Evening Standard*

'A pungent thesis, argued with verve and an abundance of telling detail' *Observer*

'Well and clearly written. The absence of jargon is especially welcome and makes the ideological debate it presents highly accessible' *Independent*

'In what [Kampfner] calls "the pact", he traces how economic prosperity has bribed populations around the world, lulling them with material goods and promises of national security to reduce resistance while people's rights are stripped away . . . Engrossing' *Metro*

'Compelling . . . Fascinating . . . Kampfner has produced a powerful account of our contemporary unfreedom, stuffed with invaluable anecdotes, and written with verve' *Spiked Review of Books*

Praise for *Blair's Wars*:

'Brilliant . . . highly perceptive' Anthony Howard, *Sunday Times* Books of the Year

'A brilliant book by one of Britain's most distinguished political writers' *Mail on Sunday*

'The book everyone in London is talking about . . . by the current star of British political journalism' *Le Figaro*

'Assiduous and highly readable' Michael Portillo, *Sunday Telegraph*

'Kampfner's revelations have already made headlines. But the value of the book goes deeper . . . I strongly recommend *Blair's Wars*' Clare Short, *New Statesman*

'One of the weightiest books yet about the New Labour government' David Robson, *Sunday Telegraph* Books of the Year

'Treads a lovely balance, and should help to usher [Kampfner's] subject from our stage' John Le Carré, *Observer* Books of the Year

'The most perceptive book about the Blair government to appear since Andrew Rawnsley's *Servants of the People*' *Sunday Times*

'Kampfner has some excellent sources and there is at least one revealing moment every few pages . . . [A] must-read book about New Labour' Johann Hari, *Independent on Sunday*

'An essential book, taking us into the thick of Downing Street, at Westminster and abroad . . . Full of facts, it is well researched, fast and gripping' Matthew Parris, *The Times*

'A fascinating insight into the personal networks through which geopolitics are conducted, and an intriguing, if not always reassuring, portrayal of a Prime Minister whose extraordinary enthusiasm for military adventures may well be what ends up defining him' Andrew Mueller, *Time Out*

'As Kampfner rightly points out, the fascinating aspect of all Blair's campaigns was their motivation. He sums it up in one glorious paragraph: "A combination of self-confidence and fear, or Atlanticism, evangelism and Gladstonian idealism, pursued when necessary through murky means" . . . Kampfner's analysis is beyond dispute' Roy Hattersley, *Guardian*

'This is instant history at its best. John Kampfner, the *New Statesman*'s political editor, is well versed in the intricacies of recent British foreign policy as biographer of Robin Cook. His range of political and diplomatic contacts has ensured we have a compelling and often devastating exposure of what is increasingly becoming the tragedy of Tony Blair and his "New" Labour project' Robert Taylor, *Tribune*

'Kampfner [traces] the steps that led to war while explaining the historic context that impelled us towards it . . . Insiders' conversations with key players provide a treasure trove for future historians' Alan Milburn, *The Times*

'Excellent . . . Blair doesn't come at all well out of Kampfner's book, which is forever putting him on the rack without having to do much more than spell out the unfavourable facts. A fair number of these were already public knowledge, but many others – and very telling they frequently are – have been extracted from unnamed insider sources . . . A truly disturbing story' John Sturrock, *London Review of Books*

'The best political book of the year . . . A dispassionate and fair-minded account of the Manichaean mindset that has led the Prime Minister to involve the UK in five conflicts in six years, it provides an entirely new perspective on the meaning of New Labour' Anthony Howard, *New Statesman* Books of the Year

Also by John Kampfner

BLAIR'S WARS

FREEDOM
FOR SALE

*How we made money
and lost our liberty*

JOHN KAMPFNER

POCKET
BOOKS

LONDON • SYDNEY • NEW YORK • TORONTO

Fir published in Great Britain by Simon & Schuster UK Ltd, 2009
This edition published by Pocket Books, 2010
An imprint of Simon & Schuster UK Ltd
A CBS COMPANY

1 3 5 7 9 10 8 6 4 2

Simon & Schuster UK Ltd
1st Floor
222 Gray's Inn Road
London WC1X 8HB

www.simonandschuster.co.uk

Simon & Schuster Australia
Sydney

A CIP catalogue for this book is available
from the British Library.

ISBN: 978-1-41652-604-9

Typeset by M Rules
Printed by CPI Cox & Wyman, Reading, Berkshire RG1 8EX

To Constance, Alex and Lucy

CONTENTS

INTRODUCTION

Why is it that so many people around the world appear willing to give up freedoms in return for either security or prosperity? From John Stuart Mill to Jeremy Bentham, from Sigmund Freud to Franklin Roosevelt, this question has been posed down the generations. Invariably we are told that it is either an obvious choice or a false choice. "Those who would give up essential liberty to purchase a little temporary safety deserve neither liberty nor safety," declared Benjamin Franklin in 1755.

If only it was as simple as that. The first part of my journalistic career was spent in the 1980s in the former Soviet Union and other countries that were generally described as "dictatorships". Freedom of expression, movement and association were heavily curtailed. These restrictions affected every part of people's lives, although they varied from country to country and from regime to regime. The lack of private freedoms was as vivid as the more politically charged restrictions on the press and politics. Citizens had no ability, and no right, to decide on where they lived, what they could buy and, in some cases, the relationships they could enter into. The dividing lines with the West, with democracies no matter how imperfect, were clear.

I witnessed first-hand the fall of the Berlin Wall and the collapse of the USSR. I remember spending the evening of 25
December 1991, when the Soviet flag was lowered from the Kremlin
and replaced by the tricolour of the new Russia, in the company of
Lev Kerbel, a much-decorated sculptor. Kerbel was born on the day
of the Bolshevik revolution in 1917. He made his name creating
giant monuments to Lenin and Marx from Prague to Pyongyang. I
had first met him in the autumn of 1985, just as his last great offering to the people of Moscow had been unveiled, the marble and
granite monument to Lenin dominating October Square. The floor
space of his studio was crammed with Lenins and Marxes, along
with a Stalin lying in state, Italian Communists, Bashkirian poets,
composers, soldiers and female collective farm workers with their
headscarves signifying youthful purpose. The wall in his kitchen
became a visitors' book. When I returned many years later I saw that
Boris Yeltsin had signed his name close to mine.

Over tea and brandy, watching the television coverage of that
momentous December night on his small, flickering screen, Kerbel
reminisced about a system in which he and millions of others had
been cocooned. He was fearful of the future, but over the coming
months he settled into the new world of the *rynok*, the market, with
reasonable ease. He learned about commercial contracts, and started
producing sculptures for the new generation of oligarchs, either of
themselves, their wives or their mistresses. His daughters began to
work for American television and he went on holiday to the Canary
Islands.

The enduring ideological divide since the Enlightenment, the
battle between liberalism and autocracy that had split Europe in
the twentieth century, had been won. The end of the Cold War and
the collapse of Communism would, Francis Fukuyama predicted,
lead to the "end of history" and "the universalisation of Western
liberal democracy as the final form of human government".
Fukuyama's argument was always more complex than is usually represented, but for more than a decade the debate about democracy

and democratisation was reduced to this simple matrix. Throughout this period it was assumed that freedom, liberty and human rights were intertwined with democracy, and that democracy was inextricably linked to the free market. They not only thrived together, but they needed each other to survive.

The West's "victory" in the Cold War appeared to confirm the supremacy of both ideology and business model. As Margaret Thatcher had once promised, it did not matter whether you started with political freedom or economic freedom: you would end up sooner or later with both. Thatcher was tapping into a rich vein of Anglo-Saxon thinking, which saw free markets and liberal democracy as mutually reinforcing. Capitalism is "compatible only with democracy", wrote the American Christian social theorist Michael Novak in 1982 in his book *The Spirit of Democratic Capitalism*. "While bastard forms of capitalism do seem able for a time to endure without democracy, the natural logic of capitalism leads to democracy." Under Communism neither the Soviet Union, nor China, nor their satellites had posed an economic threat, let alone a meaningful ideological one. The assumption was that post-Communist Russia and China would move warmly into the West's economic and political embrace.

The number of countries embracing multi-party elections and other facets of democracy had already begun to increase. By the time the so-called "third wave" of democratisation began in 1974 in Portugal, barely a quarter of the world's states met the minimal test: a place where the people were able, through universal suffrage, to choose and replace their leaders in regular, free and fair elections. Over the course of the next two decades, dictatorships gave way to freely elected governments in southern Europe, Latin America, then in East Asia. Finally, an explosion of freedom in the early 1990s liberated Eastern Europe and spread democracy from Moscow to Pretoria. This shift coincided with an unprecedented moment of US military, economic and cultural dominance. Arguably, this movement reached its peak in June 2000 at the first meeting, in

Warsaw, of the grandly titled Community of Democracies. Spearheaded by the Clinton administration, states as disparate as Chile, the Czech Republic, India, Mali, Portugal and South Korea vowed "to respect and uphold core democratic principles and practices" of free and fair elections, freedom of speech and expression, equal access to education, rule of law, and freedom of peaceful assembly.

Representative democracy expanded rapidly; by 2000, 120 out of the 192 nation states of the UN could broadly be defined as democratic. For the first time democracy had acquired majority status in the world. Yet, as the writer Paul Ginsborg points out, at the very time it appeared to be dominant, liberal democracy had actually entered a profound crisis. "This was not a crisis of *quantity*; quite the opposite. The crisis, rather, was one of *quality*," Ginsborg writes. "While formal electoral democracy expanded with great rapidity all over the world, disaffection grew in democracy's traditional heartlands. It was expressed in a number of different ways – declining voter turnout, declining political participation (more people were likely to be members of civil action groups like Greenpeace than of a mainstream party) and a loss of faith in democratic institutions and in the political class in general." A new German word meaning disenchantment with politics, *Politikverdrossenheit*, officially entered the lexicon in 1994. The concept was expressed in other, more dramatic ways, such as the anti-globalisation protests of Seattle and Genoa. Tellingly, the gulf between rulers and ruled was treated by the elites with relative equanimity. Politicians made speeches about the democrat deficit, but appeared comfortable with a status quo that rendered to them notional constitutional legitimacy – or, in the case of George W. Bush in the election of 2000, a dubious judicial legitimacy.

By the start of the twenty-first century, the rise of China and the resurgence of Russia posed a new and immediate challenge. Capitalism had been embraced beyond the West, and adapted to purpose. As a mechanism for the acquisition of wealth, it was proving remarkably malleable. Authoritarian capitalism was becoming a formidable adversary. The market had been decoupled from democracy; more than that, it was embraced with alacrity by those very elites the West thought it had defeated. The forces of globalisation and unrestricted transfers of wealth and assets reinforced the hubris of the new and old capitalists.

The terrorist attacks of 9/11 shattered comfortable assumptions about the balance between security and liberty. The resurgent autocrats drew strength from two forces playing out at the same time – the inherent weaknesses of democratic systems, and the actions of Western leaderships in their "war on terror". They exploited the mismatch between the rhetorical exhortations of the Bush administration, as it pursued its "democratisation" agenda around the world, and the tawdry practices it indulged in – from the manipulation of evidence leading up to the Iraq war, to the humiliations of prisoners at Abu Ghraib, the systematic use of torture in secret jails around the world, illegal "rendition flights" and the extra-territorial incarceration of hundreds of terrorist suspects at Guantánamo Bay.

In order to succeed in this moral void, the new authoritarians came to a pact with their peoples. The specific rules varied between countries, but the template was similar. Repression was selective, confined to those who openly challenged the status quo. The number of people who fell into that category was actually very few – journalists who criticised the state or published information that cast the powerful in a negative light; lawyers who defended these agitators; and politicians and others who publicly went out of their way to "cause trouble". The rest of the population could enjoy freedom to travel, to live more or less as they wished and to make and spend their money. This was the difference between *public* freedoms and *private*, or privatised, freedoms. For many people this presented an attractive proposition. After all, how many members of the public, going about their daily lives, wish to challenge the structures of power? One can more easily than one realises be lulled into thinking that one is *sufficiently* free.

The model is Singapore, the state in which I was born, and which has long intrigued me. I am constantly struck by the number of people there I know – very well travelled with long stints at Western universities – who are keen to defend a system that requires an almost complete abrogation of freedom of expression in return for a very good material life. *This is the pact.* In each country it varies; citizens hand over different freedoms in accordance with their own customs and priorities. In some it is press freedom; in some it is the right to vote out their government; in some it is an impartial judiciary; in others it is the ability to get on with their lives without being spied upon. In many it is a combination of these and more.

In the global order of the past two decades, the alliance of political leaders, business and the middle classes was the key. The arrangement was built on a clear, but usually discreet set of understandings. What mattered in all these societies was that the number of people who benefited from this deal gradually increased, and that the state remained flexible enough to meet their various needs. These needs could be summarised as: property rights, contract law, environmental protection, lifestyle choices, the right to travel, and the right to earn money – and keep it. The people who mattered – the wealthy and the aspiring wealthy – were to be protected against the use of arbitrary state power. But could such protection be provided without the tools of conventional democracy, such as free elections and open media? That was the conundrum that authoritarian capitalists faced.

The most obvious practitioners were countries such as China and Russia, where a critical mass of people (perhaps a minority, but a sizeable one none the less) believed that an excess of freedoms would damage economic growth, political stability or social harmony. The state, if it was clever, provided limited, but visible outlets for dissent – the arts, perhaps, or newspapers with small circulations – while maintaining its grip on mass audiences. Its most important task was to co-opt vested interests, the most important of which was business, both domestic and international. As Chris

Patten recalled from his experience as governor of Hong Kong, the most persistent critics of his attempts to bring an element of democracy to the colony before its handover to China were US and UK business leaders in the region. Why rock the boat?

I remember hearing similar voices of resistance in Russia. I lost count of the number of Western bankers and others who were genuinely disdainful of the democratic changes that were introduced in the 1990s. Why, they wondered, jeopardise potentially lucrative contracts for the sake of an experiment inimical to Russian history?

Western business found common cause with a new generation of Western-educated counterparts in Russia and China. Many would insist that an authoritarian regime, as long as it was stable, provided an attractive proposition for wealth creation. The corporate elite helped sustain the political elite. This was Deng Xiaoping's compact with the post-Tiananmen generation. The debate on political reform of the 1980s gave way to more consideration of how best to open up the ruling Communist Party to greater scrutiny and accountability, without "destabilising" a political structure that had delivered three decades of high growth.

The pact belonged not just to states in transition such as these. It belonged also far closer to home, to the so-called democracies. It was played out in different circumstances and cultures, and at different speeds. We all did it. We are all still doing it. We each choose different freedoms we are prepared to cede. Citizens in both systems have colluded, but those in the West have colluded the most. They had the choice to demand more of their governments, to rebalance the pact between liberty, security and prosperity, but for as long as the going was good they chose not to exercise it.

The context changed during 2008 as years of steady growth ended spectacularly. The collapse of the banks led not only to economic crisis but called into question the future of governments that had derived their legitimacy through securing sustained well-being for their peoples. Yet far from unravelling the pact, the global financial collapse enhanced it. Western countries that had dismissed the idea of the state as an economic force were forced to rehabilitate it. In conditions of insecurity, and with the state once again intervening wherever it saw fit, the conditions were propitious for it to assume even greater control over other aspects of people's day-to-day lives. The clamour for security that was exploited after the terrorist attacks on New York in 2001 was adapted for the new "emergency".

This book does not look at tyrannical regimes that rule by the barrel of a gun, where families and parents denounce each other, where the state is an unambiguously malevolent force and there is no element of consent. This is not about Zimbabwe or North Korea or Burma. In these countries there is no pact between the government and the people, but an instinct simply to survive. Nor do I focus on countries with their own particularities, such as Israel, or Hugo Chávez's Venezuela or post-apartheid South Africa.

Instead, in the course of a year's travels, I focused on countries that, whatever their political hue, had accepted the terms of globalisation. As a result their priorities began to merge into one. I talked to intellectuals, journalists, lawyers, cultural figures, politicians, and ordinary people I happened to come across, asking them the same question that I framed at the start of this chapter: why have freedoms been so easily traded in return for security or prosperity?

I begin with Singapore, with the remarkable socio-economic experiment of Lee Kuan Yew. Singapore is often perceived as a one-dimensional consumer paradise. It may in part be that, but it also asks more fundamental questions about our priorities. On independence from Britain, it had the same per capita GDP as Ghana. In the past forty years it has grown to become one of the world's economic miracles, an island of stability in a region of upheaval. I look at the vicious defamation culture, in which the authorities prosecute local citizens and foreigners alike for the slightest criticism; I assess an electoral system in which constituency boundaries are rigged and opposition activists are regularly jailed. Yet the achievements are striking. Previously fractious ethnic groups – the majority Chinese, Malays and Indians – live in relative harmony; through remarkable social housing and public services, all the population is well catered for. The pivot is a middle class that, with some exceptions, is comfortable with a pact in which their private space is unimpeded, as long as they do not interfere with the public realm.

In China, the officially described "century of humiliation" at the hands of foreigners was followed by the Maoist era of uniformity and seclusion. Progress has been remarkable in the past three decades and it has taken place within a system that interprets the theory of democracy in accordance with its needs. Corruption, human rights abuses and environmental degradation have accompanied a one-party structure that has depended on economic growth to keep itself in power. Yet, in my various trips, I noted the porous nature of the pact. Free speech, even if formally circumscribed in China, particularly on the internet, is alive and well on the street and in semi-private situations. The government is trying to manage and channel it, through a combination of technology, modern-day "spin" techniques and brute force. However, the middle classes have no vested interest in granting the vote to hundreds of millions of poorer people with different political priorities. The lack of democracy is, for the moment at least, part of the deal. The government knows that the delivery of comforts to the private realm will determine its success.

I move on to Russia, which I have been visiting regularly for thirty years. I focus on people I have known from a time when the expression "to get hold of" was more important than "to buy", when foreign travel was allowed only through officially sanctioned groups. These friends celebrated the failure of the coup of 1991 and the subsequent collapse of their autocratic system. They discovered new freedoms and revelled in them, before Boris Yeltsin consolidated his power by manipulating an election with the tacit approval of the West. Democracy became associated with chaos and sleaze. The ascent of Vladimir Putin in 2000 was in keeping with his time, his security clampdown coinciding with a surge of wealth thanks to the global price of oil and gas. As their country became richer and more assertive, my friends would recite a slogan of the only three Cs that were important to the New Russians – Chelsea, Courchevel and Cartier. While doughty journalists and human rights campaigners continued to ask questions, the vast majority acquiesced in the pact. These jet-setters continued to fear that their fortunes and their properties could at any point be seized. That is why they took their money abroad. But they enjoyed the fruits of their private freedoms, and left the *siloviki* – the politicians who hailed from the security elite – to rule unimpeded.

The next chapter looks at the most curious symbol of the global pact – the United Arab Emirates, specifically the brazen and gaudy city of Dubai and the more discreet and oil-rich Abu Dhabi. A saying during the boom times on the floors of finance houses went: "Shanghai, Mumbai, Dubai or goodbye". From young British traders, to Russian mobsters and B-list celebrities, the ruling sheikhs offered steady wealth from property deals to tax-free salaries in return for keeping out of trouble. In Dubai they were even more accommodating, putting religious concerns to one side to allow Westerners to lead their lives as they wished, prosecuting them for sexual or drunken displays only *in extremis*. Monuments to conspicuous wealth sprung up all around, as hotels and apartment blocks vied with each other for luxury. The sheikhs believed their model was immune to the Western economic crisis. Dubai, in particular, took a major hit. So what will come out of a pact that was built purely on money?

The second part of the book looks at the countries that profess adherence to democracy. I begin with India, which prides itself on having the world's most populous multi-party system. As China's economy soared ahead, parts of India's corporate elite wondered whether their form of governance was an impediment to prosperity. India's rich devised its own pact. It would provide for itself the basic services that the state had failed to deliver; it would make few demands. In return, it would require the government to leave it alone to make money, and to keep the poor away from its door. This arrangement was challenged less by the global economic crash, more by the terrorist attacks in Mumbai in late 2008. For the first time, the affluent classes were caught up en masse in the violence that has long afflicted India. They demanded protection.

Of all the countries in the world, why choose Italy? It matters, not because of any geo-strategic relevance, but because it serves as an example of a sham democracy. In terms of its institutions, Italy fails on almost every count. The three checks on the executive – parliament, the media and the judiciary – have seen their independence and authority eroded. Corruption is rampant. And yet, three times its voters have chosen in Silvio Berlusconi a man noted for his financial irregularities, his affection for autocrats like Putin and his general vulgarity. He has outwitted his opponents with consummate ease, and is seeking to expand his powers. It is easy to dismiss Berlusconi and his antics. But his enduring popularity among a large swathe of the population highlights the extent to which notional democracies can thrive and even depend on the same exercise of arbitrary power that authoritarian states are criticised for.

In 1997, the accession of a centre-left government in the UK that prided itself on its liberties should have been an inspiring moment. Yet, in a decade, Britain has gone a long way to dismantling its liberties. It now possesses a fifth of the world's closed-circuit television cameras; it has some of the world's most punitive libel laws, and has recently imposed a law, under the guise of anti-terrorism, that allows for the arrest of anyone taking photographs of the police or members of the armed forces. A government that was seeking one of the longest terms of pre-trial custody for terrorist suspects proudly brandishes its authoritarian credentials, arguing that they are generally well received by the public. In many cases they are, particularly before they are closely analysed. I look at a government that confused the benign role of the state in producing a more equitable society with the malign role of the state in seeking to clamp down on public freedoms. I am keen to understand how British society seems so ready to acquiesce in the erosion of those freedoms until rather late in the day.

My last destination is the United States, where the pact has been played out most visibly. The chapter traces the effects on society, at home and abroad, of 9/11, the Iraq war and the abuses that surrounded the "war on terror". Bush's neo-Conservative mission had grown out of a mixture of hubris and frustration. The removal of Saddam Hussein would be the catalyst for the overthrow of dictators in the Middle East and beyond. That it failed was the result not just of double standards but of a deeper confusion about "democracy promotion". Was democracy an end in itself? Or was it a means to an end? Should multi-party elections be encouraged in states where the outcome might produce regimes hostile to the West and to the concept of liberal democracy, or might internally produce ethnic or political instability? Domestically, Bush presided over a security clampdown that was rarely challenged by mainstream politicians or public opinion. The US media showed itself to be supine, failing to hold power to account on many of the gravest issues.

To what extent would the arrival of Barack Obama reverse the democratic erosion at home, and America's loss of democratic credibility abroad? Certainly, the nature of his election victory provided a much-needed boost to the credentials of America's constitutional democracy. Yet those hopes for a fresh start were offset by the dramatic collapse in the US and global financial systems. The cruel irony was that a new administration, in which many around the world had pinned their faith, began its work just at a time of eroding American power.

In a different age, Oswald Spengler famously predicted that "the era of individualism, liberalism and democracy, of humanitarianism and freedom is nearing its end". *The Decline of the West* was written some ninety years ago, in the fallout from the First World War, the humiliations of the Treaty of Versailles and the start of the Great Depression. The masses, he wrote, "will accept with resignation the victory of the Caesars, the strong men, and will obey them". With global markets in the throes of fresh decline, and with the old certainties destroyed, is the Spengler vision about to haunt us again? The challenge this time around is more subtle and sophisticated; the world is less fiercely differentiated between opposing systems. For twenty years the Washington Consensus proselytised the mutually reinforcing creeds of free markets and liberal democracy. The rise of authoritarian capitalism removed the link between them. Then, from mid-2007, the collapse of the neo-liberal Anglo-Saxon financial school became as much a crisis for the Western political system as it did for economics.

The events of the past decade have surely undermined the claim that the enrichment of a country, or the growth of a middle class, provide an impulse towards greater liberty. Barrington Moore's theories of "no bourgeoisie, no democracy" have surely been refuted by the past twenty years of materialist aspiration. During this period, people in all countries found a way to disengage from the political process while living in comfort. Consumerism provided the ultimate anaesthetic for the brain. What happens when the wealth disappears and the anaesthetic wears off?

My discoveries are discomforting but it is more useful to understand than to judge. It has always been the instinct of the politician to seek power and to hold on to it, by fair means or foul. Less understood are the reasons why so many of us – in authoritarian and democratic states alike – succumb, and why so few of us ask why we do it. Whatever systems we happen to live under, our priorities are more similar than we would ever want to admit.

1

SINGAPORE:
COMFORTABLE MODEL

*"Understanding the limits to freedom is what makes
freedom possible"* – Chua Beng Huat

"SINGAPORE IS QUITE SIMPLY THE MOST SUCCESSFUL SOCIETY
in the history of humanity." I scratch my head and take a large gulp
of my ice-cold water. I am sitting in the office of Professor Kishore
Mahbubani, Singapore's leading public intellectual, a man who travels the world telling doubters that countries can be harmonious and
prosperous without succumbing to Western liberal democracy. Dean
of the Lee Kuan Yew School of Public Policy at the National
University, Mahbubani is always a good person to visit to test the
political temperature. He plays host to a stream of visitors from
around the world. Before me a delegation of Chinese breezes past.
After me comes the Swiss Ambassador. They are all keen to learn the
secret of the success of an island state that is both economic miracle
and social test bed.

I am taken aback by the hubris of my host. But I am wary of
being dismissive, of falling into the trap of the "Western mindset", a
term used to dismiss criticisms levelled by foreigners. For me it is
more than idle curiosity. I was born in Singapore, and although I left

when I was young, my parents lived in the city state for fifteen years. Each time I return I invest in a new map, as streets are torn down and replaced by ever higher monuments to money and one version of progress. Nostalgia for the past is one of the few luxuries people here cannot afford. I have also kept up with a number of sons and daughters of my parents' friends, some Indian, some Malay, most Chinese. They are established doctors, lawyers, financiers, musicians. They went to university in Britain, the US or Australia, but most came back. They treat Singapore's gleaming Changi airport as a bus stop, hopping on and off planes without thinking twice. In their day-to-day lives they are able to do whatever they please. They enjoy their private freedoms, but free speech and political activism are things they express when they are abroad. I remember, as a student, going on demonstrations with several of my friends when they were in London. Back home they button their lips. They can take it or leave it, they say. They do it out of choice.

The term "pact" was made for Singapore. The state provides one of the highest per capita GDPs in the world, equivalent to the best in the West. In return the citizenry avoid causing trouble. The city state has become a monument to wealth creation. It is both beguiling and alarming. Everything works spectacularly well. The rich are exceedingly rich. The poor are exceedingly comfortable. The Singapore experiment has been conducted by Lee Kuan Yew, its Prime Minister for thirty years, and its supreme leader since relinquishing that office. Although he dominates the stage, the Singapore pact is about much more than one man. It requires, and receives, the willing cooperation of the vast majority of the people.

It is easy to forget, when one surveys the skyline of Singapore, the glistening office buildings, the state-of-the-art hospitals and the efficient social housing, that it could have turned out very differently. Singapore was a backwater, a swampy island populated by a few fishermen when it was founded in 1819 by Stamford Raffles, a British trader looking for a new foothold for the East India

Company along the spice route. As the free port became more successful, so traders and their coolies from around the region began to appear, up to 10,000 new arrivals in the first five years. Singapore became a melting pot for Chinese, Malays, Indians, Armenians, Europeans and anyone keen to make money. British control effectively came to an end with the invasion by the Japanese in 1942. Over the next three years, up to 50,000 Chinese were killed in the "purification through purge" campaigns.

The young Lee was a clerk during the Japanese occupation. He, like others of his generation, was profoundly influenced by that experience. At the end of the war, he went to Cambridge University to study law. From there he was called to the Bar. During his time in England, he was heavily influenced by anti-colonial politics, as well as by the Fabian socialism of the Labour Party. He studied the Fabians' thinking on the role of the state as an engineer of social change and provider of services. He became a believer in the "socialisation" of land. On his return to Singapore in 1949 he became involved in the fledgling independence movements that had taken hold across South-East Asia. In Malaya this took the form of armed resistance. The British declared an emergency and for twelve years were engaged in protracted fighting in the jungle. Lee, although he considered himself of the Left, argued that more would be achieved through negotiation, founding his People's Action Party (PAP) in 1954 as a mixture of democratic socialism and nationalism.

Three years later, Singapore gained full self-government from Britain, and in 1959 Lee became its first Prime Minister. In 1963, Singapore joined the Federation of Malaya, in a bid to provide greater security and tackle economic hardship. But the union was immediately threatened by ideological division and ethnic tension. Twenty-three people were killed and hundreds injured during race riots the following year. Lee hurriedly withdrew his tiny city state from the federation and started out on his own. His task was unenviable. With few resources and in the middle of an unstable region, Singapore faced acute unemployment and housing shortages, with potential for inter-communal strife on an even greater scale. One magazine at the time described the city as a "cesspool of squalor and degradation". Most of the population lived in ramshackle wooden *kampong* (Malay for village) houses. The country had no advantages beyond the position of its port and the enterprise of its population.

Lee sought to invent a new nation as a geographical and cultural entity. While his South-East Asian neighbours lurched between dictatorship and brief flirtations with democracy, never quite succeeding at either, he created something in between. He saw state-funded regeneration as key, introducing laws that annexed large swathes of land for social housing and other infrastructure projects such as roads, schools and hospitals. At the time of independence, more than half the workers had no formal education; by 1990 two thirds had completed secondary education. Between 1965 and 1995 the economy grew a remarkable 9 per cent per year, three times as fast as the US. Per capita income grew at 7 per cent on average, doubling roughly every decade. Gross National Income went from $US 1 billion to $86 billion. Across the city, new schools and colleges quickly produced spectacular results. Healthcare became the envy of Asia. Lee took to calling his small country a "first world oasis in a third world region".

For half a century, he has micro-managed his state, seeking to determine outcomes down to the smallest detail. He has personally vetted the suitability of marriage partners for government servants (usually on the basis of IQ) and decreed the number of children they should have. Through public information campaigns, he has exhorted his citizens to behave in accordance with his strictures. Instructions were issued on everything from hygiene to courtesy. In the 1970s, the "Stop at two" campaign proved so successful in curbing the birth rate that it had to be followed by a reverse campaign entitled "Have three or more if you can afford it".

I have lived in, and travelled to, many dictatorships over the years, where you look under the tables for bugging devices and assume that the man in the reflector shades lurking at the street corner is out to get you. In Singapore, the surveillance is more subtle, but it is a system that few people are sufficiently bothered about to change. It is easy to understand why. Three-quarters of the workforce does not pay income tax and nobody pays more than 20 per cent. Such is the demand for real estate, as foreign companies continue to pour in, that many people appear content to have their block of flats knocked down in order to build higher, and reap the profits. Almost none of the traditional Singapore remains. The very last village, Kampong Buangkok, just twenty-eight houses hidden away in the north of the island, is being gobbled up.

Nothing is allowed to stand in the way of wealth creation – the ultimate patriotic duty. Shopping has become the national pastime. Every time I wander down Orchard Road, the main shopping drag, I see happy consumers and happy eaters. This is a foodies' paradise, where you find some of the most inventive cuisine, fusions of different cultures alongside high-quality basic food at hawker centres dotted around the city. In one particular week, I eat Sichuan, different types of Japanese, South Indian (eating with my hands, off a banana leaf) or North Indian. I stop in food courts (cheap and cheerful). I am invited to formal English surroundings (the Singapore Cricket Club, of course), I even manage German sausages washed down with Riesling. Then there are the tennis and swimming clubs, and the drinking haunts, in the artificially created "entertainment zones" of Clarke Quay and Robinson Quay. Surely people, especially those who know the world, cannot be bought off as easily as this?

To understand the other Singapore, the less affluent Singapore, you have to visit any of the HDB high-rise developments in the "heartland". Since the 1960s, almost 90 per cent of the population has been moved into well-maintained and scrupulously clean apartments in government-built blocks. The Housing and Development Board was granted wide powers of compulsory purchase and forced resettlement. One of its missions was to break up communities that were ethnically separated between Chinese, Malays and Indians. In the brave new world that followed, the ethnic composition of every apartment block was required to mirror the country as a whole. People of different nationality were instructed to share the same stairwells, community centres, swimming pools, bus stops. Given the inter-communal strife of the 1960s, the enforced harmony that followed produced results that were nothing short of remarkable. Inter-communal differences are simply not allowed to happen.

Everything is set out in law. Citizens receive priority if they seek an apartment within a mile of their parents; this is to make it easier to look after the elderly. People can buy on the primary market – at below-market rates, with easy access to interest-free loans – but only if they are married. They must keep the flat for ten years, in order to cut down on speculation; then they can sell it on at market prices to anyone. Toa Payoh is the second oldest of these experiments. From the top floor of one block, forty storeys high, I enjoy a panoramic view of the city – a series of high rises as far as the eye can see. Everything is catered for in the surrounding streets – from little fabric stalls to tiny kiosks selling the latest 46-inch plasma TV screens or floor-to-ceiling fridges. By the lifts of one building – no graffiti or urine smells – I walk past a citizens' notice board. One flyer reminds residents that they can join a group walk at the nearby Chinese garden. Another announces a bird-singing competition – a popular pastime in which local people can spend up to a month's salary on caged birds. Another notice advertises for "volunteers", a neighbourhood watch scheme in which you are encouraged to snitch on anyone guilty of anti-social behaviour. The complex boasts excellent sporting facilities, including a stadium, an indoor sports hall and the country's best swimming pool, where national competitions are held.

On the main concourse I watch a group of old men, Chinese, Malay and Indians, playing chequers boisterously. It is Friday afternoon, and I suspect they have downed a whisky or two. They invite me to join them. We chat. I struggle to understand their Singlish, the curious hybrid that is most frequently spoken. I ask them about their lives, their aspirations. They have no complaints, they say. Thanks to the global crash, the economy is not what it was, but it will improve. They would, in any case, rather be here than anywhere else in Asia. Meaningful opinion polls do not exist. People confide only in their good friends. It is invariably hard, therefore, to work out whether people are minding what they say, knowing that criticism will land them in trouble, or expressing genuine appreciation. I suspect in the case of these men, that both suppositions are true.

The longer he stayed in office, the more convinced Lee became that he had found the model for Asia's progress. From his earliest days, he saw public criticism as an impediment. He brought the media under the control of two state companies, Singapore Press Holdings Ltd (which runs the newspapers) and MediaCorp (which deals with broadcasting). Elections are held every five years and opposition parties are theoretically allowed to compete. However, any politician or any journalist who says anything controversial about those in power is open to arrest and the subsequent charge of defamation. If they run out of money, they are declared bankrupt and may be sent to jail.

Even the minimalist democratic procedures have been "modified" to the advantage of Lee's PAP. Constituencies that vote significantly for opposition candidates tend to disappear at the next election, subsumed into existing seats. When they do opt for the wrong candidate, the voters are reminded of the errors of their ways. Not far from loyal Toa Payoh, the neighbourhood of Potong Pasir was for many years an anomaly in that it did not have an operating MRT underground station. The station did exist, but it was kept closed. Various "technical" reasons were given, but the locals knew the real reason. Potong Pasir is notorious for being the longest-held opposition ward in one-party-dominant Singapore, and dissent is not rewarded. Chiam See Tong, of the Democratic Party, has held the ward since 1984, staving off PAP candidates for six successive elections by the sheer power of his personality. No amount of inducements or threats has deterred local voters from irritating the powers that be. Locals are understandably reluctant to give their reasons for voting for Chiam, but they seem mainly to be out of long-standing loyalty. The more the government tries both carrot and stick to coax them from him, the more defiant they become. This small episode helps make Singapore's claims to being a democracy such a curiosity. Usually it is not a democracy, but very occasionally it is.

The PAP has been in power since 1959 and currently holds 82 of the 84 seats in parliament, even though at the last elections, in May 2006, it captured only 67 per cent of the vote. In other words, a more representative form of democracy should not be beyond the grasp of a highly educated electorate. By voting for the opposition, people are therefore choosing to complain. Yet at the same time they know their vote will not make the slightest difference, and they do not seem unduly concerned. Is everyone going through the motions for the sake of democracy?

Those who actually represent the opposition know what will happen to them. Chee Soon Juan and J. B. Jeyaretnam were harassed for years. Jeyaretnam became the country's first opposition MP in 1981, for the Workers Party, and ended up serving two five-year terms. On each occasion he was charged with an array of offences, ranging from slander to misuse of funds. After his second victory in 1997, he was served with eleven defamation suits, forcing him eventually to declare himself bankrupt. In his final years, Jeyaretnam – once a wealthy, flamboyant and high-profile lawyer – took to standing on street corners and outside metro stations to peddle his own books about Singapore politics because no retailer would stock them. He said he had lost count of the number of times he had been sued for defamation. He died in September 2008, aged ninety-two. The government sent his family polite but cold condolences. The blogosphere commented on it, with several people providing sympathetic assessments. The rest of the public quickly moved on. In the world's media the event passed with barely a mention. For all its efforts, Singapore's opposition has been almost completely ignored by Western governments. They choose to berate the Chinese or the Russians for their treatment of critics, but in Singapore there is too much money to be made to bother about such issues.

The longest serving prisoner of conscience was Chia Thye Poh, who spent nearly twenty-three years in jail, making his term in incarceration second only internationally to Nelson Mandela's. Dubbed the "gentle revolutionary", he was arrested in 1966 under the Internal Security Act (ISA), and spent much of the next two decades in solitary confinement, without charge. For most of that time the government gave no explanation for his imprisonment, eventually accusing him of having led a call for the violent over-throw of the leadership. On his release in 1989, he was placed under internal exile on Sentosa, Singapore's "holiday" island to the south. The ISA, which gives the security forces the right to make arrests without having warrants, was one of several repressive laws bequeathed to Singapore by the British. Others have been created more recently. They all share colourfully Orwellian titles, such as the Criminal Law Temporary Provisions Act, which allows for the jailing of dissidents, the Undesirable Publications Act, which clamps down on free speech, and the Public Entertainments and Meetings Act, which proscribes any unauthorised gathering of more than four people. Little is left to chance. In 2007 the Workers Party, the oppo-sition group previously led by Jeyaretnam, was refused permission to celebrate its fiftieth anniversary with a bicycle party in a public park.

Although capital punishment figures are regarded as secret, according to Amnesty International 420 people were hanged between 1991 and 2005, mainly for murder and drug trafficking, giving Singapore the highest execution rate in the world relative to population. During 2007, more than six thousand convicted persons were sentenced to caning. The criminal code allows caning for more than thirty offences, including robbery, vandalism and rioting. The practice is a mandatory prison punishment for rapists, drug traf-fickers and visiting foreigners who overstay their visa. The regulations are published, presumably as a deterrent. They stipulate the cane should be made out of rattan. It is soaked in water beforehand to prevent it from splitting when it comes into contact with the prisoner's buttocks, as well as to make it more flexible. It is treated with antiseptic before use to prevent infection. A lighter cane is used for juvenile offenders.

It is not just human rights groups that highlight Singapore's record. The US State Department identifies, among other things, preventive detention, executive influence over the judiciary, infringement of citizens' privacy rights, restriction of speech and press freedom and self-censorship by journalists. Its annual reports are available to the public, but they are not discussed in Singapore, nor are they advertised by American administrations that have long seen the city state as a reliable strategic partner. The British government's annual human rights report does not usually mention the performance of its former colony. As ever, realpolitik sets the terms for the West's critique of others' state of democracy and civil liberty.

It is midday, and I am standing on a patch of grass near City Hall. A sign tells me that this is Speakers Corner. It was established in 2001 to counter international criticism that Singapore is a dictatorship. The government insists that people can say whatever they want, but they must stay inside the law. That is not so easy. The instructions on the notice board list the following rules: you must register at the police station around the corner; you must fill in forms and wait for permission; if it is granted, your speech is recorded and kept for six years. Your speech can be held against you in any defamation or other trials. You are not allowed to raise any issues of religion or race – and you must not insult anyone in authority. Just in any case anyone might be tempted, the sign then helpfully lists the full provisions of all the various laws that might be infringed. I pop into the police station to ask the officer when the next speaker is likely to appear. Not for some time, the man tells me. Nor can he remember the last person who applied.

The views of most people I know in Singapore range from

mild disapproval at the state of affairs to something a little stronger. But they do not agitate publicly. The most risqué course of action tends to be sending emails, without comment, with links to opposition activities on the internet. The absence of an open media or political discourse has bred a flourishing rumour mill. Singapore-based websites are vibrant, often posting video or audio of tiny gatherings that were broken up, or other criticisms of the regime. Popular subjects for debate are aired on the internet. What exactly does the US military get up to in the giant Changi naval base? Does it contain submarine nuclear missiles? What happened to an Indonesian terrorist who disappeared from a high-security jail? How far do Singapore's financial links extend with Burma's ruling junta? Is it true Singapore provides communications equipment for the Burmese army? Is it true the elderly junta leader, Than Shwe, was secretly given cancer treatment at a Singapore governmental hospital? How many of them siphon their money through Singapore? The discussion will be vigorous on the sites of the Workers Party, the more recently formed Social Democrats (SDP) and on a number of online citizens' forums.

The authorities trawl the internet to look for potential troublemakers but have been reluctant to shut down offending sites. Several of them, including the SDP's, have posted a forty-minute video about free expression and dictatorship. Entitled *One Nation Under Lee*, the film has, according to the opposition, been viewed more than 40,000 times on YouTube and has been screened at festivals, including in neighbouring Malaysia. It was first screened in Singapore at the Excelsior Hotel. Even though the event was a private one and only invited guests were allowed, officials from the Media Development Authority made their way into the function and demanded that the film and the projector be handed over. Those proceedings were also caught on camera and are available for viewing. The film is a primer for young oppositionists, somewhat innocent but determined in tone. It cites Burma's detained opposition leader, Aung San Suu Kyi, as a model, extolling the virtues of civil disobedience. It says the Singapore government is incessantly warning of the "havoc and chaos" that would result from protest. It argues that dissident voices may be fearful, but they do have power to bring about change. Then it goes to the heart of the matter: "The only question is: do we want to exercise it?"

That question, for the moment, seems rhetorical. Demonstrations are extremely rare, and, when they do take place, the gaggle of protesters (usually fewer than ten) offer no resistance as they are quickly swept up into police vans. Seah Chiang Nee, a veteran political commentator, charts political dissent, or lack of it, on his cyber journal. He wrote of a recent, tiny, rally in favour of Burma's pro-democracy movement. "I cannot foresee 2,000 students carrying Armani handbags and iPods marching around Orchard Road throwing Molotov cocktails."

In the newspapers, and particularly on television, none of these issues is mentioned. The press does broach some social and economic problems. It is reasonably open about foreign crises; it exhorts communities and individuals to behave better. But the motivation must be self-improvement or patriotism. I remember a few years ago a government notice in the *Straits Times*, Singapore's most important paper, advising citizens of the punishments they would incur if they failed to trade in their old air-conditioning machines for new ones by a certain date. Criticism of the government, particularly of named ministers and officials, is frowned upon. It is deeply unacceptable if made by foreigners. International newspapers that criticise Lee or his underlings are hounded in the courts. Under new rules, in order to operate in Singapore foreign media must submit a hefty deposit and appoint a local representative who could be answerable in court. The list of illustrious international publications that have incurred the wrath of the authorities includes the *Far Eastern Economic Review*, the *Wall Street Journal* and the *Financial Times*. At various points they have been forced to apologise for running critical articles about Singapore. To do anything else would make no business sense.

One think-tank, officially sanctioned or at least thus far officially tolerated, is Think Centre, which was approved in October 2001 as an independent NGO. Its president, Sinapan Samydorai, sets out the ground rules: "You can talk about government policies, you can criticise government-linked companies for not being transparent or accountable, but if you talk about an individual within them and say he has family members there, and describe him by name, then you will be in danger of being sued for defamation."

Sometimes individual controversies are aired. In 2005, parliament approved a plan to legalise casino gambling, paving the way for the construction of two multi-billion dollar resorts in Marina Bay, in the centre of the city, and on Sentosa Island. Many people were furious, arguing that they did not want Singapore to become a mini Las Vegas or a rival to Macau. They did not want the low life that they feared would arrive with gambling. For a while the debate was aired, until it was decreed that it was time to stop. On one of my visits, I went to see the construction site for myself. Accompanied by a photographer, I made my way past the cement mixers and heavy trucks as they plunged through the mud. No sooner had we started taking pictures than we were "invited" into the site office to explain ourselves. A Scotsman who did not introduce himself asked for our permits, and we were politely escorted off.

Occasionally, major crises take place that cannot be kept from public view. In 2004 one of the top charities, the National Kidney Foundation, was discovered to be paying its chief executive for first-class flights, maintenance of his Mercedes and gold-plated fixtures for his private office bathroom. This came on top of an annual salary of nearly £200,000. The patron of the charity, who happened to be the wife of the former Prime Minister, declared that she could not understand what all the fuss was about as his salary was "peanuts". When the story was run by the normally cautious Straits Times, the foundation inevitably began proceedings for defamation; but the case collapsed amid a rare display of public outrage. The chief executive and the board of the foundation resigned. The Singapore version of the pact requires top officials to be seen to be acting with probity. In this case it was broken, and so punishment had to be seen to be done. Still, they would rather it had not been leaked in the first place.

Singapore is proud of the amount it pays its top officials. At the last count the Prime Minister earned $US 2.6 million a year, while the most junior member of the cabinet took a mere $1.3 million. To get the best to serve as Administrative Service Officers, the government pays as much as the private sector. In April 2007, the head of the civil service received $1.5 million a year, more than the salaries of the US President and British Prime Minister combined. It is, I am told, a small price to pay if a country wants to progress. The idea is to ensure that the most talented, including potentially the most outspoken, can be absorbed, or co-opted, by the state.

The search for talent is an officially sanctioned policy. The government does whatever it takes to attract new blood into Singapore, as long as it fills a skills gap. Officials are sent to small towns in Malaysia and India. Increasingly, they are scouring China. The Singapore government regards ethnic cohesion as one of its top goals. Any remarks considered racially inflammatory are expressly banned. However, discreetly, the domination of the Chinese, over the large Malay and Indian minorities, is maintained. The recent arrival of thousands of new people from "the mainland", many of whom cannot speak English, which remains Singapore's lingua franca, is making its mark.

There is a second reason for treating government servants so well. This to ensure that, at every link in the chain, corruption is fought off, that with such high earnings the benefit of lining one's own pockets is not worth the risk. But with so little investigative journalism, the absence of large scale corruption is something the people have to take on trust. As for nepotism, this would be regarded negatively only if the person concerned were seen as unworthy of the job. Indeed, the appointment as Prime Minister in 2004 of Lee Hsien Loong, Lee Kuan Yew's oldest son, was portrayed as playing well to

Confucian values. "Familialism", as it is called, or *guan xi*, the Chinese notion of personal relationships or connections, do not, officials say, equate to cronyism.

In the course of 2008 Singapore was the first country in the region officially to go into recession. Its reliance on exports had left it particularly vulnerable. But, in my sparring sessions at the National University and elsewhere, I saw little sign that the downturn was challenging the fundamental trade-off on which society is ordered. Mahbubani goes further, arguing that Asia is better placed economically and politically than the West to rebuild after the crisis. Asia, he says, is making progress to its eventual goal of practising democracy more harmoniously than the West. It is a variation on the theme, a results-based form of democracy. The demands of the individual are subordinated to those of the collective, and yet the individual is free in most areas of life. Anyone with any talent is co-opted into the system. "Why are Brazilians best at football? They look in the barrios for six-year-old talent. We do the same with the state. We cherry-pick the best," he says. "If you think you can run something better, we give you the chance to prove it. We absorb dissent. The stupidest thing is to crush it. No brain is wasted. The political competence of our founding fathers was extraordinary. I find that very rarely in my travels around the world." Mahbubani's thesis, which he has set out in a recent book, has gone down well in Asia, less so in Europe and America. He is not surprised. "The West is becoming the problem. You don't want to give up the space. You're also proving increasingly incompetent at government." He concludes: "By every indicator Singapore is the most successful nation. It is not just the wealth we have created; it is how we take care of people at the bottom of the pile."

One of the most intriguing aspects of Lee's authoritarian blend is his eagerness to defend it wherever he goes around the world, particularly on the lecture circuit. In a debate with Harvard's Lawrence Summers in 2006, he insisted that his aim was not to sustain the PAP in power, but to ensure stability more broadly, long after he has gone. "At the end of the day," he declared, "we offer what every citizen wants – a good life, security, good education, and a future for their children. That is good governance." During a visit to Australia that same year, he juxtaposed his way with that of his hosts. Although their politics may be more exciting, "endless debates are seldom about achieving a better grasp of the issue but scoring political points". He said of the then Australian Prime Minister: he "spends all his time dealing with this party politics. The result is you don't have a lot of time to worry about the long-term future."

The responsibility of the government is therefore a largely technical one of delivering the good life, in return for the endorsement of the electorate. Elections are in essence a report card. I promise, I deliver, you vote for me. Democracy is used to legitimise the formula. Democracy has been shifted away from any liberal assumptions, without apologies, from representation to trusteeship, from individual rights to collective wellbeing. This is what it boils down to.

Singaporeans defend their own version of democracy by comparing and contrasting it with neighbours. Some countries in the region may in theory have a more democratic system, but in most areas of life, from the economy to security, they have tended to fare worse. Take the Philippines, they say, a country that in political terms is one of the freest in the region. Guns are freely available; terrorism is rife, while the economy has slumped from being one of the most promising in the 1950s to a basket case today. There is still not one functioning liberal democracy in South-East Asia. Burma's tragic story is well known. Vietnam, Cambodia and Laos are only beginning to recover from the decades when Communists of various shades, supported by both China and the USSR, wreaked havoc throughout Indochina; Vietnam and Laos are still nominally Communist today, while Cambodia's Prime Minister is a former member of the Khmer Rouge. Thailand continues its well-worn pattern of oscillating between tentative democracy and army-led coups, with the monarchy all-powerful but also unaccountable thanks to stifling *lèse-majesté* laws. The rigidity of Malaysia's political system has been highlighted recently by the response of the governing coalition to the prospect of losing power for the first time, provoking a crisis in which the opposition leader, Anwar Ibrahim, was framed for sexual assault. In Indonesia, a supposed democracy since the fall of General Suharto, elections are so marred by corruption and vote-rigging that it would be a joke to suggest they merit the description "free and fair".

Now from Indonesia to Malaysia, from Kazakhstan to Russia to the United Arab Emirates, governments are seeking to learn from Singapore. The most important pupil is China. Progress coupled with order and limited freedom has been the maxim of those who have ruled since Mao's death; it is a philosophy whose modern origins have their roots in Singapore. With their horror of chaos, or *luan*, China's leaders have come to learn and admire the Singapore approach, and their first port of call is invariably Mahbubani's department, which has become a centre for the country's public diplomacy. The party boss in Jiangsu province sent over all his local party secretaries, up to seventy of them, for a fortnight's stay.

Lee has frequently insisted that the Singapore model is not available for export as it is applicable only to small countries or city states. In the detail, he is clearly right. Obviously no system can be ordered off the shelf. He contradicts himself, however, by making the case for "Asian values", a concept that was very much in vogue in the 1990s and is still popular in some quarters today. It promotes notions of collective wellbeing over individualism, social harmony over dissent and socio-economic progress over human rights. Lee set out his thinking on this in Tokyo in 1992: "With few exceptions, democracy has not brought good government to new developing countries. What Asians value may not necessarily be what Americans, or Europeans, value; Westerners value the freedoms and liberties of the individual. As an Asian of Chinese cultural background, my values are for a government which is honest, effective and efficient."

The counterpoint has been put most eloquently by the economist and philosopher Amartya Sen. He argued that Asian values are invoked to justify authoritarianism that is not specific to Asia. "The championing of Asian values is often associated with the need to resist Western hegemony. The linkage of the two issues, which has increasingly occurred in recent years, uses the political force of anti-colonialism to buttress the assault on civil and political rights in post-colonial Asia. This linkage, though quite artificial, can be rhetorically quite effective," Sen wrote back in 1997.

What if the model of material authoritarianism is neither the product of post-colonial reaction, nor is Asia-specific? What if it can be applied universally? I came across the following compelling observation by a young Israeli academic and anti-globalisation activist, Uri Gordon. He likens Lee's Asian values to Machiavelli's *virtù*. "Just as Machiavelli set Roman Virtue in opposition to his contemporary Christian morality, thus Lee can be seen as having chosen Asian values for Singapore as an alternative to the West's liberal democracy. Subduing the population to a comfortable life of self-censorship, Lee and his aides can be seen as devout disciples of the Florentine."

Rather than creating a greater sense of emancipation and self-awareness, Singapore has led the way in persuading the middle class to remove itself from the public realm. Why cause trouble when you have so many comforts to lose? Keen to develop this thinking with other professors in Mahbubani's department, I ask Professor Wang Gungwu, head of the East Asia Institute, to explain the philosophical underpinnings of the Singapore experiment. He describes it as a "Hobbesian contract". According to Thomas Hobbes's theory of social contract, unrestricted freedoms produce a "war of all against all". We need, we want, restrictions to save ourselves from our dark sides. "People in Singapore have mastered a range of skills. These include control and freedom." Chinese officials, he adds, are impressed. "They want their cities run like this. They have a strong fear of mass revolt that would not take much to galvanise in China."

I turn to a sociologist. "In Singapore, democratisation theories and activists meet their nemesis", says Professor Chua Beng Huat. "Singapore could not have done it without some restrictions on free speech. It would not have worked with a set of adversarial institutions." He disputes my notion of a conscious pact. Personal freedom, he says, "improves through the alleviation of poverty. Therefore you don't feel you're making a bargain." The PAP has been attempting to establish a "political culturalism", he says, that promotes the notion of the individual as "cultural citizen" in contrast to the "liberal citizen" associated with liberal democracies. Through this, the PAP has redefined the structures of political representation and participation. At stake is no less than the shaping of the boundaries and meaning of politics. A genial and highly articulate man, he leaves me to ponder this thought. "Understanding the limits to freedom is what makes freedom possible. The greater good is impossible without some constraint on individualism. The weakness of liberalism is the unwillingness to pay the cost of membership."

Perhaps it depends on which freedoms and which limits. It is in the social realm, the battle between the traditional and the modern, that the Singapore pact is most vulnerable. Lee spent years creating a state in his image. Consumer comforts do not appear to have instilled yearnings for major political change. The pressure is taking a different form. In return for ceding the public realm entirely to the government, citizens are now seeking complete control of the private sphere. The promised social liberalism has come in fits and starts. It is here that the boundaries are being most actively tested. Lee's more prescriptive views on marriage, sex and other issues are not shared by others in government. Here is a genuine divide, largely along generational lines, that is hard to conceal. I smiled when I was told that the limits on free expression are commonly known as "out-of-bounds markers". The obsession with golf, tennis and other more harmless forms of recreation is strong.

Since Lee went into "retirement" in 1990 (he is now called the Minister Mentor), some of the more idiosyncratic restrictions have been toned down. Old laws, such as the one determining the length of men's hair, have been abolished, although others punishing public spitting and failure to flush toilets properly remain in place. The law outlawing the chewing of gum was "relaxed" in 2004 to allow the use of "therapeutic" gum, in order to comply with a free trade agreement with the US. Cultural life is loosening – a little. The Audience Development Fund has been established to "educate" public taste in art, to encourage artistic risk-taking, within limits. Design, particularly fashion, is booming. At the La Salle arts school, a glass and steel structure in Little India, a group of students are rehearsing a play in Mandarin on a piece of artificial grass in the main lobby. Grace, the director, tells me they are allowed to choose from a pool of scripts. The theme of this short play is about meeting different people on a bus. Grace says it is a metaphor for life. One of the actors is wearing a T-shirt that says: "We make money, not art". He asks me if I appreciate the irony.

Occasionally, candid conversations do take place, usually with people who are not worried about their career development in the private or public sector. I discuss nepotism, corruption, secrecy and sex with a writer called Gerrie Lim. He used to live in Los Angeles, where he wrote books about art and sex. He tells me about "NUTS", an acronym that stands for the "No U-Turn Syndrome". Unlike drivers in other countries, Singaporeans will not turn their cars round at junctions unless there is a sign telling them they can. They assume that something is forbidden unless expressly told otherwise. When he submitted his last book – on the sex industry – to the Media Development Authority, the censor did not respond for over a month. He had no idea where he stood, but eventually he was given the go-ahead. "I've never come under overt pressure, but there's always a sense that you're waiting for the call," he says. "People always ask me how I get away with it. I suppose I'm harmless."

As each year goes by, the out-of-bounds markers on moral issues become harder to locate. After it came out in 1998, the American television series *Sex and the City* was banned. When the film was released in 2008, advertising hoardings of the sassy quartet marching through Manhattan adorned billboards across Singapore's shopping streets. In 2005, Singapore hosted its first Sexpo exhibition. The authorities justified it by arguing that there was much to be gained for couples to spice up their sex lives; they were not, however, encouraging promiscuity. Strict rules were applied and enforced. Nothing was allowed that "bears a resemblance to any genitalia". Nothing was allowed that encouraged oral or anal sex, both of which are strictly prohibited.

In October 2007, parliament rejected a proposal to repeal a law which outlaws private and consensual sexual relations between men. Although prosecutions have been rare, those found in violation can be jailed for up to two years on charges of "gross indecency". Homosexuality is banned on television. One station was fined for showing two fully clothed men in the same bedroom in a home furnishing programme. And yet the censors did allow the film *Brokeback Mountain* to be shown in the cinema. "Many of my colleagues in parliament were keenly aware of Singapore's reputation as a nanny state and would have readily relaxed the restrictions," the MP told me. But they were wary of loosening restrictions for fear of antagonising the "heartlanders", such as those I had met in Toa Payoh. This, she emphasised, was surely an example of "consultative democracy" in action.

With Lee in his mid-eighties, Singaporeans find it hard to imagine life without the man who has guided them all the way since independence. The vast majority of his subjects – including the people I know who are in a position to make informed comparisons – have accepted his argument that only by acting the way it has done has Singapore become so orderly and prosperous. Such is the emphasis on consumer comfort that the previous economic downturns – the 1997 Asian crash and the 2003 Sars virus – were regarded as deeply shocking. If anything, they reinforced a yearning for political stability. Many people speak of wanting the newspapers to be more open, their politicians to be less prescriptive, but at the same time they do not wish to sacrifice any of the good life – the endless shopping, the cornucopia of excellent restaurants and bars, the tennis and swimming clubs, the Mercedes and the BMWs.

The government is caught in a bind. It is worried by the number of Western-educated students who choose to live abroad for long periods after graduation. It is constantly replenishing them with graduates from China and elsewhere, but it would keenly like to entice back its own citizens. It knows that a limited loosening up of society would help. At the same time it is frightened of what that might unleash, and is seeking to confine any liberalisation to specific economic and cultural areas. It does not want to relax its control of the political or public realm.

The use of defamation suits has actually increased in recent years. Singapore is constantly seeking international acceptance for its institutions, and therefore it came as a welcome sign when it invited the International Bar Association to hold its annual conference in the city in October 2007. A few months later, the IBA's Human Rights Institute issued a report criticising the use of defamation suits by PAP to silence the opposition and the press, and expressing concerns about the independence and impartiality of Singapore's judges. Instead of tackling the detail, the authorities resorted to their customary mix of legal sanction and fury. Lee accused human rights organisations of "a conspiracy to do us in". He said that the West realised how Russia and China had been studying Singapore's success, and increasingly regarded it as a threat.

The debate about the Singapore model, such as it is, is often reduced to easy points' scoring on both sides. Many writers focus on the obsessive state and the obsessive consumer, seeing little beyond. When in 1993 the writer William Gibson coined the phrase "Disneyland with the death penalty", it jarred. It is cited by detractors of Singapore as a good summary of its human rights record and by supporters of the country as an example of foreign high-handedness. Gibson's label is neat and witty. But it is also much more complicated than that.

Will Lee's passing lead to a relaxation of both the private and the public realm or will the government seek to crack down even harder? One argument for loosening up is economic self-interest. In a rare public criticism made from inside the country, the Managing Director of the World Bank, Juan José Daboub, warned in May 2008 that Singapore would suffer economically if it did not loosen up. "One such challenge is the tricky task of balancing a desire for social order and stability – for many years a defining quality of Singapore's growth – with a need to allow more innovation and creativity to produce high-value goods and services in a more competitive global economy," he said. "Innovation and creativity are, by definition, not orderly and not regulated. As Singapore looks to a growing and prosperous future, striking the right balance will call for some skilled stewardship and probably some risk-taking."

As Singapore's economy nose-dived (growth plunged by nearly 20 per cent in the first quarter of 2009, the largest fall ever recorded there) some began to argue more forcefully that the very nature of its authoritarian politics would act as an impediment to recovery. This argument, taking its cue from experts such as Daboub, was that Singapore's state-guided economy was more vulnerable than was officially admitted and that a lack of open debate had exacerbated the problem. The heavily controlled media had also failed to act as a check on the state's two main investment funds, Temasek and GIC, which ended up with billions of losses from poor acquisitions.

The chances of the crisis leading to a new candour appear, for the moment at least, illusory. Shortly after returning from one trip to the country, I penned a blog for the *Guardian* introducing discussion of the "pact". Entitled "the new authoritarianism", it cited the examples of several of the countries I discuss in the book. My references to Singapore, though, were brief. I spoke of the people I knew, adding that "they are well versed in international politics, but are perfectly content with the situation back home. I used to reassure myself with the old certainty that this model was not applicable to larger, more diverse states. I now believe this to be incorrect." I went on to talk about increased threats to civil liberties in countries ranging from Russia to Italy to the UK, before concluding: "A modern form of authoritarianism, quite distinct from Soviet Communism, Maoism or Fascism, is being born. It is providing a modicum of a good life, and a quiet life, the ultimate anaesthetic for the brain." The following day the *Guardian* called. The Singaporean government was demanding a right of reply. I had no objection to a response to my piece – that, after all, is what commentary is all about – but I could not for the life of me imagine what I had done to earn their ire. Indeed, before sending my piece my main concern was that I might be attacked by bloggers for being too generous to the country of my birth.

The piece duly appeared, in the name of the High Commissioner to the UK, Michael Teo. It was mainly a restatement of the philosophy of Singapore's political system, before concluding: "Every society has to strike its own balance between individual liberties and the common good. Some in the west like John Kampfner feel a calling to go forth and convert the heathen to western liberal democracy. But the true test is what works in the real world, with real societies. To worship a western model as the only way, and dismiss all other solutions as authoritarian or undemocratic, is surely the ultimate anaesthetic for the brain." On the following day, the *Straits Times* carried Teo's article in full, under the captivating headline "Singapore Ticks Off British Writer".

The spat left me with a series of conflicting emotions. One was fear: would I be refused entry into the country – or perhaps locked up on my arrival? Another was concern among my Singapore friends. Several had forwarded me the various blog references, usually without comment. Another was surprise. I was more concerned that the article would be seen as too soft on Singapore, rather than the opposite. That gave rise to disappointment. Why, I wondered, cannot Singapore engage? Six months later I was back at Changi airport, with just a hint of trepidation, for an academic conference. I was allowed in, with a speedy smile from the immigration officer. Everyone I met – politicians, academics, journalists and financiers – mentioned, awkwardly, that they had read the piece. We all laughed it off. I talked, publicly, about my views of the "pact", which led to vigorous but friendly sparring. At the Raffles Bar I spent an enjoyable evening with a senior newspaper executive. He, too, mentioned it, embarrassedly, but assured me there had been nothing special in my treatment. This kind of thing, he said, happens all the time. By way of reassurance, he suggested that the Foreign Ministry must have gone into one of its "habitual bouts of group think" in which an order is handed down from on high and is obeyed without discussion. What does it say about the fragility of a regime if it goes into paroxysms of fury about any old blog? Regimes on the verge of falling are often the most extreme in their response to criticism, so maybe change is on its way. It might be, but from all that I have seen such change will be confined to the private realm, and not the public. That seems to be what most people I spoke to are seeking.

I asked my drinking partner if he saw any prospect of the defamation culture being softened. No chance, he said. The law of contempt had been designed to protect public confidence in state institutions, in good times and in bad. Most people – Singapore citizens, international businesses, foreign governments – had a vested interest in preserving the status quo. Why else, he suggested, would Singapore have done so well for so long? For me, someone who has spent much of his career seeking to cause trouble for politicians, this was an unpalatable thought.

Even more horrifying is the thought that plenty more people around the world, irrespective of their political culture, have also been contentedly anaesthetised. Singapore may be the home of the trade-off in its purest form, but are we all more Singaporean than we realise?

2

CHINA: DISCREET PLAYER

*"With the vote in the wrong hands, the wrong people get
selected who then manipulate the electorate"* – Kevin Ao

WHAT COULD BE MORE PLEASANT THAN SPENDING A BRIGHT
morning sitting by the water drinking an espresso and listening to
the chiming of church bells? I was in Portofino, so that might
explain my tranquil demeanour. Except this wasn't the Italian port
frequented by the rich and famous. This Portofino was an artificial
village built around a lake in Shenzhen, a southern city in China that
is a monument to the free market. More precisely I was in an area
called OCT, Overseas Chinese Town. The lake I was looking on to
was man-made; the clock tower I was sitting under was modern, but
what did it matter? "You have the American dream, we have the
Shenzhen dream," said my host.

Lanciel Cui is the manager in this region of China for a large
Israeli shipping firm. Unlike many Chinese, she has already travelled the world. She regaled me with her experiences of the Faroe
Islands and of the northern English town of Grimsby ("why," she
wondered, "are the school kids roaming around the shopping
mall in the daytime?" and "why does everyone look so pasty?"). Her
parents typify the modern Chinese success story. Both came from
peasant farming stock; her father rose to become a university dean,

her mother served as a military doctor. Neither would now recognise their country. Lanciel is the quintessential Western-style career woman in her forties, a single mother juggling to maintain a work–life balance. She flies regularly to Beijing and Shanghai for meetings and knows the airline schedules by heart, seeking to ensure that she catches the last flight home whenever she can. She, like everyone in Shenzhen, is an "immigrant". While Hong Kong, just across the harbour, was still in British hands, this place was a sleepy fishing village. Its population has soared to a staggering thirteen million. The economy increased at an average of 28 per cent per year for more than two decades. In the early 1990s Chinese planners believed their country's main economic centres – Shanghai, Shenzhen and others – would take fifty years to overtake Singapore. That has already happened. As for Hong Kong, plans are already being discussed to merge the "backwater" that was once considered a global financial hub with Shenzhen.

Shenzhen was therefore as good a place as any for me to look at the Chinese version of the pact. The first free economic zone, it was the test bed for Deng Xiaoping's economic reforms, the laboratory for the post-Maoist embrace of capitalism. It was a tour of South-East Asia that alerted Deng in the late 1970s to the urgent need for change. He was shocked by the modernity of cities such as Bangkok, Kuala Lumpur and Singapore. On his return to China he said: "Singapore enjoys good social order and is well managed. We should tap their experience and learn how to manage things better than they do."

From the moment Deng launched his "Open Door" policy and his "four modernisations" programme – agriculture, industry, science and technology, and the military – China has sought to find a way of reconciling open markets with closed politics. The last major Marxist-Leninist dictatorship stayed in power, but only by embracing capitalism.

Lanciel has taken the day off to show me around. Keen to start

my tour of the city, I decline the offer of cheesecake or other delights
from the Austrian-style *konditorei*, and jump into her 4x4. We drive
down manicured, tree-lined streets, with bright red cycle lanes that
would not be out of place in a provincial German town, past a gated
community and plush condominiums. In front of me is Window of
the World, a replica theme park with its own Eiffel Tower, Leaning
Tower of Pisa and Egyptian Pyramids, plus a 4,000-square-metre
indoor ski resort. It takes us the best part of an hour to drive from
one end of the city, from the modern centre of Futian, to the old
heart. Lanciel points out a small quaint building on our left. The
Skylight Hotel was once one of the city's tallest buildings. Now it
would barely make it into the top one hundred. It also once marked
the edge of the city; now millions live beyond it. Nearby are two
more firsts that Shenzhen can boast – the first stock exchange in
China (there are now two) and the first McDonald's (there are now
more than a thousand). We drive past a giant picture of a smiling
Deng, with the city's modern skyline superimposed behind him.
Lanciel points out that a few years ago the memorial was moved
back several metres to allow the highway, Shennan Boulevard, to be
widened. "Even after his death he didn't stand in the way of
progress," she says with a smile.

On each day of my trip newspapers across China and in Hong
Kong carry articles extolling the marvels of the great leap into capitalism, marking its thirtieth anniversary. Many of the pieces are
strangely gripping, a mix of bombast and self-effacement, of personal anecdote and national endeavour. As he sought to reassert his
control in 1991 after the Tiananmen crisis, the ailing Deng
famously said (or was supposed to have said) "to get rich is glorious". He urged China to "create more Hong Kongs". At least two
thousand Special Economic Zones opened up in the early 1990s,
concentrated in the Pearl River Delta of Guangdong province in the
south, with Shenzhen at its heart. Eventually, there were many more
experimental cities, motors for the most extensive and ambitious
programme of profit-driven economics yet produced. "Some must

get rich first," Deng proclaimed, arguing that the different regions should "eat in different kitchens" rather than putting their resources in a "common pot".

We stop at Coastal City, a shopping mall that had opened only nine months earlier, the latest of thousands of palaces of consumerism scattered across China. I walk past a succession of shopfronts and cannot find a single person buying anything. The global economic downturn has already hit the city, but store owners are trying not to show it. They are keen not to lose face. At lunch, in a Taiwanese restaurant overlooking the mall's indoor skating rink, Lanciel introduces me to her friend Peter. His company exports household goods around the world. My hosts say several thousand factories have closed in Guangdong province, more than has been officially acknowledged. Peter says he can now reach the nearby city of Guangzhou in little over an hour. Before, the journey down the 150-kilometre stretch of motorway would have taken him at least twice as long.

Peter points out that property prices in Shenzhen have fallen by at least 40 per cent. A downturn in the market, he says, was inevitable. Prices had been based on speculation, propped up by local government officials, many of whom had made a fast buck. Wealth creation has relied on several multipliers: commercial bank lending, privatisation of the entire housing stock, and, more recently, the limited privatisation of land. Peter says the central government had been worried for some time about the cavalier approach in regions such as Guangdong, and had been trying, with limited effect, to bring local officials into line. "Beijing saw the problems well before the hierarchies in Shenzhen and Shanghai. They wanted far greater controls on property prices, but the politicians are in bed with the developers." The figures bear out their concern. Corruption among "red barons" in the regions is said to cost around 15 per cent of China's GDP every year. Some 90 per cent of China's richest three thousand businessmen are related to party figures. Fewer than half of the high court's judgements on corruption are enforced.

I am struck by the candour of my two hosts ("everyone knows what goes on with corruption and local officials, but there's no point in going public with it"), and their knowledge of the world. They talk about shopping trends at Wal-Mart and Tesco, about the collapse in the US and European housing sectors, and the effect on specific factories in Shenzhen that have supplied them. We talk about interest rates and about inflation ("our government puts our inflation rate at 5 per cent, but as soon as you look around you realise those figures must be made up"). There is no sense of isolation here, rather the opposite. And yet, no matter how much they criticise the practices of the Communist Party, particularly the local party, they see little reason to change the political status quo. "How could you possibly give the vote to nearly 800 million uneducated peasants and expect the country to remain peaceful and stable?" I hear this refrain repeatedly during my travels.

Resuming our tour, Lanciel points out some of Shenzhen's striking modern buildings. As town halls go, I have never seen anything like Citizens' Plaza, a glass structure that occupies an entire block, with a roof undulating like a wave. The Boaon and Longgang districts on the northern outskirts contain no such delights – only vast concrete warehouses and factories belching out thick smoke.

What remains of the countryside has been destroyed. The ground seems a mixture of mud, sand and scrub. A number of the hills surrounding these industrial behemoths have had their peaks chopped off, in order to provide the sand for land to be reclaimed. Throughout this period, people were told the same thing: Shenzhen must not stop growing. Wealth or clean air: in the headlong rush to modernisation, the people were told they could not have both. The government chose for them. The economic crisis now has its compensations. The skies are much clearer than normal, Lanciel tells me, because output has fallen. She says that until a few days before we met she had not seen the sun for months. The cost of China's headlong growth has long been evident. The World Bank estimates that over the past decade around 750,000 people have died prematurely each year from pollution. It estimates that health costs of environmental damage account for about 5 per cent of GDP. Of the Bank's list of the twenty cities around the world with the worst air, sixteen are in China. Most of the people I talk to are guided by their personal experience, not by government statements or foreign statistics.

We stop at a traffic light in the middle of this industrial jungle. On the other side of the road, a dozen or so young female workers, all in identical red overalls, emerge from one industrial monstrosity, darting across a dangerous four-lane highway to get to their bus stop. Here is the epicentre of the "Wal-Mart miracle" – the low-margin, high-production revolution that supplied China with unparalleled wealth and the West with goods at unparalleled low prices. At the peak of the cheap output boom, half the world's jeans, air-conditioning machines, furniture, textiles and shoes were made here. The relaxation of the long-standing *hukou* system of residency permits was a key factor. More than 100 million people, officially deemed to be rural dwellers, flooded into urban areas. Shenzhen alone was said, at the peak, to have eight million temporary migrant workers. By the middle of this decade, some had begun to organise, seeking to form non-official trade unions, and to protest at living conditions. Partly as a result of local agitation, and partly to counter international consumer concerns about "sweat shop" labour, a new employment law introduced in January 2008 raised the minimum wage.

Then came the collapse in consumer demand in the West and the ensuing sharp fall in exports on which China and this region especially depend. Locals insist that the most cavalier managers in Shenzhen are not from the region, but from Hong Kong and Taiwan. Several cases have been recorded of factory owners suddenly locking out their workforce and then disappearing out of China's legal jurisdiction. With no job and no compensation, the workers have no choice but to return to the countryside. By the start of 2009, some 600,000 migrant workers from Guangdong province had been forced to leave, according to official figures. The Chinese Academy of

Social Sciences put the rising urban jobless rate at nearly 10 per cent – more than double the government's published rate. Given the propensity to understate problems, these totals could also be appreciably higher.

The most recent figure for "mass incidents", the official euphemism for protests, is put at 87,000 a year. With a small number of exceptions, most protests were linked to specific grievances, such as job losses or concerns about corruption or exploitation. They were not overtly political in tone. Officials are nervous, but they are keen to point out what happened last time around. In the mid-1990s, during the rapid liberalisation of the economy introduced by the then Prime Minister Zhu Rongji, some fifty million workers in state-owned enterprises were laid off. Protests did take place, but they eventually fizzled out.

Publicly a number of different messages are being put out by the party. The government's information strategy is dogged, but also subtle and sophisticated. The state-run central media seems to do little to play down the protest movement. The explanation I am given is that this has less to do with the principle of free expression, more with expediency. The national media have been using it to demonstrate the perfidy of local administrators, and the need for the central government to keep corrupt officials in the hinterland in check. But there is a further message, and it goes to the heart of the pact between the Chinese Communist Party and the middle class. If you value your new comforts, do not encourage the mob. Your lifestyles will be guaranteed only through central control, which should not be challenged, particularly in a time of adversity. For years, annual growth averaged more than 9 per cent. It began to be taken for granted on both sides, so the sudden fall in 2008–9 was bound to leave people nervous. But insecurity can be as strong a social adhesive as optimism once was.

When *Hurun*, a lifestyle magazine-cum-research institute, began its first annual Chinese "rich list" in 1999, it required a personal fortune of just $6 million to make it into the top fifty. By the time of its 2007 report, it included five hundred individuals and the minimum requirement was $100 million. Even more remarkable has been the dramatic rise in the number of billionaires: according to *Hurun*, the number of dollar billionaires jumped from seven in 2004 to 106. Below this level emerged a rapidly expanding class of millionaires. In 2008, at the height of the boom, China had 415,000 people with $1 million dollars in disposable assets. This made the country home to more millionaires in real terms than any other in the world. With inequality also among the highest in the world, the social ramifications were not lost on the party top brass. Already in 2005, the priority, as set out in the eleventh five-year plan, had shifted to "scientific development" – the idea that the quality of growth was as important as the amount of growth, that inequalities within regions and between regions needed to be tackled. The Jiang Xemin exhortation to build the "well-off society", *xiaokang shehui*, was followed by the move towards the "harmonious society", *hexie shehui*. The new generation of the Chinese super-rich adopted a lower public profile than their Russian counterparts; they kept their luxuries out of view of the rest of the population. Their acquisitiveness is no less pronounced, but China's wealthy were set one further stipulation: be careful to flaunt your riches less and be seen to contribute more to the broader society.

The earthquake in Sichuan province provided them with one such test. Within a week of the disaster in May 2008, *Hurun* estimated that the top one hundred richest people in the country had already donated $120 million collectively. As with Russia, as with Singapore, as with many countries, those who had done well for themselves in China knew what they needed to do to keep on the right side of the authorities. They made sure that their newly won private freedoms were not endangered by any temptation to interfere in the public arena.

The Chinese trade-off is the easiest of all to understand. I first visited the country in the mid-1980s. Then, most aspects of life were still rigidly controlled. People had little choice of where to live, what kind of job to seek, even in some cases what clothes to wear or whom to marry. For the middle classes (although by no means for the rest) all that has long gone.

These freedoms are not trivial. They are the ones that are experienced day-to-day. They have meaning and value, especially if they have not been experienced before. Many Chinese adopted the ubiquitous symbols of luxury that globalisation brought them – Armani, Mercedes and golf. Shenzhen is at the forefront of the Asian infatuation with the sport, and would not countenance anything that is second best. The city has at least a dozen exclusive golf clubs, attracting players from across Asia on tailor-made weekends or holidays. The Mission Hills Golf Club is the biggest in the world, including no fewer than twelve courses designed by some of the world's top professional players, eight restaurants, a hotel, private residences and two swimming pools.

I have little interest in the sport, so it was with a wry smile that I saw that the destination for my final meeting of the day was the Noble Merchant Golf Club. Lanciel tells me her brother-in-law, a lawyer, has assembled some friends and business contacts for a dinner in my honour. We are led to a banqueting room that overlooks one of the holes. I pick up a brochure from reception on my way: "NM-Golf's another superiority [sic] is the complete lighting system for the 18 holes. The system makes night daytime so that the busy members can enjoy playing golf comfortablly [sic] and conveniently whenever they have spare time," it tells me. "It is good to know that the State Guest House of NM-Golf is the first luxurious clubhouse in Shenzhen, providing state banquet series dishes only."

I am greeted by our host, Wang Heping of the Shenzhen Lawyers Association. A kindly, animated man, he introduces me to the assembled guests, waiting for me on the veranda of our private dining suite. The group includes several local journalists, two industrialists, an asset manager, an architect, a philosophy professor from Nanjing University who has flown down especially, and two senior figures from the Shenzhen Municipal Bureau of Culture. The occasion does not begin auspiciously. I make a rather limp attempt at a joke about football being the international language, at which the other guests try valiantly to laugh. Mr Wang gets straight down to business and asks me for my assessment of the current state of China. I reply that I would not presume an opinion as I am there to learn. This is deemed to be not good enough, and so I proffer my thoughts about the "pact". Just how far were they all prepared to sacrifice their freedoms in return for prosperity and security? From that point, aided by good red wine, the evening takes off.

The conversation is a mix of the impassioned, the philosophical and the quizzical. We discuss the importance of family, the election of Barack Obama, the global downturn and the possible remedies. One guest takes a pessimistic view of China's economic prospects. "Everyone is blindly waiting for a recovery. They think the ship has a small leak. But it's going to take in a lot of water before this is done." Naval metaphors are apparently in vogue, and another is used about political reform: "This is like a long boat journey on the ocean. There is no destination. We must listen to the passengers." I interpret that as a call for more democracy, but I am not absolutely sure, so I press them on the West's approach to civil liberties and its application in China. "This is a dilemma for people like us," says one. "We know the value of democracy and freedom, but how do we achieve this?" Another counters that China will embrace "universal values of human rights, democracy and that sort of thing in ten years from now", before adding, "We don't believe in fundamentalism. We are more opportunistic and pragmatic."

Only occasionally is nationalism allowed to intrude. The dinner coincides with an emergency summit in Washington of the G20 to discuss the financial crisis. We all agree that this marks the first, belated, official recognition of China's place at the economic top table. At this point the architect produces a sheaf of papers and proceeds to read out a prepared speech. The others guffaw at his earnestness, but he is not to be denied his moment. He talks of

China's humiliation at the hands of foreign powers and how "we couldn't have dared dream about this life ten years ago". The prosperity of the economy was due not to the opening up of political reform, but to the nature of the Chinese people, their entrepreneurialism and industriousness. It was unfair of other countries to dictate any particular course of action on China, particularly environmental restrictions that would curb its growth. "The world is small; its resources are limited. You [the West] have already eaten most of the good food." This, I thought to myself, was a variation on another such line I had heard: "America eats tomorrow's lunch today. China eats the lunch it failed to eat 150 years ago."

As for my own eating, during the architect's discourse I am making a hash of extracting anything from an extremely expensive crab. My embarrassment is alleviated somewhat as one guest chips in: "Chinese reform is just like that. It's delicate, difficult and messy." Everyone descends into laughter. The mood darkens again when the subject moves to the identity of modern China. "We don't know who we are," suggests one of the journalists. "People are trying to believe in something." The Chinese people, he says, are "trapped in transition". He is citing the title of a book written by a Chinese-American academic, Minxin Pei, in 2006, which has galvanised the debate about the political and economic trade-off. Pei argues that strong economic growth has diminished the chance of political reform. Through a process of "illiberal adaptation", the ruling elites have entrenched their power, and will continue to do so. Another of the guests turns to me and adds: "We are different from you. We are a flock of sheep; we follow the deep grass, and the whip of our rulers." Finally, one of the assembled, who until this point has not spoken, offers a brief thought: "The only thing we have left is our traditions, and our only tradition left is the family." During the dinner, each point is made forcefully and rebutted equally forcefully by someone else around the table. Even the men from the local culture bureau lose their reserve and weigh in. The subject turns to the Olympics, overwhelmingly regarded as a great display of Chinese professionalism and pride. Not so, says one guest. "The opening ceremony might not have been Communist, but it was collectivist. We were embarrassed, humiliated. It was too regimented."

It is late into the night. We leave with handshakes and bear hugs. As he walks me to our car, my host, Mr Wang, asks me for my impressions. I tell him I found the evening remarkable for its candour. I suggest that I will not quote any of the attendees by name, just to make sure. He says he hadn't thought of that, but does not protest. I ask him how he had organised the gathering. He said he had invited three or four of them, and asked them to bring people they knew. In other words, everyone was speaking without knowing whether they could trust others around the table. "We talk openly in our close circles, but never at formal gatherings such as these." For him and his friends, it is a venture into the unknown, a break with the convention that has left them contented and safe. He insists he is pleased it happened. I am not sure whether to believe him, but for my own purposes I am very pleased it did.

In Beijing, for all the superficial attempts at cosmopolitanism, political discussions remain more guarded. That is no particular surprise, as it is the seat of power, and many of those I speak to have ambitions that would not be enhanced by an excess of criticism. I am sitting in the Zi Guang café, near the east gate of Tsing Hua University, with a collection of half a dozen scholars. One of them, a teacher in literature and translator from the central Communist Party School, has brought her laptop for the conversation, which unnerves me a little. Is she blogging our conversation (in which case, fine)? Or is she noting it for official use (in which case my interlocutors are hardly going to open up)? When it comes to the economy, the discussion is candid. The group talk about friends who have lost money on the Shanghai stock market (which by this point had shed two-thirds of its value). One person speaks of a friend who had sold his home in order to invest in shares several years ago. For some people like this, it was a calculated gamble. For others it became a social security fund, which they have now been deprived of.

For years, China's global advance had been watched with trepidation in the West. By the middle of the decade, Chinese money,
through its Sovereign Wealth Funds, was reaching parts of America
that the American government could no longer reach. By 2007,
China had accumulated a staggering $1.2 trillion of foreign
exchange reserves to invest, much of which had been placed in US
Treasuries or government bonds. Some of that was done in con-
junction with Singapore funds, as the links between those two
governments increased. Between 2006 and 2007 alone, Chinese stake
holdings in US corporations had risen by sixteenfold. In the minds
of some American politicians, China's rise was as threatening as
Japan's had been in the 1970s and 1980s. Specific deals were blocked;
tariffs were set at prohibitively high rates. In 2005, Congress ensured
that the proposed takeover of the energy giant Unocal by the China
National Offshore Oil Corporation (CNOOC) was abandoned. A
later attempt to buy the telecoms firm 3Com was blocked, amid
Pentagon fears that Beijing would gain access to sensitive US military technology.

Initially, Chinese inroads into Western economies were popular back home. But when the results went wrong, a backlash began.
In May 2007, China invested $3 billion in the New York-based pri-
vate equity firm Blackstone. The symbolism of the Communist state
buying into one of Wall Street's rising stars, in the expectation of a
more professional handling of its investments, was strong. Within
weeks, however, its shares plummeted. Bloggers piled in to criticise,
and the authorities did nothing to stop them, suggesting a certain
tolerance for open discussion expressed in patriotic terms. "The foreign reserves are the product of the sweat and blood of the people of
China, please invest them with more care," proclaimed one comment on sina.com, a popular site. Overall, the media debate about
the economy has been relatively open.

When we move off finance and on to politics, my university
group becomes more circumspect. A young man who has just
returned from a year at Cornell insists that China can continue to

"combine the collectivist social and economic model with a high degree of consumerism" (a variation on the established Leninism-plus-market-economy idea). I tell them that I have just been browsing at a nearby bookshop, where I find on the counter the assembled works of Milton Friedman alongside Chairman Mao. They see this as unsurprising. So I ask whether they detect any link between material comfort and a demand for more freedom. "Definitely," says one. "Affluence leads to demands for more personal autonomy," she says, before adding quickly that this could and would be accommodated through debate within the Communist Party.

The students admit that they exchange information with their friends about technical wizardry that allows them to bypass the latest internet firewalls. Yet they insist that certain checks should remain in place, for the sake of social stability, adding that the main goal of a relaxation in censorship should be greater efficiency and probity. "We need transparency of reporting to improve our accountability system and anti-corruption drive and identify mistakes in decision making." They develop the argument by means of proverbs: "How does a patient cure himself?" And another one: "How will a horse run fast if it is the only one in the race?"

Their solution, it seems to me, is based around pragmatic statecraft, a variation on Singapore's view of elections as a form of referendum or a simple performance indicator on government. Democracy is thus defined purely in terms of technocratic accountability. The forum for such assessments lies within officially sanctioned structures – public consultations, expert meetings, surveys, and, most of all, intra-party discussions that can accommodate different viewpoints. All these fall into the term, so fashionable in Chinese intellectual circles, of "deliberative democracy".

Can these be achieved through a single party? The Communist leadership has yet to embrace the "soft" institutional infrastructure that, to a greater or lesser extent, has featured in Western systems: independent courts, clear property rights, a free press, independent trade unions, effective corporate governance, transparent anti-monopoly rules, free intellectual inquiry and even a properly functioning welfare system. My student interlocutors are convinced China will adopt such mechanisms, but can absorb them into the existing system. They use as a reference point the Sichuan earthquake. "We could not have reacted as quickly as we did to Sichuan if we had had multi-party democracy. This natural disaster rekindled our confidence in the necessity of consistency, which only the collectivist model can provide," one of them tells me. They contrast Sichuan with Hurricane Katrina. Later on they might have added the Indian authorities' response to the Mumbai terrorist attacks.

The Sichuan tragedy marked an important moment. It reflected the various contradictions at play, as the Chinese authorities struggled to keep pace with both the opening up of society and the demands of digital technology. They began in time-honoured fashion, trying to play down the extent of the damage and prevent on-the-spot reporting. With the Olympics only three months away, the government was particularly keen to control the message. However, when reports and video began to emerge around the world via the internet, before any opportunity to censor the information, the strategy started to collapse. The authorities quickly relented and were surprised to see that the immediate consequences were the opposite of their fears. Footage of Prime Minister Wen Jiabao in his scuffed shoes and drab suit, clambering over debris to meet victims and to exhort the emergency services to greater efforts, proved an instant hit. "Grandpa Wen" became the global face of China's grief. For a brief moment it became distasteful to criticise China, as the actress Sharon Stone found out when she suggested the disaster had been due to the bad "karma" caused by its government's human rights record. Wen made several more visits to the area. He even acquired his own Facebook site, which became one of the most popular of its kind.

The carefully news-managed images of the quake helped reinforce a sense of national solidarity throughout 2008, one of the most important years in China's modern history. Across Beijing and other cities advertising hoardings on the sides of buses or in underground stations a picture of either a panda or a pretty girl appeared with the slogan: "All because of you, Chengdu will be better". However, as criticism grew of the long-term measures being taken, reporting restrictions were tightened again. The Propaganda Ministry issued directives to state-run news outlets setting out forbidden topics. These included: questions about school construction, whether government rescue efforts were too slow, and whether Beijing knew in advance that the quake would happen, but failed to warn inhabitants (as the rumour mill was alleging). Several groups of bereaved parents, who had lost their only child in a collapsed school, were prevented from travelling to Beijing to lobby the government. Journalists who asked too many questions were told to "emphasise positive propaganda" and "uphold unity, stability and encouragement".

Almost nobody I spoke to was content with the large amount of censorship of the media, although suggested alternatives varied considerably. The thousands of newspapers, magazines, television and radio stations across China's provinces are all to a greater or lesser extent under the watchful eye of the party. (Business journalism has, in recent years, been the most dynamic and outspoken.) According to the International Committee to Protect Journalists, as of December 2008, China had twenty-eight journalists in jail, consistently the highest number in the world (followed by Cuba). The most common convictions are for divulging state secrets, subversion and defamation – charges that are regularly used to silence the most outspoken critics.

The party's greatest concern now is the internet. In 2008, China passed the US to become home to the biggest population of users – up to 200 million regulars at the latest count. The authorities have tried to block sensitive discussions, using keyword filters and an army of "net nannies" employed by portals and service providers. This "great firewall of China" is manned by 100,000 monitors, or "cyber cops", or "chat room mamas". Foreign sites, ranging from the BBC to Wikipedia, are regularly blocked. The government has developed some of the most sophisticated technology in the world for

spotting dangerous sites, developing algorithms to weed out post-
ings that include words like "democracy", "Dalai Lama" or
"Tiananmen massacre". Both sides play an elaborate game of cat
and mouse, with savvy users quickly finding ways of circumventing
government blocks. One clever technique has been to use online
software to render Chinese-language script vertically instead of hor-
izontally. This, for a while, baffled the keyword detectors. One of the
tricks employed by the state is to use thousands of paid commentators who pose as ordinary web users to counter criticism of the
government. They are known by independent bloggers as "50 Cent
Party members", because of the small sum, fifty Chinese cents, they
are said to be paid for every posting.

Sometimes the central government encourages bloggers to vent
their spleen. It has allowed a sense of "people power" to emerge to
serve as vigilantes against wrongdoing among local officials. This
then strengthens the credibility of the federal authorities that move
quickly to punish the miscreants. In one case, an ostensibly harmless
photograph of a Nanjing housing official found its way on to the
web. Sharp-eyed bloggers could not help noticing the $15,000 Swiss
watch on his wrist. Two weeks later, he was fired after investigators
determined that he had led an improbably lavish lifestyle for a modestly salaried civil servant.

The border between the private and the public space is the
fault line in defining and determining freedom in China. This line is
constantly changing, and defies easy labels. Many of the students I
spoke to were frustrated by the authorities' censorship efforts that
they saw as both aggressive and desperate. Yet they are keen to point
out that the torrent of information now accessible online has given
many young urban Chinese a sense of freedom that their parents
could only have dreamed of. They resent suggestions that they are
brainwashed, or that their access to information is any less complete
than that in the West.

The political scientist Anne-Marie Brady suggests that China's
central propagandists have studied the theories of "manufacturing

consent" by Edward Bernays, regarded as the originator of modern public relations, and Walter Lippmann. In his seminal 1922 book, *Public Opinion*, Lippmann said democracy and the media operated in an environment of low attention spans and the inability of the "bewildered herd" to come to intelligent conclusions without prompting. This herd, he argued, must be governed by "a specialised class". That class would be composed of experts, otherwise known as elites, whose role would be to circumvent the primary defect of democracy, the impossible ideal of the "omni-competent citizen". Brady points out how governments decree which subjects are open to discussion, and which are rendered impermissible. They are then placed outside the perimeter. The state intervenes at all levels of the media hierarchy through a system of news guidance, post-publication review and reward and punishment. Its most effective tool is a traditional Chinese invention rather than a Western import, a "you know what we mean" style of regulation that allows experimentation, tolerates ambiguity and then punishes retroactively and arbitrarily. This is the Singapore model adapted for a larger canvas, with less emphasis on defamation suits (the accused in China would rarely have the money to pay), and more on other forms of sanction, from peer pressure to imprisonment.

Then there are the cultural outlets. In many ways Beijing is more avant-garde than Singapore or other Asian cities. A walk around the area of Sanlitun attests to lively visual arts and music scenes, crowded bookstores, stylish street designer clothing and more. In the academic world, several professors I spoke to who had worked across Asia said they enjoyed at least as much freedom of intellectual inquiry in the Chinese capital as elsewhere. This is opening up with a distinct purpose, as the long-time China watcher Andrew Nathan writes: "This lightly patrolled free zone is not the antithesis but the twin of the permanent crackdown on the political frontier, where the few who insist on testing the regime are crowded to the cultural margin and generally ignored."

This tap was ostentatiously turned off in the immediate run-up to and during the Olympics. Back in 1993, China was embarrassed before the world when its bid to host the games in 2000 was defeated amid public criticism of its human rights record. When it later submitted its application for 2008, the Chinese government promised to be "open in every aspect" and to improve civil liberties. This provided a face-saver for all concerned. The international community could claim to be working towards universal human rights, although everyone knew that China's enhanced global status was the real cause of the change of heart.

In many ways, the Chinese system had been ideally suited for such a grand venture. With no budget constraints, no transparent tendering and a large pool of docile migrant labour, the authorities completed, on time, not only the thirty-one Olympic venues, but also three new subway lines and the largest airport terminal in the world.

With so much to do, the government saw manifestations of dissent during this period as especially inefficient and harmful. Repression was intensified to ensure "order". Human rights groups reported the imprisonment of activists campaigning for causes from land rights to AIDS. Several dissidents were punished by "re-education through labour", sent to prison camps without trial. A number of ordinary citizens who used the traditional and permitted method of petitioning over local grievances were detained. Arrests for "endangering state security" rose to their highest level in eight years. Lawyers defending activists in court were subjected to detentions, beatings and threats. "It was hoped that the Games would act as a catalyst for reform but much of the current wave of repression against activists and journalists is occurring not in spite of, but actually because of the Olympics," Amnesty International reported.

The Chinese assumed that with so much global political and corporate investment already committed for the Beijing games, protests from Western governments would be muted. They were mainly right and a little wrong. A number of incidents took place that proved deeply embarrassing. But in the end the West did what it usually does. It went with the money.

At the start of the year the film director Steven Spielberg resigned as artistic adviser to the Games in protest at China's role in the humanitarian crisis in Darfur. China had long dismissed international concern over its support for Sudan's tyrannical government, which is accused of fomenting a conflict in which at least 200,000 people have been killed and two million forced from their homes. Spielberg declared that he and other Hollywood stars would have no involvement in the "genocide Olympics". That condemnation was by no means misplaced, but human rights groups have been equally frustrated with the West's consistently weak response to the long conflict.

Tibet was another area where China's record has come under sustained scrutiny. In March 2008, five months before the Games, Chinese forces broke up protests by some three hundred Buddhist monks in the capital, Lhasa, that had been called to mark the anniversary of the failed uprising of 1959. More than a thousand Tibetans were detained. The Chinese government said rioters killed at least nineteen people. Tibetan exiles said soldiers killed dozens of civilians. Many Chinese responded furiously to Western coverage, or what they were told of Western coverage. On the MSN message board "I love China" was a popular posting, alongside "I hate CNN".

What ensued on the streets of European capitals further inflamed such thinking. In London, on 6 April 2008 protesters disrupted the processional Olympic torch as it was taken through the city. The scenes in Paris the following day were even more chaotic. The Chinese government encouraged a mood of wounded patriotic pride. Many Chinese were told that Western television had deliberately doctored coverage. One student regaled me over the coverage of Tibet by the BBC: "It might as well have been written by the Dalai Lama." Another, who had been studying in London on the day of the torch protest, said she had taken part in a counter-protest by pro-government Chinese students. "There were thousands of us defending our country, but we simply disappeared from your screens." My protestations that she might have been misinformed fell on deaf ears.

This was a defining period for Western governments. Should they take a stand on civil liberties? Or should they try to keep their powder dry in order not to risk the strategic and business relationship with the world's third largest economy? In the end they did a bit of both, managing to frustrate human rights groups and enrage the Chinese government.

The German Chancellor, Angela Merkel, caused fury by meeting the Dalai Lama in Berlin. Her predecessor, Gerhard Schröder, said of Merkel's decision: "Some recent situations have hurt Chinese people's feelings, and I regret it." He was speaking at a seminar in Beijing on "China's development and world harmony". Within a year, relations had "returned to normal", after Merkel followed up her attendance at the Games with another visit to China. Britain's Gordon Brown appeared consistently confused. On his first visit to Beijing, he focused almost exclusively on trade, barely mentioning human rights. As the Tibet riots escalated, he declared that he would not be going to the opening ceremony, but he would attend the closing festivities. Nobody quite knew what that denoted. When the battered Olympic torch reached Downing Street on that chaotic day in April, he agreed to receive it, to be photographed next to it, but would not touch it.

It was the French who suffered most. Their President, Nicolas Sarkozy, initially decided that he would infuse his country's foreign policy with new concern for human rights. He suggested he might pull out from the opening ceremony unless "progress" was made over Tibet. That threat, and the torch protests in Paris, led to an extraordinary anti-French backlash. China's government successfully mobilised a popular campaign against Western interference. The main target was the French supermarket chain Carrefour, the most successful foreign store in China. For several days in April it was subjected to a series of noisy protests. The Chinese government was quite happy to advertise the wrath of the people on national and international news, and to allow its citizens to use the internet to exhort each other to join in. The goal was threefold: to play to a swelling patriotism ahead of the Games, to punish France and to warn off future miscreants.

The Chinese government is a past master in the exercise of implicit power. Unlike Russia, it tries to avoid bellicose language. Its speciality is controlled menace, reinforced in the knowledge of its growing economic strength. On the eve of the Olympics, countries that treated China with "respect" were told that they would benefit as a result. The "skip France" campaign succeeded in all its goals. On departing Beijing after the opening ceremony, Sarkozy sought to ingratiate himself with his hosts, declaring the games deserved a "gold medal", only to swing back again, meeting the Dalai Lama in December. France's business leaders fumed at the lost opportunities, and their counterparts in other countries were excited at the prospect of snapping up an extra contract or two at the expense of the French. This competitive bidding over human rights was not new: it was done with as much alacrity during the Cold War. The British corporate lobby was given a further boost when David Miliband slipped in a change in relations with Tibet just when everyone's backs were turned. On the eve of the American elections that autumn, the Foreign Secretary issued a written parliamentary statement formally recognising Chinese sovereignty over the disputed region. Miliband argued that he was only bringing the UK into line with the US and the EU and he was only removing an anomaly, both of which were true. But the point was made. The Chinese were pleased.

The Olympics produced a huge surge in patriotic ardour, and by extension an endorsement of the pact. Some Western diplomats point out that the more they or NGOs or journalists criticise the Chinese leadership, the more it seems to bolster rather than undermine the regime's popularity at home. In July 2008, the Pew Research Center published a survey that was widely reported back in China. Pew summarised it thus: "As they eagerly await the Beijing

Olympics, the Chinese people express extraordinary levels of satisfaction with the way things are going in their country and with their
nation's economy. With more than eight in ten having a positive
view of both, China ranks number one among 24 countries on both
measures in the 2008 survey. These findings represent a dramatic
improvement in national contentment from earlier in the decade."

Chinese state media and the blogosphere seized on these findings. They were equally enamoured of a book published at the time
of the Olympics, *How East Asians View Democracy*. Published by
Columbia University, the book compared and contrasted eight East
Asian countries, and concluded that public satisfaction with the
regime was highest in China. Satisfaction was less pronounced in
countries more associated with democracy – South Korea, Taiwan,
the Philippines, Hong Kong and Japan, which scored lowest. Few
questioned the methodology of these surveys. They appeared to
reflect the mood at the time, one of defiance in the face of criticism
and pride in the wake of success. That pride was reinforced by
the table-topping fifty-one gold medals the host country won at
the games.

Yet throughout the month of sporting action, much of Beijing
resembled a ghost town. Many people who normally received visas
were refused entry. Hotels, at least those not close to the Olympic
Village, reported lower than usual occupancy. A helpful "legal guide"
advised athletes, officials, reporters and spectators on how to behave.
They were told to avoid "subversive activities" or the "display of religious, political or racial banners". Sporadic protests did take place,
among followers of the Falun Gong sect and the "Free Tibet" movement, but, in front of Western camera crews, the demonstrators
were summarily hauled away. Some websites were blocked; others
were unblocked after official representations were made via the IOC,
only for most of those to be blocked again after the Games.
Residents reported that a number of eccentric regulations suddenly
applied. Restaurants were prevented from serving dog meat, for fear
of upsetting foreigners, while a number of shops were not allowed to

sell gin, as officials said it could be used in the making of Molotov cocktails.

One of the first things I do on my arrival in Beijing on a cold November day is to take a walk around the Olympic Stadium, the Birds Nest. I want to get a flavour of what it must have been like. I sense a slight hangover. The building itself, only a few months on, already looks a little tatty. The price of admission hardly justifies a desultory costume exhibition on one corner of the ground. Police warily guard the home straight of the running track, for reasons I cannot fathom. Still, the tourists continue to come, particularly from other regions of China, cameras at the ready to capture a shot of their national stadium.

I wonder whether the Olympics really did mark China's successful arrival on the world stage or whether they merely provided a brief fillip before a harsher reality dawned. Nicholas Bequelin of Human Rights Watch reminds me that China continues to have more than sixty capital offences, among them non-violent crimes such as tax fraud. It executes more people than the rest of the world combined. That practice has also become big business: up to 95 per cent of commercial organ transplants are obtained from executed prisoners. Then there is the one-child policy, the most vivid area where the state continues to intrude into the private realm. The official line is that the policy, introduced thirty years ago, has prevented 400 million extra births, which would have stymied China's economic growth and damaged social stability. Economists predict a major workforce shortage in the medium term as the present population ages. That part is discussed relatively openly. What is rarely mentioned are the human rights consequences – the infanticides, forced adoptions and various other abuses arising from the policy.

We discuss the tortuous path trodden by the West. Bequelin suggests politicians are not exclusively culpable. They take their lead from major corporations. International law firms, he says, are increasingly loath to criticise China for fear of losing business. The same goes for media conglomerates, indeed for just about all commercial companies. The underlying problem, he suggests, is not one of principle – China has signed fourteen international treaties enshrining human rights and continues to insist on "progress" – but the need to save face. The reason the authorities clamp down so hard on dissidents is their propensity to criticise China in front of foreigners. The task is to find a new language and new mechanisms with which to address these problems. The old Cold War agenda, with its easy certitudes about one system blazing a trail and the other languishing in moral degradation, has long gone. Issues such as multi-party elections and free expression – and the relationship of the population to them – are far more complex, less black and white in contemporary and more affluent China. "The human rights industry needs to evolve," Bequelin says. "We need to find a new language which talks to people who have grown used to consumerism and a one-party system."

Many unsavoury practices seemed to have returned. Corruption scandals continued unabated. The most damaging was one in which several children died and thousands were made ill from drinking milk formula adulterated with melamine, an industrial compound used to cheat nutrition tests. The official media, once again, began by trying to play down the affair, until the full extent was exposed. The affair caused further damage to the reputation of Chinese products worldwide. Officials warned food and drugs makers of the punishments, including the death sentence, if they used the economic crisis to cut corners.

The global downturn is top of the agenda when I meet Michael Pettis and his students. Pettis is a professor at Peking University's Guanghua School of Management. Even though it is Saturday evening, he is conducting a seminar on macro-economics with eleven young men in a corridor meeting area of the economics block. Pettis nominates one of his pupils to lead the discussion. The students talk variously about the predictions of the depth of the recession, fiscal reform, banking liquidity and the pitfalls of both inflation and deflation. They discuss the extent to which the crisis is already affecting China and how far the growth rate might fall. Pettis leaves them to it, only occasionally chipping in. He asks his charges if they have seen a recent television interview with the Prime Minister about the state of the economy. "Wen looked really terrified. They are really afraid of something," he remarks. They nod in agreement. "What is it?" No answer is offered.

We walk down the road and through a narrow doorway into a large windowless cavern, a club called D22. Pettis combines his specialism in financial markets with running one of the capital's most vibrant music venues. As he fixes me a gin and tonic, he points out that the current crop of students is the first in a long while that will struggle. Some 80 per cent of the students who completed university in the summer of 2008 did not have jobs to go to on graduation, and many have still not found work long after. So worried have they become about finding jobs in the private sector that up to one million students have taken the civil service exam to compete for government jobs, a rise of 25 per cent on the previous year. With each position receiving an average of eighty graduate applications, the frustrations are great. According to the newspaper of the People's Liberation Army, applications to join the military are the highest for a generation.

For many young people, influenced by their parents' harrowing tales of life during the Cultural Revolution, the ability to be apolitical is seen as a privilege. They are keen to get good marks and to enjoy what little free time their busy timetables permit. Everything else is considered a distraction, even a danger. With employment prospects contracting, it comes as little surprise that people have become even more circumspect about "causing trouble". A popular saying goes: "No one will smash his own foot with a rock." Pettis talks of the mismatch between a "dramatic cultural liberalisation similar to that of the US in the 1960s" alongside "the worst education system for the smartest kids" that remains rooted in the old practice of very long hours and learning by rote. "They are the world's greatest test takers, but the complaints I hear from financial services managers is that many of the Chinese graduates they hire can't cope with ideas outside the box."

Caution may be one explanation for the reluctance among some to criticise, but there is invariably a more confident justification, too. The following day I am in a private room in a venerable, one hundred-year-old tea shop, Sheng Xi Fu, drinking extraordinary gold tea from Yunnan province. I am with two young entrepreneurs, Chenggen Hu and Kevin Ao. Both are part of a trend of returnees from Silicon Valley, people who have honed their business skills in the US and are seeking to put them to good use in their home country, investing in semi-conductor companies. Although they would not describe themselves as such, they could be considered converts to the "new left" movement in China that even before the economic crisis had become concerned about the unquestioning adoration of free market theories. "For the past ten to fifteen years we just copied the West. Until recently, I thought China would be a purely capitalist society. But the crisis shows that the US is not a good example," Chenggen says. "Before now, you would have been denounced in academic circles if you advocated economic intervention. I suppose China is lucky that the government was not so pro-market. Now even those professors who graduated in the US are questioning the American model." What of the social system? "The Chinese middle class has always wanted to live the American life – a house, car, kids, dogs, that kind of thing. But it isn't open to all of society."

In spite of the startling demographic shift from countryside to cities of the past two decades, China's 1.3 billion population still comprises, by most estimates, around 800 million peasants, most of them poorly educated. The self-proclaimed middle class may be growing fast, and in sheer numbers it may even have reached 200 million, but it is still a fraction of the total. "Free elections are good in theory, but not now," says Kevin. "With the vote in the wrong hands, the wrong people get selected who then manipulate the electorate." I protest the rather obvious point that this is the last refuge of the elite that wishes not to share power, that this is just what was said in the West before suffrage became universal. It is, he counters, a matter of education and a sense of responsibility. The issue of ethnicity is also cited. Some fifty-five minorities are represented across China. "It is only a short step to imagining how China would break apart if it became a democracy," says Chenggen. "There are too many examples of political change that bring division. Chinese people want a stable life."

I question them about the specifics of China's human rights record. I start with Tiananmen Square, a subject that until now I have been wary of pushing. Kevin says his brother-in-law was one of the protesters, but left the scene the day before the crackdown. He has a good friend who stayed, and who subsequently spent a year in prison. He is now a successful businessman who lives abroad, even though apparently he has the right to return. "The students were good-hearted but misguided," he says. He recalls a dispute in his family at the time: "My father was against the students. Everyone else was in favour. History will prove him right." Kevin says his brother is a senior party figure who has been responsible for the reconstruction of Chengdu, the capital of Sichuan province, after the quake. Many local people complained about the lack of compensation. Kevin says that while their grievances may have been justified, they should not have protested during the Olympics, insulting their country.

Before I mention Singapore, he gets in there first. "The Singapore model is best for us. In many ways Singaporeans are more Chinese than we are. They want even more control than we do." I cite three alternative models that China might have adopted. One is the brief liberal experiment in the Russia of the late Gorbachev and early Yeltsin years. Another is the tumultuous democracy of Taiwan. The third is India, the world's most populous democracy. Each produces pained expressions. Just look at the economic performance of these countries and compare them to China, they say. "Western people are not open-minded about political systems," Chenggen says. "They can't accept that other systems might be good."

Chenggen and Kevin may not be as well travelled as my Singapore friends, but they appear to be drawing similar conclusions. Again I am confronted by the realisation that some of the most pro-government elements are those with the strongest Western educations. Perhaps I should not be surprised. I had seen enough evidence of the "MBA crowd" in London, Europe and in the US, people of all manner of nationalities, who for two decades defined themselves through the global power of money rather than any issues of political engagement or protest. Their Chinese counterparts are merely seeking to emulate them.

The Olympics had shown how far China had modernised, but just not in the direction of liberal democracy. The state still tells people how many children they can have. It still restricts movements for the urban and rural poor. But otherwise it has largely withdrawn from people's everyday lives, giving Chinese citizens unprecedented freedoms to consume and to organise their professional and personal development. This increased personal freedom has been matched with ever more sophisticated control of the public sphere. In the 1980s, many Chinese intellectuals supported multiparty elections. Since Tiananmen Square, political reform has been redefined. While there are still prominent thinkers who believe in the country's incremental embrace of democracy, many modern intellectuals argue that China would do better to avoid elections altogether and focus rather on making the one-party state more rules based and more responsive. The party is nothing if not thorough. It has begun to rely on opinion polls, focus groups, the internet and other consultations to keep it in touch with public opinion. A model of "deliberative authoritarianism" has emerged that for the moment at least appears to have increased the legitimacy of the one-party state and lessened calls within the mainstream population for what it understands to be Western-style democracy.

What of those small offshoots of China that have had more experience of what we think of as democracy? Hong Kong may not be as bustling as it once was. Perhaps it no longer feels it can compete with the economic might of Shanghai and Shenzhen. In certain respects the "one country, two systems" pledge of the Chinese, as they ushered the British out in 1997, has been preserved. Although the press has clipped its own wings, newspapers and television are still more inquiring than those on the mainland. The standard for trouble-making is set by the ever vibrant *Apple Daily*. Its owner, the entrepreneur Jimmy Lai, has resisted all cajoling and threats to tone down his tabloid, including an officially encouraged boycott by advertisers. Talk of Tiananmen Square does not have to take place in hushed tones; religion is openly practised. It is remarkable to see followers of the Falun Gong, banned and persecuted just a few miles away across the bay, mounting noisy protests. The original Joint Declaration signed in 1984 guaranteed the "Hong Kong way of life". The Chinese authorities regarded the later pro-democracy changes introduced by Chris Patten, the outgoing governor, as contradicting what London had agreed to. Chinese academics are keen to argue that, even until the early 1980s, the colonial rulers of Hong Kong were less amenable to democratic representation, free expression and free association than Chinese rule is now.

For activists, journalists, academics and others who are politically engaged in Hong Kong, the danger lies less in codified law and more in self-censorship, in fear of the more subtle consequences of speaking out. Joseph Cheng is one of a dwindling band of Hong Kong-based academics prepared to agitate openly for the pro-democracy movement. "I am an activist, I'll remain an activist, but I cannot be optimistic," says Cheng, who is Professor of Political Science at Hong Kong's City University. "Most people, even here, think that there is no obvious alternative. People are afraid of change, particularly in difficult times. They think that if you get rid of the party you will get chaos."

Deeply rooted in the minds of the rulers, and in the burgeoning middle classes, is this fear of *luan*, chaos. The authorities thoroughly research the potential sources of trouble. "Party officials are assiduous in studying historical comparisons," Cheng says. "For example, they have looked at the Solidarity experience in Poland in dealing with their own trade unions; they compare the worship of the 'Polish Pope' with Falun Gong." The political opening of the past ten years has been heavily circumscribed. The day-to-day administrator of Hong Kong, the Chief Executive, is appointed, not elected. Parliament consists of ordinary constituencies and "functional constituencies", constructs created to give the business community disproportionate influence over parliament. As in mainland China, the Hong Kong business elite have worked closely with the Communist Party. These two forces have seen eye to eye on the dangerous potential of a fully functioning democracy, ever fearful that it could provide the catalyst for unrest. Cheng is writing a book about Tiananmen Square and takes part in rallies and other activities organised by the Hong Kong Alliance in support of human rights. He notes that the annual vigil in June 2008 was smaller and more muted than before. Part of that could be explained by the Sichuan earthquake and enthusiasm for the Olympics. But researchers at the rival Hong Kong University detect a slight shift in the public mood. Its survey found that the majority of Hong Kong residents still believe that the Chinese students were right to protest in 1989 and that the government was wrong to crack down so hard. But the proportion of respondents who believed that human rights in China had improved since 1989 had risen steadily, to 85 per cent. Some 77 per cent expected those rights to improve further in the future.

Cheng says everyone is being more careful, even in the comparatively freer environment of Hong Kong. "Covert pressure is now strong. I am the only senior professor who organises things. Even here you don't become a dean or a president, and you don't receive research funds if you speak out too much. During 1989 intellectuals had low living standards, so they felt they had less to lose. Since then the party has been very skilful in co-opting the elites, and now many academics here and in China are also doing quite well."

Academics are just one of several groups that have been successfully co-opted by the regime. I recount to Cheng the conversations I have had in China about the uprising of 1989 and the choices made after. They are, he says, fairly representative of the consensus. People have reconciled themselves to their political defeat, because they have succeeded economically, he says. "The post-Tiananmen generation has made peace with the government. The general view now is that the students were right in principle, but got it wrong in practice. By confronting the regime so directly, they gave it no wriggle room. A lot will say gradual reforms are best." Cheng predicts no major ructions in a system that "still functions sufficiently well" and does not disparage the "deliberative" approach of the Communist Party. "They are experimenting with political reforms within the party. They are trying to be more responsive. Because the leadership doesn't want to give democracy, as we understand it, it must be more responsive." That is surely, then, another variation on the pact, I suggest. "There is, even in a financial downturn, a chance of improvement in living standards if you don't challenge the authorities. As long as you don't cause trouble you are quite free. If you do, you quickly become an outcast. The police come for you, the tax authorities come for you, your friends and colleagues are more wary of returning your calls." It comes down, Cheng says, to a "simple cost benefit analysis". The costs are high, but the benefits are high, too. But what happens, I wonder, if the benefits start to drop?

My final stop is Taipei, capital of Taiwan, or the Republic of China, or the twenty-third province of the People's Republic of China, depending on your point of view. I had come to look at the pact from the opposite end of the telescope, at a country which, from a Western "democratisation" agenda, ticks all the boxes.

After forty years of martial law, Taiwanese have for more than a decade enjoyed a period of turbulent freedom. For many foreigners, their only knowledge of Taiwanese politics is television footage of members of parliament embroiled in punch-ups. For many Chinese, Taiwan provides the perfect advertisement for the perils of democracy. Eight years of rule by the Democratic People's Party (DPP) have just come to an end. The long-time party of power, the Kuomintang, or KMT, is firmly back in charge, having reinvented itself, at least for the purpose of the election, as a force for democracy. Yet, just days before I arrive, the former DPP Prime Minister, Chen Shui-Bian, is led from his home in handcuffs on embezzlement charges. His party protests that this will be a show trial, arguing that the judges have never come down hard on KMT politicians whenever they put their hands into the till. It was no coincidence, after all, that Taiwan's former leader, Chiang Kai Shek, was known as Cash My Cheque.

I decide that I should first pay homage to the man himself. When I arrive at the Chiang Kai Shek memorial hall I am told its name has been changed. The DPP government tried to remove as many monuments as it could of Chiang. Eventually, it was forced to reinstate the statue of the man who took on Mao in the Chinese Civil War, lost and fled to Taiwan in 1949, from where he ruled a government in exile for twenty-five years. The National Taiwan Democracy Monument, as it is now called, is housed in lavish grounds that also accommodate the National Theatre and National Concert Hall – shades of the Lincoln Memorial and the Mall in Washington, DC. It is no surprise that so much of modern Taiwan is modelled on America, for years the sponsor and paymaster of a dictatorial regime. What mattered was that Chiang was anti-Communist.

I walk the eighty-nine steps (eighty-nine being Chiang's age at his death) to reach the gargantuan marble figure of a man seated, smiling and holding a walking stick. The same pose is replicated in other statues around the island. The museum downstairs is equally beguiling. The walls are covered with photographs showing Chiang meeting world leaders (or at least those few that recognised Taiwan after Richard Nixon had famously gone to mainland China for a spot of ping-pong diplomacy in 1972). Chiang's statesmen friends included Nicaragua's General Somoza, Augusto Pinochet of Chile and other unsavoury types. The museum's *pièces de résistance* are the two shining black Cadillac Fleetwoods, one from the 1950s, the other from the 1970s, gleaming three-ton monsters of limousines from which Chiang would survey his island.

Taiwan's fraught history casts an intriguing light on the double standards of the Cold War. As long as a country was pro-Western in its geo-strategic loyalties, its approach to democracy and human rights internally was glossed over. That much applied to Chiang and his declaration of martial law. Then, just as Taiwan introduced real freedoms, it was abandoned by the West as it threw in its lot with the authoritarian Chinese mainland.

This point is emphasised repeatedly by Dennis Engbarth, an American journalist and long-time resident. He has spent much of his life trying to persuade anyone who will listen that Taiwan's democracy is setting an example for others to follow, and that it should not be abandoned. Few people are listening. Engbarth then embarks on an impassioned defence of Taiwan's independence which he and other supporters of the DPP see as imperilled by the advance of China, its money and Western ambivalence. He reminds me that when the Taiwanese held their first fully democratic elections in 1996, the Americans then still professed to care. The Chinese government tried to prevent the impending democratic experiment by conducting military exercises just off the coast. President Clinton sent two aircraft carriers to ensure the elections proceeded. In little over a decade, Engbarth says, Taiwan has come a long way, overtaking Hong Kong in the democratic stakes, and serving as a beacon for others to follow. Which other country can boast multi-party elections, freedom of speech, a growing human rights culture and a per capita GDP of $30,000 a year so soon after being ruled by a dictatorship for half a century? "It's a rare case of bottom-up democracy, although some people don't realise it is." None of this, he says, is thanks to the international community. The more Taiwan democratises, the less anyone seems to care. The double standards were most acute during the Bush administration. For all the neo-Conservatives' ardour for "democracy promotion", the White House saw Taiwan, particularly its more obdurate DPP government, as an impediment to progress with China. "Bush was upset with Taiwan for trying to deepen democracy," Engbarth says.

Apart from a few Latin American countries – a throwback to the old dictatorships – and one or two others, nobody has an official embassy here any more. With its gleaming Taipei 101 tower, the tallest building in the world until relatively recently, parts of the city centre look modern. But compared to those in some cities in mainland China, most of the buildings seem older and shabbier. The cars are less polished. Scooters are the preferred mode of transport, giving the streets a chaotic, noisy feel. Much of the place seems like a throwback to a bygone era, an America whose priorities have moved on.

Andrew Yang, of the Chinese Council of Advanced Policy Studies, points me to some statistics. Taiwan's investment in China has just reached a staggering $70 billion, almost catching up America's. In other words, Taiwan and China are already heavily integrated, and that is just the way Taiwan's business community wants it. Yang insists there is no appetite for going back. According to a recent opinion poll, although fewer than 12 per cent of the population are in favour of political unification, only 17 per cent now support independence. Change will come slowly, but it will come, and economic interests will take the lead. "Most people want the status quo, in order to let the next generation determine Taiwan's status," Yang says. "For the moment people are keen to develop other links with the mainland."

That is the strategy of the new Taiwanese government, which has unashamedly developed warm ties with the Chinese Communists. Secure a military truce and pursue financial ties. Yang insists that neither of the two main parties will barter Taiwan's civil liberties in return for economic gain. "We have ninety-eight political parties here, including our very own Communist Party. I love taking

Chinese officials to the Central Administration building, and showing the Falun Gong lot protesting outside. I tell them that when they allow that and religion, then they will make progress." But with so many Taiwanese now travelling to and working on the mainland – more than a million regular travellers or short-term residents in China out of Taiwan's population of twenty-three million – I have my doubts. Such rights will surely prove expendable, as the mother country absorbs the tiny island.

Within weeks of the KMT's return to power, a deal was signed establishing charter flights between Taipei and mainland cities. In December 2008 those links were significantly expanded, with more than dozen routes every day to a growing number of destinations. Over time, personal experience will have a more pronounced influence than the politics, as people see the economic benefits of assimilation into the mainland, probably sweetened by a promise of autonomy of sorts – not unlike Hong Kong. Will Taiwan stay as it is, a strange mixture of 1950s Americana, ancient Chinese custom, Japanese tradition and a sense of defiance that isolation often brings? I doubt it. Is this a case of Cuba in reverse, a case of catch it while you can, before China's inexorable power absorbs this island, without a shot being fired?

Such was the nervousness during the Olympics that television stations across China were ordered to delay "live" broadcasts by ten seconds, to give them a chance to abandon transmission in case Free Tibet or other protesters caused trouble. Half a year later, the authorities in Beijing expected no such embarrassment as they planned their live coverage from Washington of Barack Obama's inauguration speech. The incoming President was only a few minutes into his address when he declared: "Recall that earlier generations faced down fascism and communism not just with missiles and tanks, but with sturdy alliances and enduring convictions." The broadcast abruptly cut away from the lectern, leaving the anchorwoman in Beijing and the Washington correspondent on the studio screen mumbling a conversation together about Obama's economic policy, in a desperate attempt to fill the airtime. They made valiant efforts over several minutes to ensure that viewers did not hear the President's thoughts about liberty, particularly his sentence "those who cling to power through corruption and deceit and the silencing of dissent, know that you are on the wrong side of history". The time difference – it was 1.00 a.m. in Beijing – ensured that not as many people were watching as might have been. Just to be sure, the official censors deleted these and other offending remarks from the translations that followed later in the day. It did not take long, however, for the internet to be filled with comment about the ultra-sensitivity of the state. More people than before went to other sites to watch the speech in full.

Any hopes that the clampdown during the Olympics would be relaxed once the foreign guests had all gone home had proven illusory. Censorship, particularly on the internet, increased. A number of campaigns were launched against what the authorities called dangerous or vulgar websites. In one move, nineteen sites were shut down for failing to censor inappropriate content which was considered harmful to young people's physical and mental health. A top official in China's Internet Affairs Bureau warned colleagues to be vigilant: "You have to check the channels one by one, the programs one by one, the pages one by one," he said. "You must not miss any step. You must not leave any unchecked corners."

In December 2008, some three hundred intellectuals had caused a stir when they posted an online political manifesto they called Charter 08. It was issued to mark the sixtieth anniversary of the UN Declaration on Human Rights. The name was intended to recall that of Charter 77, the human rights manifesto circulated by dissidents in Communist Czechoslovakia in 1997. This new document called for everything from private ownership of land to multi-party democracy; it said social tensions and protests were increasing, "indicating a tendency towards a disastrous loss of control". Democratisation, it concluded, could "no longer be delayed".

The Communist Party's success, and comparative popularity, has rested on four pillars: a military security blanket presence, control over the media, the co-opting of the most important groups in society (particularly the middle class) and double-digit economic growth. Is the edifice that transformed China's place in the world and sustained the party in power about to founder as the economy falters? Many intellectuals and members of the middle class – on whom the party depended for its support – had adopted a purely pragmatic view of one-party rule. They had seen it as the best means of ensuring security and prosperity, and they had seen it succeed. So, is the pact beginning to break? It is certainly facing its most severe test since 1989. The dilemma for the leadership is acute. If the party loosens up too much it could unleash a repeat of the protests that shook the state at Tiananmen. If it does not provide enough safety valves for the discontented, it could break apart under the strain.

Such predictions were reinforced not just by the economic data – the sudden fall in growth rates, the rise in unemployment and the potentially dangerous demographic shifts involved. With tens of millions of workers no longer required in the cities, what would happen if many of them refused to go home and stay in their home villages? Those fears were reinforced by attempts of dissidents to organise. Yet stability will be most threatened only if a large enough section of the population concludes that it cannot afford to sit out the crisis and that political change would be worth the upheaval. For many Chinese, particularly those who remember the old days under Mao, what matters is that they have more freedom to determine the course of their own lives than they had before.

The pact made with the post-Tiananmen generation, and the political and human rights clampdown that accompanied it, has been remarkably successful in delivering Chinese from the chaos they so fear. Yet this pact is not static. It is dynamic and uncertain. Those who have been co-opted into it have yet to determine whether it is temporary – the "China isn't ready for greater public freedoms" school of thought – or whether it marks a principled and long-term view that such rights are inimical to China's needs. In other words, are the human rights set out in the UN declaration a Western construct, as ultra-nationalists argue, or will China, in time, begin to adopt them? For the moment, though, many Chinese believe that only by keeping out of the public realm have they won more liberty in the private realm. They ask if they could have achieved the prosperity and security that they demanded from the pact by any other means.

In any case, the West's performance has surely not convinced them of another route. When Zhou Xiaochuan, the Governor of the People's Bank of China, spoke of "the inherent vulnerabilities and systemic risks" in the dollar-based global economy, chancelleries around the world took note, and took fright. They could see that he was talking about more than currencies. They knew that, whatever the short-term turbulence that lay ahead, he was reflecting China's greater assertiveness about its role in the world and its greater confidence in the political model it had chosen to adopt.

3

RUSSIA: ANGRY CAPITALIST

*"Ordinary people wearied of their unprecedented freedom
to criticise the government because it had brought no
improvement"* – Lilia Shevtsova

IT IS A SUMMER SATURDAY AFTERNOON AT THE MOSCOW
Beach Club. The sand has been imported from the Maldives.
Champagne and fresh lobsters are being served, and we're invited
outside for the entertainment. Two MCs are extolling the virtues of
a luxury car, while pole dancers are gyrating on a platform. It is
drizzling. I enter into conversation with a young man who works for
the British department store B&Q. He berates me over the UK's
"aggressive" foreign policy towards Russia, while munching on and
slurping his seafood. I can't be bothered to answer and make my
excuses. I start talking to Russia's top television football commentator, Viktor Gusev, and we engage in a more enjoyable exchange
about the relative merits of each of our countries' national teams.

My spirits lighten further when the band topping the bill
begins its set. Mumi Troll have been around for years, with their mix
of rock and balladeering. My friend Art Troitsky, Russia's top rock
promoter, is invited on to the stage to introduce them, and, as they
play their hour-long set, I understand why they are so popular. I
make out some of the lyrics, from the comprehensible "I left my

motherland behind" in one song to the incomprehensible "don't inject yourself with a school of dolphins" in another. Later, Art takes me backstage. This time it's not fancy cocktails, but malt whisky served in plastic cups and some very good chat with the band, and their lead singer, Ilya Lagutenko. They leave on their coach. It is midnight. We move on, out of town, to another beach party, at Rublyovka beach. Normal-looking young Russians – no swagger, no bling – dance to a Brazilian samba band. Others are swimming in the river. As ever with Russia, I am disheartened and heartened in quick succession.

Russia's embracing of conspicuous consumption was the most pronounced of any emerging market. I first went to the country in the late 1970s, and have been a regular visitor since, including two spells of working as a correspondent, in the mid-eighties, and during the heady years of the early nineties. I saw the Soviet Union in stagnation and not-so-blissful isolation. The joke was "we pretend to work, they pretend to pay us". I saw it in the turbulent years of Mikhail Gorbachev's opening up through *glasnost* and *perestroika*, returning to see his plans first undermined, then accelerated by Boris Yeltsin. After the unsuccessful putsch of 1991 and the collapse of the USSR that it precipitated, the new Russia underwent a new revolution. It was as much a revolution of the individual mind as it was of the political world. Millions of Russians lost their fear, began questioning authority and embraced the free expression that blossomed.

That is, of course, not how this era was subsequently portrayed by Vladimir Putin. Instead, the 1990s were to become known as "the decade of chaos". Such thinking revolves around a narrative of "the Russia we lost" (a term used at the time from the title of a popular and compelling film by Stanislav Govorukhin). Many Russians see this as the era of a gold-digging elite combining with the criminal underworld to divide up the spoils; many in the West berate themselves for losing the opportunity to consolidate Russia's move towards democracy. The greater Western error, which was manifested around the world, was to see free markets and democracy as indistinguishable. It began with "shock therapy", the monetarist theory that decreed the privatisation of almost anything that belonged to the state. I remember attending countless press conferences held by the economics and finance ministers, watching as their Western advisers acted as their puppet masters. These Westerners displayed an excess of zeal and a shortage of political foresight. The West's overall approach during the 1990s was a mix of condescension, ingratiation and insensitivity. Russian liberals responded with a cultural obeisance that would later transform itself into resentment.

An entire country's natural resources, mainly oil and gas, were put up for sale, at rock-bottom prices. They were snapped up by those in power, close to power, lucky or smart. The first generation of oligarchs arose in a society almost free of rules. Between 1991 and 1996, the Russian state effectively absented itself from the policing of society. Distinctions between legality and illegality, morality and immorality barely existed. There were no hard and fast definitions of organised crime, money laundering or extortion; by implication, all commercial transactions were illegal and legal at the same time. These people worked in tandem with the political and security elite, all of whom shared in the spoils.

The first phase of the embrace of capitalism came to a sudden halt in 1998 as "pyramid" investments and other wealth-siphoning schemes came crashing down. Russia stunned international investors by defaulting on its debts and triggering a run on the rouble. As Yeltsin's authority collapsed, the oligarchs consolidated their position. The most important of these oligarchs was Boris Berezovsky. He had taken control of Channel One television, called ORT, and had open access to the people who counted – Yeltsin's daughter and her husband. Together they orchestrated the government, chopping and changing prime ministers (in Yeltsin's eight years as President he appointed five prime ministers). All the while, even as a tiny minority enriched itself, infrastructure collapsed. Tens of millions of state workers – from soldiers, to police, doctors and teachers – saw their already worthless salaries fail to be paid for months on end. Life expectancy declined; several contagious diseases that had been eliminated in the USSR returned, schools and hospitals were dilapidated.

Of the people I knew, those who had dealt with money did well. Those with talent in other areas, from science to the arts, teachers and doctors, saw not just their living standards collapse but their sense of pride and identity wither. They had invested many hopes in the new order, and had felt let down. Yet for all the disappointments, Russians enjoyed unprecedented freedoms. The country opened up dramatically. I visited several previously closed regions, in one trip meeting a suspicious military top brass at the Arctic nuclear base at Novaya Zemlya, in another hiring a military helicopter in Kamchatka, close to Alaska, and inviting twenty members of the local community, including the priest, to join us. I recall hunting deer in the snows of Siberia with Mikhail Kalashnikov, the inventor of the assault rifle that bears his name. I ended up befriending, if that is the right term, one of the leaders of the 1991 coup, the former Prime Minister Valentin Pavlov, visiting him shortly after his release from Lefortovo prison. Everyone felt free to speak out. Newspapers sprang up, a whole new generation of journalists in dailies such as *Sevodnya* (Today) and *Nezavisimaya Gazeta* (the Independent) who felt unhindered by libel laws or other concerns over censorship. I got to know Svetlana Sorokina, one of Russia's best-known TV anchors, who had made her name in the late eighties, at the tail end of the Gorbachev era, by refusing to read out certain items of propaganda on the evening news. She and others like Yevgeny Kiselyov, with his Sunday night show *Itogi*, broke new ground in television news and analysis. They would talk excitedly about tough interviews they had done, or scandals that had been revealed. NTV was perhaps the biggest breakthrough, a new station funded by Vladimir Gusinsky, one of the most prominent of the first generations of oligarchs. It developed a new style of investigative reporting, political analysis – and satire.

Gusinsky epitomised the best and worst, a man of some political principle who nevertheless could not resist money. Like so many Russians of that period, he defined himself through his rapid accumulation of wealth. I got to know him and his wife quite well, and it was curious to watch an intelligent but unflamboyant theatre director succumb to the excesses of bling. In Moscow, an ordinary dinner would have to be a lavish banquet presided over by white-gloved waiters. In London, he could not resist showing me the swimming pool in his Chelsea mansion. In restaurants, he would enjoy sending back the lobster he had ordered, complaining that it was too small. At the same time, through NTV and *Sevodnya* he was determined to play his part in Russia's democratisation. Most damagingly, though, he seemed to confuse the democratic process with outcome. He and six other oligarchs, including Berezovsky, bankrolled Yeltsin's re-election campaign in 1996, allowing television to become propaganda tools again. The President's alcoholism and deteriorating health were not mentioned by Russian liberals, or by Western embassies. They knew exactly what was going on but decided that free expression should not get in the way of electoral success. They insisted that the ends justified the means, that if Yeltsin was forced out, Russia would return to a dark age of repression. Free expression was abused in the apparent cause of liberal democracy.

As the nineties drew to a close, Yeltsin had become a source of derision. The more his drinking bouts and the weaknesses of the economy were exposed, the louder the clamour became for "stability". Those same oligarchs who had manipulated the process to extend Yeltsin's tenure now saw the need for a quick and orderly succession. They trawled through a list of possible candidates, alighting on Putin, an undistinguished former KGB officer, who they had recently installed as the latest of their prime ministers. He performed well in that post for them, displaying a tough professionalism. His decision to wage war on rebels in Chechnya was proving popular. Russia was beginning to assert itself again.

On millennium night, Yeltsin startled his country by announcing that he was handing over to his Prime Minister, with immediate effect. Putin's rise met the needs not only of many ordinary Russians, but of corporate interest, too. In any case, democracy had been bankrupted well before he assumed his powers. Three months later, Putin secured the necessary "endorsement" of the people, thanks to an election that had been fixed by the oligarchs. They threw money at the campaign, just as they had done in 1996, and ensured that Putin's opponents were denounced at every turn. His more serious rivals such as the Mayor of Moscow, Yuri Luzhkov, and the former Prime Minister, Yevgeny Primakov, had been "encouraged" not to stand. Vladimir Potanin, one of the most prominent tycoons, said during the campaign of Putin: "We'll see if he delivers on his promises." Those promises were to restore order, but also to leave their respective business empires alone. That was their pact with him. This pact was more invidious than that in China and other states in transition because it was portrayed as being in the interests of democracy.

Putin did not take long to assert his authority, or to alter the terms of engagement with those who had installed him. Within weeks of taking over, and even before his "election", the Kremlin ordered the arrest of a well-known reporter from Radio Liberty. Andrei Babitsky's despatches from Chechnya posed a direct threat to Putin. One of the pretexts for the second Chechen war was the bombing of apartment blocks in three Russian cities, in which three hundred people were killed. Babitsky was one of those who investigated claims that the terrorist attacks could have been ordered by the Russian security forces. He was charged with spying, held in an isolation cell, interrogated and then handed over to the Chechen rebels, like a terrorist in exchange for a Russian soldier.

Putin's message was clear: the media must see itself as a mechanism for delivery, not as an outlet for criticism, least of all as a plaything for business. He then turned on the oligarchs. Gusinsky was detained, before he left for the UK, then Spain, then Israel. Then he went for Berezovsky, who hopped on his private jet and headed for Britain. Putin could have stopped them both, but appeared content to see the back of them. He assumed they would trouble him less from afar. Berezovsky did not oblige him. From his mansion outside London, he led a personal campaign against Putin and was the object of repeated extradition requests from the Kremlin. What mattered most to Putin was that Gusinsky and Berezovsky had been forced to give up their media power bases. Their stations and newspapers became organs of the Kremlin, but Putin had calculated that any damage to his reputation from the takeovers would be limited. He was right. In the height of this first purge, in November 2000, one poll found that only 7 per cent of Russians thought that the main networks were independent to begin with, against 79 per cent who thought they were dependent on the oligarchs. In other words, many wondered whether what they saw of democracy was worth saving.

Putin had changed the terms of his pact with the first generation of oligarchs; even though they had put him in power, he summoned several of them to a meeting within months of taking over and made the position plain. He had consolidated his power and rewritten the rules. These rules now read: I will leave you alone to make money; make sure I enjoy my cut, but steer well away from the public realm, unless I tell you otherwise. Those who challenged him would come to regret it.

In 2003, Mikhail Khodorkovsky, an oligarch who had become one of the major players with his oil corporation, Yukos, was seized on charges of fraud and tax evasion. He had riled the Kremlin not with his business expansion, but with his political ambitions, advertising his credentials as a potential rival to Putin and financing opposition parties in the lower house of parliament, the Duma. The arrest and subsequent trial sent shock waves through Russia and the international financial community. Putin wanted it known that nobody was above the law, his law. "We have a category of people who have become billionaires, as we say, overnight," he declared.

"They got the impression that the gods themselves slept on their heads and that everything is permitted to them." Khodorkovsky was sentenced to nine years in a Siberian labour camp.

Putin knew, and he knew that everyone knew, that he had chosen a single scapegoat. He could have chosen to make an example of any of several oligarchs, but Khodorkovsky's ambitions had been the most brazen. Putin also knew that nobody with serious business ambitions would complain. The Khodorkovsky case led not just to the silencing of dissenting voices in business, but also to the takeover of private enterprise by the security and intelligence elite, the *siloviki*. In short, it dictated the country's entire economic and political course. The robber baron capitalism of the early Yeltsin years had been brought firmly under the Kremlin's control. Key to that was the consolidation of the lucrative energy sector. Under what came to be known as "velvet re-privatisation", the boards of Russia's biggest companies – from the oil and gas giants, to airlines, to railways – were now dominated by Putin's allies. Everyone did well, politically and financially, out of the arrangement, particularly the President. It was dubbed "Kremlin Inc.".

In 2004, I was invited to meet Putin. It was part of the inaugural meeting of the Valdai Club, which aimed to become an annual discussion group of experts from Russia and the West. Our arrival coincided with the start of the Beslan school massacre in the northern Caucasus. It was impossible not to feel revulsion at the ruthlessness of the killers unfolding before everyone's eyes on live TV. But my discussions with politicians, journalists and academics in those fraught few days were dispiriting. One or two editors showed courage, such as Raf Shakirov of *Izvestiya* – once a government mouthpiece but which had become a serious and critical voice – who was sacked after his paper reported that the number of hostages in the school was much greater than officials had said. Others whom I had previously regarded as liberals had transformed into nationalistic xenophobes, blaming outsiders for their country's ills and refusing to consider the context for Beslan (two bloody

Russian incursions into Chechnya). Was this a genuine ideological conversion, a case of second-guessing their masters or an attempt to deflect attention from the incompetence of the security forces? The politics of grievance, one of the least attractive facets of Soviet political life, remained as ingrained as ever in capitalist Russia. Someone else was always to blame for the country's woes. It was a gut instinct that seemed to be shared as much by the rich as by the poor, as much by those who knew the West well as those who did not.

I assumed that, with a national terrorist emergency raging, a social gathering with a group of foreigners might not be top of the President's agenda. When word came that it had not been cancelled, I surmised that it would be a cursory handshake in the Kremlin. Instead, we were bussed to his official suburban residence. As we arrived in Novo-Ogarevo, past the opulent homes of the new suburban elite, we were taken to an anteroom containing a pool table and a plasma television set. There, we watched the eight o'clock news on Channel 2, which had now become the most loyal of all the loyal Russian channels. It failed to ask any of the hard questions about how the Beslan rescue attempt had been so botched, about why the authorities had underestimated the numbers inside the school, about why Chechnya is the way it is. What we did see was image after image of bodies being buried, of mothers and fathers wailing uncontrollably in the pouring rain, of a boy singing "Ave Maria" to a silent crowd in St Petersburg.

Eventually we were taken upstairs, with the warning that the President was in no mood for this meeting. With a wave of the hand, he beckoned us to a long, rectangular table covered with a white cloth. We were seated in alphabetical order and, as Putin invited questions, I was one of those who tentatively raised their hands. He pointed across the table at me. By way of introduction, I offered our collective condolences. I did not wish to sound insensitive, I ventured, but surely his policy towards Chechnya had some bearing on the broader problem? For the next thirty minutes, Putin gave an uninterrupted exegesis of Russia's recent history. His eyes were fixed and expressionless; he never hesitated or looked at notes. He conceded that the Chechens had suffered terrible hardship during Stalin's deportations. They had fought more valiantly than anyone else in defence of the Soviet motherland against fascism. He also suggested that he might not have done what Boris Yeltsin did in 1994 when he unleashed the first of the modern Chechen wars. "I don't know how I would have acted; maybe yes, maybe no. But mistakes were made."

Putin explained that, after the Russians withdrew, Chechnya received what it wanted: "de facto independence". But local leaders allowed it to be run down, encouraged extremism and turned it into a launch pad for terrorists across Russia. "The vacuum was filled by radical fundamentalism of the worst kind," he said. Men and women were shot by firing squad and beaten with sticks. In 1999, by which point he was Prime Minister, the Russian government had no choice but to go back in, if only to prevent violence spreading beyond Chechnya's border into neighbouring Dagestan. All the while, Russia searched for political leaders to talk to: "We even tried to deal with people who were bearing arms against us. We have done what you asked for." The status of Chechnya was not the issue, he said. The independence question had been subverted by Islamists with a bigger goal.

His arguments, if selective in their use of history, were carefully framed and fluently put. It was only when he referred to Beslan that he allowed his emotions to show. Even at his angriest, however, he appeared always in control. He finished his treatise – we were still on question number one – by inviting me to ask myself: "Would you like it if people who shoot children in the back come to power, anywhere on this planet? If you asked yourself that, you wouldn't ask any more questions about Russian policy."

Chechnya, Putin told us, was not Iraq. "It is not a faraway land. It is a crucial part of our territory. This is about Russia's territorial integrity." It was now being used as a launch pad, he said, and "certain foreign" elements were encouraging the violence. "We've observed incidents. It's a replay of the mentality of the Cold War. There are certain people who want us to be focused purely on our internal problems. They pull strings here so that we don't raise our heads internationally." Russia, he insisted, no longer had "imperial" pretensions beyond its border. It was not comfortable with NATO enlargement into the once-Soviet Baltic states. He did not see why so-called partners wanted to fly fighter jets alongside Russian airspace. This, he added, resorting to another Soviet word, was nothing but a "provocation". His country did not have the resources to guard its borders properly. A weak and unstable Russia was in nobody's interests. "Has anyone given a thought to what would happen if Russia were eliminated?"

It was hard not to sympathise with much of what he said. Putin's growing hostility was largely the result of the West's failed analysis of the psychology of modern Russia, and a strongly held Russian anger at Western double standards following the help rendered by Moscow to Washington after 9/11. Consider the Russian concessions: the closing of an intelligence-gathering post in Cuba and a naval base in Vietnam and the green light for the US to use airbases in Central Asia to support the invasion of Afghanistan. The Kremlin assumed it would enjoy greater understanding of its concerns in return.

Putin's suspicions had been raised in November 2003 when popular protest in Georgia had forced out of office the Soviet-era President, Eduard Shevardnadze, and ushered in a pro-American administration led by the US educated Mikheil Saakashvili. The "Rose revolution" was seen in Western capitals, particularly by neo-Conservatives in Washington, as the ultimate expression of people power; for Moscow it was a flagrant example of American manipulation of public opinion and of the duplicity of democratic rhetoric. Putin's concerns would be reinforced less than a year later by similar events in Ukraine. The election campaign there of November 2004 was marred by accusations of Moscow's role in the poisoning of the pro-Western Viktor Yushchenko, and the disputed victory of the pro-Kremlin candidate, Viktor Yanukovych. After mass rallies, a run-off was ordered, and the so-called "Orange" forces took control of a deeply divided country. For East and West these two former Soviet republics became the focal point not just of a geo-strategic struggle – as NATO membership was dangled in front of Georgia and Ukraine – but an ideological one as well. It became essentially a zero-sum game. Russian resentment would grow even stronger as America developed plans for missile defence and radar systems in Poland and the Czech Republic, and supported Kosovo's declaration of independence.

But still, back then in 2004 during our session with him, Putin was prepared to give Bush the benefit of the doubt. He showed no restraint, however, when it came to critical forces within Russia itself. We asked him his views on freedom of speech. It was, he said, an essential part of a country's development, but journalists, too, had to be "efficient". He likened the relationship between state and media to something he had seen in an Italian film; he wouldn't say which. Maybe he had learnt the phrase from his friend Silvio Berlusconi. "The role of the real man is to make advances. The role of the real woman is to resist them."

We had got through several cups of black tea and finished our individual fruit sponge cakes. It was beyond midnight. We had been with our host for three and three-quarter hours. Which other world leader would have given a bunch of foreigners so much "face time", especially at the height of an emergency? Putin struck me as extraordinarily eager to be understood. Before he released us, he wanted one final word on Chechnya. He was prepared to open a dialogue, but not with "child killers", he said. "I don't advise you to meet bin Laden, to invite him to Brussels and NATO or to the White House, to hold talks with him and let him dictate what he wants so that he then leaves you alone." He simply could not understand why people abroad could see things differently. Did we have no conscience? With that he stood up and walked round the room, shaking our hands, his eyes firmly fixed on each and every one of us.

Earlier that day, I had gone to a metro station, Rizhskaya, which I had used to go to work when I first lived in Moscow in the mid-1980s. The station forecourt had become a shrine, the latest of several across Russia to victims of the new terror. Along a wall, people had placed carnations, photographs and poems to their loved ones. On the evening of 31 August 2004 a "black widow", as Chechen female suicide bombers are now called, blew herself up outside the station, by a row of shops. I took the escalator down to the train, past the advertisements for DVD players and detergents. On the intercom, a recorded message asked travellers to look out for suspicious packages and to inform on suspicious people. But to whom should they report their suspicions? Surely they wouldn't expect anything of the young policemen slouching against a railing? In the carriages, everyone looked at everyone else, wondering what they might be planning, but they all knew that they were powerless to do anything about it. My mind wandered to what Putin had said in his TV address to the nation: "We showed ourselves to be weak, and the weak get beaten." I also considered the term *zhurnalyuga*, journalist-scum, which had become popular with Putin and his entourage.

In that same week, two prominent journalists had been prevented, in suspicious circumstances, from reaching Beslan. One was held by police at Moscow's Vnukovo airport after an altercation with a drunk that seemed to have been planned. That was Radio Liberty's Babitsky, who had continued his fearless work. Another collapsed on a plane heading to the Caucasus after being given a cup of poisoned tea. That was Anna Politkovskaya, Russia's most famous investigative reporter and commentator. What mattered to Putin was that the media did not sully his reputation as the man delivering order – hence the use of the word "efficient".

Since 2003, in its worldwide press-freedom index, the organisation Reporters Without Borders has each year ranked Russia between 140th and 147th out of roughly 170 countries in the world. It usually occupied places similar to Afghanistan, Yemen, Saudi Arabia and Zimbabwe, although it has ended up marginally ahead of

Singapore and China. Unlike those countries, the Russian authorities have focused less on preventative legislation and more on punitive thuggery. The International Committee to Protect Journalists says Russia is the third most deadly country for reporters. The Russian Union of Journalists estimates that more than two hundred have been killed in ten years. In not a single case has the mastermind been arrested.

The most famous case was Politkovskaya herself, who was gunned down in the lift of her apartment block in October 2006. Her work in the Caucasus broke new ground, and infuriated the Kremlin. And yet, while lesser known writers had been killed or injured, there was a sense that her fame rendered her a little safer. Not so. Roman Shleinov, an investigative journalist at the paper where they both worked, explained why: "Journalism becomes a threat and a serious irritant when it begins to influence social dynamics. Politkovskaya's reports had this effect because they were seen by foreign human rights organisations as an alternative source of information. She had become more than a journalist: she was a social activist. It is not criticism of the Kremlin itself that endangers Russian journalists, but the threat they pose to an old system of relationships which benefits a tiny minority of people. And that will not be permitted."

Her death alarmed journalists and human rights groups around the world. In Russia, the reaction was passionate among the dwindling band of liberals, but most people seemed to take it with equanimity. When pressed to comment, Putin said Politkovskaya's influence on Russian politics had been "negligible". It took many months for an investigation to be launched. Eventually, three hit men were put on trial, but in February 2009 they were acquitted. Few were surprised, as the case against them has proven flimsy. The investigators had gone through the motions. The people who had ordered the killing were not to be touched. The involvement of the state in an assassination such as this might have been a scandal, but not under Putin's regime. When the interests of power structures are threatened by independent reporting, contract killers function as the ultimate censors.

Politkovskaya's murder was just the latest in a long line. Journalists and opposition politicians had been targeted in the Yeltsin era, too, notably Galina Starovoitova, a prominent liberal, who was gunned down in her St Petersburg apartment block back in 1998. But in Putin's time, the frequency of these killings increased, as did the confidence of those ordering them. In 2003, Yuri Shchekochikhin, deputy editor of *Novaya Gazeta*, and deputy chairman of parliament's scrutiny committee, died at the age of fifty-three of a mysterious allergy. Nobody for a moment believed it was due to natural causes. I had known him in the late eighties and early nineties when he was elected to the Congress of People's Deputies, the first and only semi-free parliament the Soviet Union ever had. Its chaotic, freewheeling style gave him a taste for trying to turn campaigning into action. Fearless but also eminently practical, Shchekochikhin was a prominent figure in the Gorbachev and Yeltsin years, joining many Muscovites in defending their fledgling democracy during the coup of 1991. Most of that crowd had since disappeared into their consumerist cocoon. He, and a few with him, kept going. As a public opponent of the Chechen war and as a scourge of the KGB and its successors, he had made many enemies.

In provincial Russia, not just reporters but anyone who gets on the wrong side of the authorities and their business and criminal associates is liable to summary punishment. "Local authorities react to publications far more ruthlessly than federal ones," says Shleinov. "The heads of local administrations have free rein in their dealings with journalists. On their own territory, they are small-time 'tsars', and they mimic the central authorities in exaggerated form." There is a certain similarity with China, where excess in the regions may be greater than in the centre, but where the national leadership sets the overall parameters.

When Putin was asked how he would respond to critics who accuse him of limiting media freedom, he once replied: "Very simply. We have never had freedom of speech in Russia, so I don't really understand what could be stifled. It seems to me that freedom is the ability to express one's opinion, but certain boundaries must exist, as laid out in the law." This is a Russian version of the Singaporean "out-of-bound markers", although usually with a stairwell as the venue and a semi-automatic as the means. Journalists such as these, along with a tiny group of human rights activists and lawyers, had broken what the commentator Masha Lipman calls Russia's equivalent of the "non-participation pact". The public agreed not to meddle in politics in exchange for the chance to take part in the consumer benefits of the Russian energy boom.

The Putin era may now be unravelling as Russia reels from the global crisis, but in his eight years as President, from 2000 to 2008, he oversaw the greatest period of economic growth and political stability his country had witnessed for a generation. And how the place boomed: a country that had almost gone bust in 1998 built up the world's third largest foreign exchange reserves. GDP per head rose from less than $2,000 in 1998 to $9,000 at the start of 2008. With income tax a flat 13 per cent, and with every Russian given their own flat free as the Soviet era ended, disposable income was higher than these figures suggested. Unlike in many Western countries, mortgages and excessive consumer debt were rare. It was all based on skyrocketing prices for commodities on global markets. Every $1 rise in the price of a barrel of oil represented a $1 billion increase in government receipts. The Kremlin was cautious in its budget preparations, assuming a fall in prices, and amassing a $160 billion stabilisation fund from surplus revenue. It thought that would be enough to protect it from any sudden shocks.

Not everyone benefited, by any means. Most pensioners struggled to make ends meet; some people had their homes snatched from them by various developers' scams; others had failed to recover from the pyramid schemes of the last economic crash. Vulnerable members of society continued to suffer, as they had done in the

1990s. But what mattered was that *enough* people were doing *sufficiently* well and considered themselves to be *sufficiently* free in their personal lives. Those doing well did extraordinarily well. Sports cars, designer shops and expensive restaurants had, by the mid-2000s, become the norm for a small, but significant proportion of the population in the big cities. Moscow was said to have the best sushi outside Japan. It boasted more 6-series BMWs than any other city in the world. It was predicted that Russia would overtake Germany to become the world's biggest market in luxury cars. This wealth helped foster a revival of national self-confidence – the belief that Russians could once again hold their heads high in international company. That self-confidence continued to be manifested in a mixture of hubris and grievance.

Putin had promised his people a new pact, or, rather, the return to an old one in a modern setting. Return the public realm to those in the know, and in return the population will receive the security it has lost. Although prosperity was the preserve of a few, the restoration of basic order meant that public sector workers and others who had not shared in the wealth would at least enjoy a stable and regular income. The main difference between Putin and the Soviet era was in the private realm. Putin had no intention of reimposing a travel ban, or dictating where people lived or worked. Individuals were free to go as they pleased and live life as they pleased, as long as they did not cause trouble.

In those terms, Putin had delivered. Wealth, which several generations of Russians had never enjoyed, was the perfect antidote to political involvement. The concentration of authority in Putin's hands and the elimination of alternative sources of power resulted in an overwhelming indifference towards politics and anaesthetisation of society through consumer goods.

Many journalists continued to take risks, even well into the Putin era. But many of the people I knew opted for a quiet life. Why rock the boat when you could enjoy the good life, paying little more than 10 per cent in tax, take your holidays in Cap Ferrat and live inside one of the many gated "villages" that were springing up on the outskirts of Moscow? Such a trade-off was similar to that of my Singapore friends, except that I had seen many of these people in the early 1990s coming out to defend Yeltsin's fledgling democracy and vigorously engaging in the political debate. Now they had decided to withdraw.

They had joined the global pact and they were enjoying the privileges it afforded. I remember one evening in Moscow in May 2008. An advertising hoarding opposite the Bolshoi Theatre reminded passers-by that Russia had just beaten Canada in the final of the World Ice Hockey Championships and that Zenit St Petersburg had just beaten Glasgow Rangers in the UEFA Cup Final in Manchester. "We do it better", the advert declared. The biggest achievement was still to come: the hosting of the dramatic Champions League showdown between Manchester United and my club, Chelsea. It marked, in the words of one Russian fellow supporter, "Moscow's coming of age". I had witnessed many dramatic changes in Russia, but I still blinked when I saw Red Square turned into a carnival, with English fans, who had been allowed to enter the country without visas, knocking footballs about outside Lenin's Tomb, and touts selling tickets. For the Kremlin, this important public relations exercise was about to be trumped by something even better.

That Saturday was the final of the Eurovision Song Contest. My rock promoter friend, Art Troitsky, had been invited on to the set of Channel 2 along with a carefully picked selection of entertainers and groupies. Live current affairs discussion programmes had long since stopped, because the authorities did not want to risk the wrong kinds of comments being aired. But this was pure fun, surely. The outdoor stage was to intersperse reaction in Moscow to the live event, which was taking place in the Serbian capital, Belgrade. I was surprised, and intrigued, to be allowed to join Troitsky, but thought that, given the hapless performance of the British entry, I should stay silent. The Brit came last, and I duly kept my head down. The

Russian entry, a solo ballad from one of the countries top stars, Dima Bilan, swept to victory. As Bilan performed his victory rendition of "Believe", draping a Russian flag across the stage, the Russian coverage switched to the Moscow studio. A succession of fur-coated, middle-aged showbiz types grabbed the microphone to proclaim how he deserved to win, how his victory proved Russia's greatness, and even how they all had their Prime Minister and President to thank for the victory. When it came to Troitsky, he said he thought the song was trash and the voting had been fixed among the Slavs and other countries of the former Soviet Union. Audible gasps all around. "Traitor," shouted one woman. "I thought you were a patriot," declared another. "I used to respect your work," said a third, "but now I see you for what you are."

Russian television has, in many respects, moved on from Soviet times. Its production values were slick. Its game shows and entertainment programmes are just as popular as any around the world. It is a past master at dumbing down, producing celebrity pap as well as any Western country. It does not, however, do spontaneous expression of contrary views. Troitsky is no naif. He knew how to play the system during Soviet times, in order to get bands promoted. He had been at the forefront of the Yeltsin revolution, being invited on to prominent shows on television and radio. Once Putin was in power editors became more suspicious of him, but it took Troitsky a while to find this out. He had been invited to take part in the celebrity edition of the show *Who Wants to Be a Millionaire?* but the day before it was due to be filmed one of the producers called to say the list of contestants had changed. He apologised awkwardly, citing a "change of circumstances". Other cases followed. His friend, the TV presenter Sorokina, asked the chairman of the station, Konstantin Ernst, what was going on. Ernst told her: "You know very well, Sveta. He's uncontrollable." Shortly afterwards, Sorokina herself was taken off air. First, she was told that her evening chat show would have to be pre-recorded, because of "dangerous" opinions by guests and members of the audience. Then it was stopped altogether. In 2008,

Novaya Gazeta published an article on blacklists on Russian TV. Troitsky was one of several people on it. The paper quoted a television source as saying one remark he had made on a show in 2004 had caused particular offence to the Kremlin. This is what he said: "People usually either trade freedom for security, or security for freedom; look at recent Russian history in this respect – under the Communists we had no freedom, but relative security; under Yeltsin we didn't have security, but there was a plenty of freedom; with Putin, we've got neither of the two."

Even as wily and prominent a figure as Troitsky was taken aback by the fury directed at him that night on the Eurovision show. This, after all, was only a question of popular music, hardly an issue of existential importance to Russia. As we drove home in the early hours, he received a succession of texts, some supportive, from friends, others threatening. He had broken the pact. The issue was not important enough to put him in harm's way, but he had been warned.

His so-called friends had not needed to react the way they did. No overt pressure had been applied. They chose to, however, seeing in their flamboyant displays of patriotism perhaps more lucrative future contracts. The new business culture was working in harmony with authoritarian thinking.

Self-censorship has become a natural instinct among journalists and others in public life. The human rights community, or what is left of it, is regarded as a bunch of incurable romantics; non-governmental organisations are seen as agents of hostile foreign forces. Russia's parliament, which throughout Putin's tenure was a rubber-stamping body for the Kremlin, has passed a series of laws clamping down on what it calls "anti-state behaviour". One piece of legislation grants the security services the right to kill enemies of the state at home and abroad. Another gives law enforcement agencies the right to view acts of dissent as forms of extremism or treason, crimes punishable by up to twenty years in prison. Treason has been redefined to include damaging Russia's constitutional order. Human rights advocates say this marks a return to Stalin's time. Again, few people complain.

As ever, Western countries displayed characteristic confusion and double standards in their dealings. One of the ironies is that throughout this period the country with which Russia had one of the worst political relationships – the UK – played host to its economic boom. Britain had by 2006 become the second leading investor in Russia. Most of the money, however, was flowing the other way. When Peter Mandelson, one of Blair's closest confidants, declared back in the mid-nineties that New Labour was "intensely relaxed about people getting filthy rich", perhaps even he did not realise quite what would ensue. London, under the Labour government, advertised itself to the new global elite as a less regulated and more tax-efficient place to do business than any of its rivals. The government provided far more attractive ways of avoiding paying tax (legally), and made it far less likely that you would be caught if you evaded paying tax (illegally). It was no wonder that Russian oligarchs made the British capital their home. The city became known among Russians as Londongrad, where "ultra-high net worth individuals", as they were branded by the real estate agents, could enjoy their luxuries undisturbed. A quarter of a million Russians settled there.

In summer 2007 I confronted Alistair Darling, the Chancellor of the Exchequer, over the "Londongrad" phenomenon. I asked him if there was anything Britain would not do to prostrate itself to the super-rich. Would the government even consider, as many had been urging, to impose a tax on non-domiciled residents? He looked bemused, confining himself to a smile. I told him many Russians I knew were perplexed at the laxity of the British government in letting in so many people with controversial records. He shrugged his shoulders, said I was "exaggerating" the problem, and murmured something about the British capital being the "world's financial hub". This was Britain's part in the pact.

British intelligence was concerned by this arrival of an entire subculture of fabulously wealthy individuals of dubious repute. There was surprise among some at the Foreign Office about the decision to grant asylum to Boris Berezovsky. The security services noted a large rise in FSB activity, pointing to an inextricable link between Russian business and political interests. In April 2006 the Serious Organised Crime Agency (SOCA) was established, along the lines of the FBI in the US. Blair promised that the new body would "make life hell" for gangsters, drug barons and people traffickers. The Russian mafia was one of the most powerful players in a crime industry said to be worth at least £20 billion in the UK. SOCA's only significant success against Russians during that period was the arrest of three small-scale computer hackers, who had been blackmailing British and Irish bookmakers. Then the trail went cold; when it came to the Russians, the British appeared reluctant to investigate all but low-grade crime such as drugs and prostitution. This reinforced a suspicion of an absence of political will in Whitehall to deal with Russian money laundering as this might undermine the City's reputation as the world's financial capital.

Everyone was getting in on the act. Public relations companies were making their money on spreading Kremlin propaganda; financiers were striking deals. The extent of the camaraderie would later be laid bare in the unlikely setting of Corfu. It transpired that Mandelson, who would later be appointed Business Secretary in the Labour government, and the Conservative Shadow Chancellor, George Osborne, had separately been ingratiating themselves with Oleg Deripaska, one of Russia's most controversial oligarchs with close links to the Kremlin. Osborne's soliciting of money for his party became the bigger controversy, but Mandelson's actions might have caused more of a stir. What was the EU's Trade Commissioner, as he was then, doing as a regular visitor on a luxury cruise ship owned by a tycoon who at that point had had his entry visa to the US withdrawn?

In the House of Lords, members queued up to take on "consultancies" for various oligarchs. They earned handsome retainers for their job of providing dubious political respectability. One told me he was advising a financier on how to sue newspapers for delving into his business practices. Journalists showed an increasing reluctance to investigate corruption, as the Russians used British legal firms to threaten them. "We've been told to steer clear of the oligarchs," one national newspaper editor told me. "It's too much trouble."

Alistair Darling's apparent equanimity that day was even more startling given that, six months earlier, in November 2006, Alexander Litvinenko, a KGB operative turned dissident, had been poisoned in the heart of London. With that murder, the Kremlin had put down another marker – of the consequences, anywhere in the world, for any Russian challenging its supremacy. Initially, the British declared that, for all their indulgence on the economic front, they would take a stand on Litvinenko. The man at the centre of this approach was Sir Anthony Brenton, the British Ambassador to Moscow. Brenton had already riled the Russians by attending opposition rallies. He urged Downing Street, in a number of private memos, to take a harder line on Putin, reporting without equivocation on the increasingly dictatorial tendencies of the Kremlin. A few weeks later, Britain said it had uncovered a plot to assassinate Berezovsky in London and announced that it was expelling four Russian diplomats in response to the Kremlin's refusal to hand over the man suspected of Litvinenko's murder. The Russians responded in kind, with tit-for-tat expulsions, while the vilification campaign against Brenton was intensified. Thugs from the Kremlin youth organisation, Nashi, took to jumping in front of his ambassadorial car, whenever it left the compound, and heckling him at public meetings. The fact that they had apparently obtained copies of the ambassador's daily appointments diary, enabling them to trail him, reinforced suspicions of FSB involvement.

Nashi was not a fringe organisation of headstrong young people. Established by Putin's deputy head of administration, Vladimir Surkov, it was central to the Kremlin's attempt to devise an ideology and a visible means of proselytising it. Surkov, whose nickname was the grey cardinal, coined the term "sovereign democracy", defining it as "a society's political life where the political powers, their authorities and decisions are decided and controlled by a diverse Russian nation for the purpose of reaching material welfare, freedom and fairness by all citizens, social groups and nationalities, by the people that formed it". This rejected the idea that there can be only one type of democracy and argued that each country should have the freedom and sovereignty to develop its own form. Its adherents defined themselves through a combination of nationalism, anti-Western rhetoric and animosity to "oligarchic capitalism" (although the cleverer oligarchs made sure they offered money to Nashi to keep its people at bay). It presented itself as young, modern and social. It combined teenage adventures and frolics, at a number of holiday camps, with the chance of a good rampage against enemies and an ideology of sorts. Within a year of its creation, it numbered over 200,000 members, of whom 10,000 were regular activists, or "commissars". Nashi thugs were increasingly used alongside Interior Ministry police to break up demonstrations. Often these took place away from Western cameras, sometimes they were filmed. On one such occasion, in May 2007, a group of protesters, who included Members of the European Parliament, tried to draw attention to increasing hostility towards homosexuals in Russia. The demonstrators, who included the British human rights campaigner Peter Tatchell, were knocked to the ground and kicked. They, rather than their assailants, were arrested.

A month later, Brenton took it on himself to fly to London the weekend after Gordon Brown had succeeded Blair in Downing Street. He insisted on briefing the new Prime Minister, and his young Foreign Secretary, David Miliband, on the dangers posed by Putin's Russia. Brenton told them that the Litvinenko killing was just the start and urged them to maintain the hard line.

Britain was involved in another, equally important, struggle – over control of Russia's vast and lucrative energy reserves. Standing

in the way of the Kremlin were the Western oil multinationals, particularly BP and Shell, which had secured a number of deals on
what the Russians later complained were absurdly generous terms.
BP had set up a joint venture, called TNK-BP, with a number of oligarchs, securing a 50 per cent share at what the Russians would
claim was a preferential rate. The Russian operation drove much of
BP's growth during this period. It made a healthy profit, and the
Kremlin wanted to grab it back for its allies. Most foreign oil companies buckled under the pressure. Shell sold a large part of its stake
in the $20 billion Sakhalin-2 project to Gazprom. BP held out. Its
executives were hounded and harassed on the streets of Moscow;
their offices were raided. Two young British-educated Russians were
charged with spying. Russia's political and business leaders held all
the cards. They knew that eventually BP would fall into line, which
is what it did. The British company knew that something was better
than nothing. It was not lost on British ministers that, no matter
how bad the diplomatic relations, business between the two countries was flourishing. The financial links were simply too close, and
too mutually beneficial, for them to be sacrificed on high politics or
principle.

British companies had rarely shown scruples when it came to
dealing with Russia. Whenever their services were required by
Russian energy giants, they were happy to oblige. When part of
Yukos, the company seized from the jailed Khodorkovsky, was floated
on the London Stock Exchange, the sale attracted a number of competing buyers. The financier George Soros had been a lone voice in
urging Western institutions to boycott the offering. Andrei Illarionov,
a former economic adviser turned critic, called the listing a "crime
against the Russian people". Such complaints fell on deaf ears. By
the end of 2007, more than twenty major Russian companies with a
combined market capitalisation of around $625 billion were listed in
London. That was far more than on the New York Stock Exchange,
where standards of disclosure were comparatively higher. The
Americans, whatever their many other failures in regulating their

financial markets, were less eager to prostrate themselves before Russian money.

Many Russians I spoke to were bemused by the complaints of unsavoury dealings involving the oligarchs. The British, they told me, had brought it on themselves. If they hadn't wanted polonium poisoning, if they hadn't wanted industrial blackmail, they should not have been so eager to welcome Russian money.

In March 2008 it was announced that Brenton would leave Moscow. The Foreign Office denied that Britain had raised the white flag, saying only that his term had come to its natural end. The Kremlin portrayed the ambassador's departure as a victory, suggesting that London wanted to adopt a more conciliatory approach. British companies operating in Russia, which had quietly expressed misgivings about the ambassador's hard line, breathed a sigh of relief.

The Londongrad phenomenon suggested that frosty political relations need not hinder warm business ties. Most Western European countries took a more indulgent approach, seeing the two as inextricably linked, and going out of their way not to antagonise. States that depended most on Russia for its oil and gas, Germany and Italy, had been the most reluctant to challenge the Kremlin's clampdown on human rights. Within months of leaving office as German Chancellor in 2005, Gerhard Schröder became supervisory board chairman of Russia's dream project, the Nord Stream gas pipeline, the most expensive ever built in the world. A few weeks before, in one of his last acts in charge of his country, Schröder had signed a $5 billion agreement to supply natural gas to Germany. When the leader of the opposition Free Democrats, Guido Westerwelle, had pointed out the strange coincidence and attacked Schröder's appointment, the former Chancellor took out an injunction to try to silence him. Schröder insisted that the two acts were a coincidence, and that he had done nothing wrong. "I cannot understand this criticism," he told a news conference at Gazprom's Moscow headquarters. A similar offer had been made to Romano

Prodi, just as he was stepping down as Italy's Prime Minister. The inducement to him was to become chairman of Gazprom's parallel South Stream project. At least Prodi turned down the job. Another to decline similar overtures was Donald Evans, a former US Trade Secretary and good friend of George Bush. He had been personally courted by Putin to take a senior position at the oil firm Rosneft, just at a time when its sequestering of Yukos assets was being investigated by the European Court of Human Rights.

What was so dispiriting is that many of the examples of authoritarian abuse were not taking place away from prying eyes, in a secret prison in the Siberian wastes. This was not Stalin's Soviet Union, but a country fully integrated into the global economy. Violence was meted out on the doorsteps of the new rich. In December 2008, police raided the small St Petersburg offices of Memorial, a human rights group and research centre that charts the victims of Communist purges. A number of riot police wearing black face masks broke into Memorial's headquarters, taking away its files. The raid coincided with an unprecedented public offensive by Kremlin-backed intellectuals who accused Memorial of distorting Russia's history in order to undermine patriotic fervour. One of Putin's chosen political scientists, Gleb Pavlovsky, complained that Russia was vulnerable to "foreign" conceptions of its history. The raid was covered only in passing by the Russian media. Most people appeared unperturbed. In any case, there was little further appetite for dredging up the abuses of the past. Opinion polls had consistently shown that voters welcomed the restoration of the old Soviet national anthem, and that at least 50 per cent viewed Stalin's role in history as positive. A new, or rather traditional, version of history was now standard fare in school textbooks.

Shortly after the Memorial raid, Anastasia Baburova, a twenty-five-year-old journalist, and Stanislav Markelov, a human rights lawyer, were shot dead, in the middle of the day on a busy street in central Moscow. Markelov had represented *Novaya Gazeta* in several court cases. But on the day of his death he had been focused on another issue – his attempt to appeal against the early release from prison of a Russian army officer convicted in the rape and murder of a young Chechen woman. Markelov was shot at point-blank range. When Baburova, who was walking with Markelov, attempted to intervene, she was shot as well, becoming the fourth of the newspaper's journalists to be murdered in a decade. They were mourned by the small human rights world, but, as ever, the vast majority of Muscovites were indifferent. "The killers have no fear because they know they will not be punished. But neither are their victims afraid, because when you defend others you cease to fear," wrote Yelena Milashina, a colleague of Markelov and Baburova. "Those today who are fearful are the people who keep out of trouble, trying to survive these bad times, when the bad times (for some reason) never seem to end."

Incidents such as these were designed to instil fear. But the overall clampdown was not comprehensive. Several newspapers, not only *Novaya Gazeta*, continue to criticise the Kremlin and to break stories that were damaging to its interests. The radio station Ekho Moskvy has for nearly two decades produced strong, independent journalism for its loyal band of listeners in the capital. Ironically, since 2001 its major shareholder has been Gazprom, the energy conglomerate that is one of the bases of Kremlin economic and political power. Throughout, market economics have informed Putin's decisions. Newspaper circulation and radio audiences are comparatively small. Therefore it has served his interests to leave certain outlets alone. He could then cite these papers and radio stations in his defence whenever Western leaders questioned him about his democratic credentials.

Curiously, in Russia the internet is less policed than its Chinese equivalent. A number of prominent bloggers have, from time to time, been told by the authorities either to stop their work or tone it down, but there has been no concerted attempt to close down sites. One apparent reason for this relatively relaxed approach is demographic. Such is Russia's ageing population (compared to

China's) that the online world is still seen as a minority pastime. Internet penetration is still under 25 per cent and is concentrated mostly in Moscow and the other more wealthy cities. For the Kremlin, only television counts. As in China, live coverage is rare, and chat shows are aired with a time delay, in case someone says something untoward. The heads of the networks are summoned to regular weekly meetings to set the news agenda; executives are provided with lists enumerating the names of political opponents who are not permitted on air. The loyalty of important anchors, station managers and star reporters is bought with unheard-of salaries. That, too, is part of the deal.

A similar calculation was made by one-time political opponents. Even as recently as the parliamentary elections in December 2003, the share of the vote garnered by liberal groupings was nearly 20 per cent. How did they and their supporters disappear so easily? Only a few sustained their challenge. For many years the best known figure was Grigory Yavlinsky. I had made a number of trips with him across the country during the 1990s when he was setting up his opposition party, Yabloko. In the Yeltsin era, Yabloko was a force to be reckoned with in parliament. Yavlinsky twice stood for President, but early into the Putin era he complained that opposition politics was becoming impossible.

Many figures stayed silent, went into business or allied themselves to the ruling camp. One of those was Pyotr Aven, a minister in one of the first post-Soviet liberal governments. He went on to become a wealthy banker, calling on Putin in March 2000 to model himself on Augusto Pinochet and suggesting that only dictatorship was capable of pursuing market reforms. Undeterred, Yavlinsky and others went through the motions, appearing on Western television stations to criticise the Kremlin, lending a veneer of credibility to the claims that Russia was developing a democracy of sorts. In the parliamentary elections of December 2007, none of the liberal parties came close to crossing the threshold required to gain seats in parliament. Shortly after, Yavlinsky decided to give up the ghost and quit the scene.

The journalist Arkady Ostrovsky commented that Russian liberals had been more active in their opposition to the invasion of Czechoslovakia in 1968 than they were to the war in Georgia.

The problem for many of these liberals is that under Yeltsin they had allowed themselves to be identified with uncaring shock-therapy capitalism. In so doing, they inadvertently undermined their notion of liberal democracy. Lilia Shevtsova, a leading chronicler of the era, sums it up like this: "The Yeltsin period gave Russia quite a few freedoms. Never had Russia been so free," she says. "But freedom in the absence of orderly habits, with a weak legal culture and ego-tistical elites, led to chaos and illegality, a disregard for all taboos and restrictions. Russians – frightened by the unfamiliar freedoms and not knowing how to deal with them – swung the pendulum back towards order." Sitting in her office on the corner of Tverskaya Street and Pushkin Square, near the old *Moscow News* office where dissidents would once gather, Shevtsova told me: "Ordinary people wearied of their unprecedented freedom to criticise the government because it had brought no improvement." In her most recent book, *Putin's Russia*, she says of the period in which he came to power: "Putin received mass support from the main forces in Russian society. The accumulated fears, the disarray, the feeling of being in danger, and the very real Russian 'Weimar syndrome' all pushed people toward a longing for order and a new face in the Kremlin." She recalled something the sociologist Yuri Levada wrote in the last edition of *Moscow News* of 1999, as he assessed the Russia that awaited Putin's leadership. "No researchers had ever seen Russian society in this state. All the fears and passions that had been biding their time came to the surface and the hidden layer of our consciousness was exposed." I was reminded of another remark, this time by Sergei Kiryenko, a former Prime Minister. He spoke of "liberalism of lifestyle". This had superseded "liberalism of outlook" which had, he said, become obsolete. That was April 2000 – even before the Putin era had begun to take hold.

Shevtsova likened Russia's new middle class to *rentiers* – people who have benefited from the state's largesse to a bloated bureaucracy. This was not dissimilar to those of the business and political elites of Latin American juntas in the 1970s and 1980s, who enjoyed a good life as long as they did not inquire too hard about the actions of the ruling juntas. Russia's elite had left one civilisation, but not arrived at another. "We are lost in transition. We may be here for some time," Shevtsova said with her usual eloquence. That seemed to me a good summary of where many Russians found themselves. They would not have seen themselves as defenders of Putin's world view, but nor did they see the need to cause trouble. For years they had done well by him, with the riches that accompanied his rule. What they wanted was less brutalism and a stricter adherence to the rule of law.

In September 2008 I returned to Russia for my first encounter with Putin in four years. This time at the Valdai conference we were given two for the price of one – Prime Minister Putin and his protégé, the new President, Dmitry Medvedev. We were curious to see how this cohabitation would work. Nobody for a minute, in Russia or abroad, doubted who was really in charge. Before those meetings we had taken part in round-table discussions in Rostov-on-Don. The consumer culture had brought at least three sushi restaurants and a number of designer clothes stores to this pleasant southern town. Yet the discussion inside the conference was all about a return to the Cold War.

A few weeks before, Georgia had launched a military offensive into the region of South Ossetia, which had long been allied to Russia. The Russians have used the date 8/8 to portray themselves as victims of terrorism. The Kremlin responded by launching a disproportionate assault on Georgia itself. Victory was quickly achieved, but at the expense of a sharp deterioration in its relations with the West. It did not take long in our discussions before the scale of the anger began to manifest itself. Vyacheslav Nikonov, grandson of Stalin's Foreign Minister, Vyacheslav Molotov, had become another of Putin's favourite "thinkers". He told our group that Russia had shown through its tough military response in Georgia that it had "never been so strong since the fall of the USSR". He added: "We are all paying the price of ten years of Western contempt for Russia." A slightly milder variation on this theme came from a young television commentator, Sergei Brylov: "The West has achieved the consolidation of the Russian political class."

For the main event, we were flown to Sochi, the Black Sea resort town that was sprucing itself up in preparation for hosting the 2014 Winter Olympics. Putin looked fit, relaxed, sarcastic, quick-witted and at times angry, as he entertained us over fine food and wine at a villa said by locals to be owned by his friend, the oligarch Deripaska. Since the Rose and Orange revolutions, the Russians had watched events unfold in Georgia and Ukraine with mounting concern. Thanks to political in-fighting and corruption, neither country had become the beacons for democracy that the US had so hoped. But they had, in the view of the Kremlin, become a geo-strategic bridgehead for America right in the heart of the former Soviet Union. Putin portrayed Russia as embattled and encircled by an aggressive West, particularly the US and UK. "What did you expect us to do – to defend ourselves with catapults?" he shouted. "If an aggressor comes into your territory you would punch him in the face and be right to do so. Should we have wiped the bloody snot away and bowed our heads?" For three hours he regaled us with his customary mix of threatening and emollient language. He said he had treated Bush "better than some Americans do", but warned America, and the West more broadly, that the time was over for unilateral action. The Romans may have destroyed Carthage, "but the Roman Empire was destroyed by barbarians. We have to look out for the barbarians." He insisted: "Russia is no threat to the US or Europe. We don't have any imperial claims any more."

As I watched, transfixed, I could not help concluding that this quintessentially Russian politics of grievance had found its apogee in this man. He no longer pleaded for understanding, as had been the message of his meeting with us during the Beslan massacre in 2004. Perhaps he felt he no longer needed it, because in the intervening years Russia had forced its way, through money and brute force, back to the top table.

Unlike Putin, who had kept us waiting for an hour and a half, the following day Medvedev breezed in, exactly on time, to meet us in the bizarre setting of a top-floor banqueting room of the Gum department store, opposite the Kremlin. After greeting all of us in turn, he told us that he had wanted to spend the month of August tackling corruption, strengthening the rule of law and reforming the economy. But war was war. "The protection of the lives and the dignity of Russia's citizens, no matter where they are, is the most important task of the Russian state. The US learnt major lessons from 9/11. The events of 8/8 have lessons for us." He made it clear he would be prepared to defend Russians militarily wherever they were in the world, and that any attempt on behalf of Georgia or Ukraine to seek membership of NATO would escalate tensions with the West. The hand of the US administration had been evident in goading the Georgians to challenge Russia.

Medvedev said he had tried several times to argue his case with the Americans, but his conversations had got nowhere. Bush had asked: "You're a young man with a liberal background. Why are you doing this?" Medvedev had replied: "I really didn't want this. But there are times when image is nothing and action is everything." The Russian President then added: "I don't want Russia to be a militarised state living inside an iron curtain. I've lived in that country and it was boring and uninteresting." He acknowledged that Russia had failed to convince much of the outside world that it was different from the old Soviet Union. "Some think that not only are we the legal successor to the USSR, but we are also the ideological heirs. This is simply not true. We have a completely different set of values." With that he toasted us with some excellent red wine (French, as Georgian has long been banned in Russia), and posed with us for a group photograph.

The following morning we had our final meeting. The timing (8.00 am) and setting (a nondescript Holiday Inn beyond the outer ring road where we had been staying) spoke volumes about the state of the Russian opposition. In order to show its adherence to free expression, the Valdai organisers had invited Garry Kasparov, the former world chess champion and Russia's most visible opposition leader, to meet our group. Kasparov said he had found it increasingly difficult to hold meetings in international hotels in the centre of the city. The managers, often Westerners, had decided it did not make commercial sense to rile the Kremlin. Kasparov told us he had been allowed to see us only after creating a scene at an international media forum a few months earlier.

Whereas our every meeting that week had been featured on prime time evening news, it came as no surprise that there was not a camera in sight for our discussion on this occasion. Kasparov spent much of his time analysing why other opposition figures and organisations had been outwitted by the Kremlin. Most of them, he said, had mistakenly believed they could influence attitudes towards freedom of expression, and human rights and democracy more generally, from within. "All the forces of liberalisation and democratisation from the top are exhausted," he said. "It's over." It was time to work "in parallel" with mainstream politics. Kasparov was adamant that the Putin era was drawing to a close and that the clamour for change was growing. He claimed that recent protests over the issue of high fuel prices had assumed a political dimension. "This regime is in a state of agony." Most of the panellists there that day quietly dismissed his analysis as wishful thinking.

In the early months of the global economic crisis, the government appeared confident that, thanks to its large stabilisation fund, Russia would emerge relatively unscathed. Some took that argument one stage further. "The United States and its ideas of the superiority of liberal capitalism and the limited role of the state in the economy have been dealt a severe blow," commented Sergei Karaganov, a veteran political scientist. "It turned out that the Old

West's model of a mature liberal-democratic capitalism, which seemed to have won for good, was no longer the only ideological benchmark for the rest of the world. States of the new capitalism – naturally more authoritarian, in line with their stage of economic and social development – offered a much more attractive and attainable political development model for lagging countries." Putin delivered a similar message in front of the world's elite at Davos.

He was quickly proven wrong. Russia's downward spiral became one of the most pronounced of any country around the world. The immediate response from the Kremlin was relatively adept. It staved off a run on the banks, a remarkable achievement given the fragility of that sector, helped by the stockpiling of gold and hard-currency reserves when times were good. Still, the stock market and the rouble plunged. Billions of dollars were wiped off share values; many people lost their savings, and millions were made unemployed. As for the oligarchs, they were said to have lost an astounding $250 billion. Many had little choice but to go the Kremlin, cap in hand, and beg for loans to save their empires.

Even during Putin's tenure, sporadic street protests had taken place. The authorities usually did not intervene, because the demonstrations were invariably called to highlight a specific grievance, such as pensions or electricity prices. Seldom were they overtly political in nature. That began gradually to change. In early 2009 a rally in Vladivostok in the Russian Far East, which had been originally called to complain about customs duties imposed on the import of foreign cars, turned into an anti-Putin rally. So worried was the Kremlin that it sent elite Interior Ministry troops thousands of miles across the country. Political opposition began to coalesce under the banner of a new organisation, Solidarity, taking its name from the 1980s Polish trade union that helped precipitate the collapse of Communism. In Boris Nemtsov, a former deputy Prime Minister, it had a charismatic figurehead. Groups such as these were an increasing irritant to the Kremlin, but were still some way off from posing a direct political threat.

During the Valdai conference, I was struck by one observation in particular. It had come from Timothy Colton, an American academic and Yeltsin's official biographer. Russia, he said, provided no model for soft power. It possessed "no ideology of global scope and appeal". That much was true, but there was an appeal of sorts domestically, and for a long time it had worked. The Russia of the Putin years had consolidated around wealth, nationalism and grievance. Putin had not derived his legitimacy from abstract concepts such as the rule of law, probity and transparency, but from two things: the regime's capacity to deliver political stability and economic growth. Had he been lucky or clever? Had he generated all that wealth during the oil boom or had he merely been its beneficiary and custodian? It did not matter. He had passed the efficiency test, a variant of the same test that was applied in Singapore and China. At least it was what people had been led to believe before much of the wealth evaporated. Putin had presided over an economy that was increasingly dependent on oil and gas. He had called for diversification into new areas, but had shown no serious intent. He did not believe he had to.

Putin's problems provided a small opening to Medvedev. He used his own increasing profile around the world to assert his own brand of what he called "rules-based" politics, to smooth some of the rougher edges of Putin's particular brand of authoritarianism. It was tempting to believe what he had implied to us that day at our meeting, that he was a genuine reformer but had been sidetracked by the war in Georgia. Medvedev gave a similar message whenever he spoke to Western audiences, and instructed his confidants to do the same on their travels. They encouraged people to read much into the President's renewed commitment to fight corruption, such as a meeting he had held with Mikhail Gorbachev to discuss civil liberties, and the reconvening of an obscure human rights body that had actually been created by Putin in 2004. Medvedev and his people bridled whenever comparisons were made with China. The age-old debate about Russia's European or Asian place has long been settled.

Russian opinion polls suggested his citizens were not so sure. Surveys showed a consistent animosity towards Western political values (as opposed to Western consumer values) that had pre-dated the Georgia crisis, but had been exacerbated by it. The New Economic School in Moscow published data collated between 2003 and 2008 on attitudes to democracy. Scepticism or hostility to the US was as pronounced among young people as among their grandparents, dipping slightly in the 35–45 age group. When asked whether Western society provided a good model for Russia, 60 per cent responded negatively, and only 7 per cent positively. This attitude, the pollsters said, had hardened each year. Disapproval among the rich was as pronounced as among the poor. The survey concluded that Russians came out among the least enthusiastic in the world, a good deal less keen even than the people of Belarus, known as Europe's last dictatorship.

In any case, the question of Russia's place misses the point. What happened in the Putin era, what happened to the people I knew might have been more dramatic, more brutal than in other countries, but the trade-off was no different from anywhere else. Money was there to be made, by Russians and foreigners alike. The pact came under strain because the anaesthetic of wealth had begun to wear off, and Russia's citizens had no other comforts to fall back on.

4

UNITED ARAB EMIRATES:
EASY MONEY

"Democracy is a system in which to provide the best possible life for people. It's not an end in itself" – Ayman Safadi

THEY WERE ALL THERE. HOLLYWOOD AND BOLLYWOOD MIXED with members of royal houses, the National Baseball Hall of Fame and other assorted celebrities. Dubai was bearing witness to the most garish party it had ever hosted. The Atlantis, a gargantuan, pink monstrosity of a hotel launched itself on the world in November 2008. Some two thousand B- and C-list celebrity guests were flown in from around the world for a feast of lobsters and a fireworks show that was heralded as seven times grander than the one that had marked the opening of the Beijing Olympics. A very particular pact was on display. In the deserts of Arabia, a traditional Bedouin state was feting a palace of greed owned by a South African Jew. The highlight of the evening was a special performance by Kylie Minogue, a global gay icon.

A business model had been built on complicity, all in the name of consumption. The United Arab Emirates had become a dream destination for those who wanted to get rich quick, but who were not required to ask too many questions. They could indulge their wildest fantasies, behind closed doors. The ruling families could click their fingers, and statesmen, entrepreneurs and artists would flock to them. Everyone was welcome, irrespective of colour or nationality, united in the goal of wealth creation. To that end, everyone would turn a blind eye to what everyone else was doing. This was a truly global dream come true, and for a decade or more everyone emerged a winner.

Then it crashed. Just as the Atlantis was opening its doors, the economic edifice collapsed. The oil price plummeted to $50 a barrel, a third of its peak value. Property prices plunged. The stock market plunged. Tens of thousands of foreigners – Britons, Indians, Russians, Americans and more – panicked. The liquidity crisis made them desperate to recapitalise, and to offload their properties at any cost. Distressed selling brought prices down even faster; in this domino effect, half of all the region's construction projects, totalling a staggering $600 billion, were put on hold or cancelled, leaving a trail of half-built towers on the outskirts of the city stretching into the sand beyond.

Thousands of foreigners who had gone out to Dubai in the hope of making an easy fortune saw themselves fall suddenly into negative equity. Jobless people lost their work visas and then had to leave the country within a month. Many decided to do so voluntarily. After falling into arrears, which is punishable by jail under UAE law, thousands literally fled the country. Airport car parks were filled with cars abandoned by their owners, keys left in the ignition and notes of apology taped to windscreens. The Atlantis, like all the hotels that had preceded it, had never imagined that business would dry up. There would be, so the marketing claimed, no shortage of people willing to pay as much as $25,000 a night for a room, to gaze at the sharks and rays in a vast glass-lined aquarium in the lobby. Within months the hotel was reduced to taking out advertisements offering cut-price package holidays.

Dubai was the playground of the Emirates. It suffered most

when the dream collapsed. Abu Dhabi was the more serious player. It did not need to try, as oil guaranteed its riches. Abu Dhabi has 95 per cent of the UAE's oil and more than half of its GDP. It has more money than it can possibly spend and over the years has sought ever more inventive ways of doling it out. "They have more oil than God has dollars," one businessman told me. Its trade-off was more sophisticated. Its rules were more complex. Its model proved to be more enduring.

"If this formula succeeds, this is the new world." Ashraf Makkar was drinking tea with me in one of Abu Dhabi's many luxury hotels alongside its tree-lined corniche. Once a correspondent with the Reuters news agency, he is now a media adviser to the Mubadala Development Company, a not insignificant job in a not insignificant company. MDC is the investment arm of the largest and wealthiest of the seven sheikhdoms that comprise the UAE. Makkar is a burly, pugnacious man, who gently berates me for a piece that had been brought to his attention. I had wondered out loud whether the Sovereign Wealth Funds established by the Gulf states, China, Singapore and others, and buying large stakes in global corpora-tions, might pose a danger to what is left of liberal democracy by dictating the terms of engagement around the world. Makkar recited whole sentences of a piece I had long forgotten. I remembered the "Singapore Ticks Off British Writer" headline. My admonishment this time was private, verbal and very discreet. I had nothing to fear, he told me. "This is the place where globalisation works." Everyone was coming to Abu Dhabi and its brasher and younger cousin down the road, Dubai, not just for the wealth but for the message the Emirates were sending as the global model of multiculturalism. "Look at the lights. Nobody does Christmas better than these guys do." It is, he insists, a model of harmony. "This is the only place you'll find Indians and Pakistanis playing cricket together. What transforms things is a sense of ownership. People have a vested interest in seeing this place succeed."

It was the present ruler's father, Sheikh Zayed bin Sultan Al Nahyan, who transformed Abu Dhabi from a few huts scattered in the desert, reliant on pearl fishing and a declining livestock trade, into this gleaming metropolis. Sheikh Zayed came to power in 1966, with the support of the outgoing British colonialists. While Bahrain and Qatar opted for independence, the sheikh enticed others to form a federation, the United Arab Emirates, promising to share his land's copious resources, but granting the other clans considerable autonomy. Having overseen his emirate's acquisition of wealth through oil, Sheikh Zayed decreed in the late 1990s that his city state should diversify into the ultimate travel destination for business, sports and arts events, and for European sun worshippers – all at the top end of the scale. He insisted that this be done without offending the indigenous Bedouin culture, and without indulging in the unregulated development and louche and flamboyant cosmopolitan society of Dubai. Zayed saw little need to open up society, let alone the royal family, to scrutiny. "Why should we abandon a system that satisfies our people in order to introduce a system that seems to engender dissent and confrontation?" he said. "Our system of government is based upon our religion and that is what our people want. Should they seek alternatives, we are ready to listen to them. We have always said that our people should voice their demands openly. We are all in the same boat, and they are both the captain and the crew."

Succeeding his father in 2004, Sheikh Khalifa bin Zayed al-Nahyan proceeded to open up Abu Dhabi further; but each step was carefully controlled. The sheikh had all the palaces and luxury hotels a monarch could wish for: what he really wanted was for his kingdom to be taken seriously, and he was determined to spend his way to that end. Culture was a commodity to be purchased. Some £20 billion was earmarked for hiring the world's best architects and licensing the best museum "brands" to establish branches in Abu Dhabi. A site was chosen. Saadiyat, "the Island of Happiness", was one of several islands being built on reclaimed land to increase the size of Abu Dhabi. Here Frank Gehry, the architect behind the renowned Guggenheim Bilbao, is building the latest – and biggest – Guggenheim. The French modernist Jean Nouvel is designing the world's first outpost of the Louvre. Each will lend works, and each museum is being paid hundreds of millions for the right to use their name. Alongside these monuments to gargantuan fantasy will be the new Sheikh Zayed National Museum designed by Norman Foster, and a six-thousand-seat performing arts centre, designed by Zaha Hadid. The cultural "hub" also contains a branch of the Sorbonne and will soon house a campus of New York University, the first American liberal arts school to be established abroad. Discussions have also taken place with the New York Public Library, among other major world libraries, and New York's Metropolitan Opera and Lincoln Center.

There was plenty of resistance, more in France than America, to the general idea of exporting culture to the desert. The sceptics' view was summed up by the Sorbonne's president, Jean-Robert Pitte: "Can we really bring culture to camel riders and carpet sellers?" Art critics accused the sheikh of "bribing" Western museums to give their seal of approval to what was merely the artistic version of the leisure theme parks being built all over the Gulf. Design critics complained of "architectural megalomania". Gehry himself condemned the decision to build so many high-profile buildings so close to each other on Saadiyat as "a group grope". A number of leading cultural figures in Europe and America complained about the sheer cheek of using money to buy culture – as if that had not originally happened in their own countries. Early in 2008, more than four thousand French academics, art historians, archaeologists and others signed a petition opposing the Louvre partnership, insisting that France's cultural patronage was "not for sale".

It took more than eighteen months for the deal with the Louvre to be settled. A former senior French diplomat, Jean d'Haussonville, was put in charge. He saw his mission in terms of France's time-honoured *mission civilisatrice*, its mission to civilise others through

French culture. French voters and art-goers, he said, would appreciate the idea of helping "to deter [Islamic] fundamentalism through
culture". Such ideals – lofty and condescending in equal measure –
disguised the real motive: cash. Abu Dhabi paid over $500 million
just to use the name "Louvre". The total package was $1.2 billion.

As a sweetener to its critics, the French government has created
an advisory board for the Louvre to ensure that artistic standards
and artistic freedom are not compromised. Critics predict that the
museum, when it opens around 2012, will have to accommodate its
socially conservative hosts. "Thank goodness Monet painted
waterlilies [and not nudes]," said the newspaper *Libération*.
D'Haussonville admitted that the final say would rest with the local
government, not the advisory board. "At the end of the day, it is
their country, and their museum, so they can refuse any pieces."

Those who attack the cultural compromises inherent in projects such as Saadiyat may have a point, but they have chosen the
wrong targets. Given the limitless depth of his pockets, Sheikh
Khalifa is not to be condemned for seeking to spend some of his
money on high art. More at issue are the morals of the Western sellers, but, as I have seen in the dealings between Western institutions
and foreign governments, rarely are ethical considerations brought
into play when it comes to a deal. The test now is whether these universities and museums bring intellectual adventure and controversy
into a land where freedom of expression is limited and democracy is
virtually non-existent.

When George W. Bush chose Abu Dhabi as the destination to
deliver a speech on "democracy and advancing freedom" in January
2008, the point was not lost on some that he had picked a nation
with one of the least developed set of political institutions in the
region. Here was the political branch of the same compromise. Since
its formation nearly forty years ago, the UAE has witnessed only
one transfer of power and has held just one national election, of
sorts. In 2006 an electoral college selected by the UAE's royal families voted for twenty people to join a Federal National Council. The

other twenty members were handpicked. That council has only consultative powers. Political parties are banned and there are restrictions on press freedom.

I discuss the extent and the manner of censorship with Martin Newland, a former editor of the *Daily Telegraph* who was lured to Abu Dhabi to start an intriguing new venture. The *National*, an English-language paper, was launched in April 2008. It was, said its chairman, the Crown Prince, "born out of a vision that recognises the key role that a free, professional and enlightened press plays in the national development process". The aim, in other words, is to bring international journalistic standards to the Emirates, without unduly the rocking the boat. This fell far short of the greater risk taken by the Qatari royal family when it established the al-Jazeera television station back in 1996. Although the channel has refrained from any form of criticism of its paymasters (entering into a pact of its own), it has blazed a trail in the Middle East in producing independent and robust journalism. Still, the *National* does mark progress of sorts. I put to Newland something that Makkar had said to me: "When you want to say something in the local press, you can say it as long as you say it in the right way." Newland develops the thought. "As a marketing principle you won't sell papers if you attack the country's leaders. But that doesn't mean you're prevented from doing strong journalism." He points out stories, that his paper has broken, on the decision to move to nuclear energy. "Maybe they don't like 20 per cent of what we do, but they appreciate the fact that we are showing Abu Dhabi as a normal society."

As in Singapore, these arrangements are left deliberately vague. Nobody quite knows when they have overstepped the mark until they have done so. Sheikh Khalifa had long decreed that journalists should not be jailed for excessive criticism, and his government had been reluctant to use defamation laws against journalists. However, as the economic crisis began to grip, so the UAE responded in the classic manner of countries where freedoms are granted instead of enshrined in law. In early 2009, a new media law was tabled that imposed new curbs on free expression. The government had become alarmed by the media's increasing criticism of its business model and by publicity surrounding a number of major corporate scandals. The law proposed that fines of up to $150,000 should be applied "to whoever publishes news misleading public opinion in such a way as to harm the national economy". Even larger fines would be imposed on journalists criticising the royal family. Ministers sought to emphasise that critical news stories would be permitted as long as they were "well-researched" and "balanced".

The new clampdown showed the fragility of the deal. It increased the already large information gap in which reliable data were hard to come by and rumours were bound to flourish. Rules governing other areas of cultural life are similarly ill-defined. Films and books are often censored if they are deemed to offend cultural taste or to indulge in excessive criticism of the government. In one recent example, publication of a book by Christopher Davidson, a lecturer at Durham University and specialist in the UAE, was delayed. Davidson accused the authorities of censorship. The National Media Council denied this, and released it for sale, while insisting that the book contained "a plethora of errors". The authorities pay huge sums to Western public relations firms to put out press releases or answer difficult questions on their behalf, leading to the strange situation of reporters in the UAE phoning London about an event taking place in Abu Dhabi or Dubai. Western corporate skills can always be called upon to do the bidding of regimes around the world, irrespective of politics or ethics.

Not just on the record, but privately, too, many Westerners I spoke to were keen to emphasise the positives of Abu Dhabi society, although often in order to contrast it with the coarseness of neighbouring Dubai. Newland stresses that 160 languages are spoken in a tiny country. "We can prove here that the clash of civilisations theory doesn't work. Here on the street you can find a Pakistani tribesman alongside a Goldman Sachs banker. People can live happily alongside each other. This is proof positive about globalisation," he says. I cannot say that I saw the said tribesman and the said banker arm in arm, but Newland is right in pointing out a cultural mix of sorts. Westerners in their shorts and locals in their dishdashas seem at ease with each other in the restaurants and shopping malls. It is the earning and spending of money that brings them together.

Ayman Safadi is head of the media company that runs the *National*. From his vantage point, he sees Abu Dhabi as a role model for the Middle East. "Look around you, and you will see that the states functioning best in the region are either monarchies [his native Jordan, for example] or emirates. Compare this place with Yemen or Egypt or Syria. The big population centres of the Arab world are no longer the power bases. I haven't met one Emirati who is unhappy about the formula here," Safadi tells me. How many businessmen in Tehran or Beirut could establish themselves with so little hassle from the authorities, clans or religious zealots? "Western judgements on Abu Dhabi are unrealistic. Here we have a different form of accountability." As for relaxing the ruling family's grip on power, or at least providing counterpoises, he says: "You have to pace democracy. Elections are a vital tool in a democracy, but you cannot reduce democracy to elections. Democracy is a system in which to provide the best possible life for people. It's not an end in itself." The establishment of the *National*, and the greater, albeit circumscribed, freedom it enjoys, is essential to this process of pacing democracy. Safadi points to a recent study on the standard of education in the Emirates, which complained about the low level of critical faculties among indigenous students. That is already working itself through into the jobs market, where local inhabitants are finding it increasingly difficult to secure, and sustain, demanding jobs.

I get a similar picture in a very different setting. I have been driven for nearly two hours along a freeway as soft as a carpet. Trees line the road, sustained by constant watering in the desert. Behind them the sand dunes gradually shift from golden to red. The city of Al Ain, on the border with Oman, is the second largest in the Abu

Dhabi emirate. It is also the centre for learning. Only three years earlier, on my previous visit, I found few buildings of more than two storeys. Now the town has expanded dramatically; high rises are springing up. But the old character has not yet been completely destroyed. The landscape, the forts, the open markets and the barren mountain of Jebel Hafeet that bestrides the town are the nearest approximation to Arabian authenticity to be found around here. I meet Donald Baker, a Canadian, who is Dean of the College of Humanities at the UAE University. He is one of a number of professors and lecturers recruited from abroad, as part of the sheikh's concerted drive to improve education standards. The student rolls have long been a cause for concern. The UAE has each year an average of 38,000 school graduates among the local population; only four thousand go on to university, of whom 80 per cent are female, a remarkable achievement. Yet many of those women come under family pressure to give up their studies early in order to start a family. At least, at government level, women's education is regarded as vital to the country's development.

The Zayed Centre for Heritage and History, a few miles up the road, is a throwback to another age, a life without foreign cultural imports, a life of material simplicity. The corridors are lined with sepia photographs of sand and souks. "If someone had asked any sheikh twenty years ago if this is how he wanted his country to turn out, he would have been shocked." Hasan Al-Naboodah teaches medieval Islamic studies, specialising in the history of Oman. "Now this development can't stop. It will have to continue until the end. Everything has gone beyond our leaders' control." He is exercised by the plight of local people, many of whom he says do not do nearly as well as one might think because of the sharply uneven distribution of wealth. What alarms him and others most, however, is the erosion of culture. A quietly spoken man who has studied for long periods in the West, he insists he is not averse to the principle of modernisation of the UAE, but to the speed and manner of its practice. He knows that criticism can lead to accusations of sympathising with

Islamists, of dragging the UAE back into the dark ages, all of which he emphatically denies. Some people are using websites to express their misgivings, anonymously, on issues ranging from the demographic imbalance, the disappearance of the Arabic language, the buying up of properties by foreigners and competition over jobs. Most stay silent.

Some get away with stark criticism. In April 2008, a warning by the head of police about social instability made headline news. "I'm afraid we are building towers but losing the Emirates," General Dhahi Khalfan Tamim told a "national identity conference" in Abu Dhabi attended by all the top figures. The very survival of the royal family was at stake, he said. While praising Sheikh Khalifa's decision to declare 2008 "national identity year", he said Emiratis had been late in tackling the demographic problem. The "demographic imbalance", as it is politely called, is stark. Less than 15 per cent of the population of the UAE are indigenous. The rest are foreigners. Al-Naboodah describes it to me like this: "Local people are hunkering down in their compounds in a state of shock. They feel marginalised. They are living through inner migration. Here in Abu Dhabi they have oil. They don't need anything else. This is what the people don't understand. They could have lived a beautiful and luxurious life. They don't need a bigger population."

Such are the underlying tensions among local people that the ruling family could not afford to introduce greater democracy, even if it wanted to, he says. He points to the contradiction at the heart of the West's emphasis on "democratisation". Free elections for the local population in the UAE would, he says, undermine the ruling family and its entire economic project of growth through foreign labour. "Imagine what would be the reaction if you had a functioning parliament here."

In Abu Dhabi I return to visit an old haunt. In March 2005 I had the dubious honour of being one of the first ever guests in the Emirates Palace hotel. To my surprise the only other person I found in the breakfast room was the German tennis star Boris Becker. I had arrived a day before an organised press trip. I remember describing in my article the sheer scale of the place – 6,000 square metres of gold leaf, has 7,000 doors, 12,000 signs and 1,002 chandeliers made with Swarovski crystals. "The centre of the palace is dominated by a grand atrium, the biggest in the world. Its gilded dome outstrips the one in St Paul's Cathedral. The public lounge is the size of two football pitches. It already employs 1,200 people from 50 countries, a veritable tower of Babel in Armani, short skirts and gold braided jackets. Even with full occupancy, that would translate into four staff for every guest," I wrote. The highest category guest enjoyed their own entrance. "Their limos sweep through the Palace's own Arc de Triomphe (inexplicably, slightly smaller than the Paris original) and up a ramp to the higher floors. That is, if they would rather not use the hotel's own helipad. The rest of us have to make do with a procession past an orgy of fountains to the main entrance."

My reaction to the place was a fairly standard mix of disdain for the excess but also a little awe, best kept to oneself in polite Western society. Who, after all, would admit to finding such a display of bling anything but vulgar? I could imagine people going there for a laugh, for a weekend of self-mocking self-indulgence, but I could not see a hotel of such great scale and small taste becoming popular. That was never the point. In the Emirates, projects such as these are individual follies. They do not conform to standard business plans. I was relieved to see in late 2008 more people frequenting the hotel than my previous time. It is now the centre of Abu Dhabi's business and diplomatic scene, with presidents, kings, chief executives and sports stars regular visitors. But I still cannot imagine how it makes ends meet.

Travelling between Abu Dhabi and Dubai has long ceased to be an exotic experience. Whereas a few years ago one might have seen, from the comfort of an air-conditioned car, the odd Bedouin walking on the sand, the vista is now dominated by buildings, cranes and more buildings. Dubai has been building, out of nothing, 120 kilometres of canal, with houses on either side. This process is now slowing down, but few doubt it will resume in earnest. Once the joint population reaches ten million, the two cities will have effectively joined together. Locals predict it will be known as Abu Dubai.

Dubai has long made its more grown-up cousin feel distinctly middle aged. The package it presented around the world – stability, property deals, high-earning potential and endless shopping and recreational opportunities – proved consistently attractive to hundreds of thousands of foreigners. Dubai was seen as one of the three links in the great globalisation miracle, as the boom-time saying went, along with Shanghai and Mumbai. London, New York and Tokyo were dismissed as yesterday's cities. Some of the more sensible in the financial community regarded this as another example of the hubris that had carried Dubai from a backwater to the construction jungle that it had become. But their voices were rarely heard. Why should they be, when people were having so much fun making so much money?

Dubai turned itself into the global hub of greed. Each symbol of luxury had to be outdone by another. The developers' thirst showed no limit. Other considerations were ignored, such as heritage or environment. Few seemed to complain when one new entrant, the Palazzo Versace hotel boasted a refrigerated 800-square-metre swimming pool and a beach with artificially cooled sand and wind machines to protect its guests from the excesses of the summer heat. "We will suck the heat out of the sand to keep it cool enough to lie on," said the president of the hotel group. "This is the kind of luxury that top people want." It seemed to matter little that, per head of population, the UAE was the second largest carbon emitter.

Sheikh Mohammed bin Rashid al-Maktoum, the ruler, affectionately known as "Sheikh Mo", turned his plot of land from a mini-kingdom to a global corporation. A decade ago, as the oil began to run out and revenues dwindle, he charted a different course for Dubai's prosperity. It was based on property, tourism, shipping (through Jebel Ali) and creating a new financial centre halfway between London and Singapore, tax free for individuals and many corporations.

The public relations talk is laden with superlatives. The Burj al Arab is the world's tallest hotel, taller than the Eiffel Tower and only slightly shorter than the Empire State Building. It was the world's first self-styled, seven-star hotel, prompting envious Abu Dhabi to build the Emirates Palace. When the Burj al Arab was built, the sail-shaped shard of steel and Teflon-coated glass became Dubai's national symbol. It has since been overtaken in height by the Burj Dubai, as the race for the gaudiest construction has gathered pace. "Monument. Jewel. Icon. Burj Dubai will be known by many names. But only a privileged group of people will call Burj Dubai home," proclaims the literature. In July 2007, a still unfinished skyscraper, it overtook Taipei 101 to become the world's tallest building.

Sheikh Mo's plans were not hard to fathom. From B-list Western celebrities, to financiers, footballers and tourists, everyone was welcome to take a slice of the pie and come and go as they pleased, as long as they abided by his rules. A sharp intake of breath accompanies the announcement of each construction project. For years the skyline has bristled with cranes – an estimated 20 percent of the world's total. Dubai has seen the first ski dome built in the desert; it has seen vast artificial islands rise from the sea, from the Palm, home to many of England's football stars, and the World, around three hundred artificial private islands, shaped like the continents of the world. Each would be owned by someone rich or famous, who would be delivered to and from the mainland by personal speedboat. Most marketing strategies were based around celebrities, who were invited to take complimentary or hugely discounted properties, to set an example. Part of the sales pitch for Burj Dubai was to seek out world statesmen like Henry Kissinger, Bill Clinton and Tony Blair so that like-minded people could meet each other in the lift, and feel comfortable in their hermetically sealed environment. It was, as one developer admitted to me, "designed to increase the brain power, along with the bling".

From on high looking down over the city, Nicholas Maclean pointed out to me all the various projects under construction. The regional head of one of the main international real estate firms, he took me through the plans for Dubai in meticulous detail. Over the next four years some 75 million square metres of office and residential space was scheduled to be built, more than trebling the total amount of land under use. The new airport site alone would have eight hundred towers. Such was the demand that the local paper, the *Gulf News*, had at one point three pullouts a day on property, partly to deal with the speculation, but mainly to accommodate the 300,000 new arrivals per year. "Build it and the people will follow" was the abiding principle. That was before the crash. They are less bullish now.

Dubai rivals anywhere in the world for the excesses of luxury coupled with the worst inequality. At any time, night and day, gangs of "guest workers" – usually from India, Pakistan or Bangladesh – can be seen pounding away on building sites. As the NGO Human Rights Watch puts it, "one of the world's largest construction booms is feeding off workers in Dubai who are treated as less than human". Employers routinely deny construction workers their wages. Officials with the UAE Permanent Committee for Labour and Immigration told the NGO that, last year alone, nearly 20,000 workers filed complaints with the government about the non-payment of wages and labour camp conditions.

Most construction workers secure work in the UAE by taking loans from recruiting agencies in their home country. A typical labourer uses a large portion of his wages (average £70 a month) towards repayment of such loans on a monthly basis, and without wages he falls further into debt. They have no access to healthcare or other basic rights. The companies that sponsor them hold on to their passports – and often a month or two of their wages to make sure that they keep working. The result is virtual debt bondage, a system of indentured labour. Industrial accidents are a regular occurrence. Independent research published in local media found that an average of two to three deaths occur every day. These labourers work in shifts and sleep in shifts, sometimes twenty to a room. Yet, according to UN agencies, there have been up to 300,000 illegal workers in the Emirates at any one time. When the going was good, some workers took part in public protests and strikes in an attempt to improve working conditions. One unpalatable truth was that most workers did everything they could to extend their stay, knowing that they were earning up to ten times what they would get back home, even after all the various deductions and humiliations. Another even more unpalatable truth was that everyone who was making money in Dubai – the real estate companies, hoteliers, tourism chiefs, the financial whizz-kids – knew they were doing it off the backs of the exploited from South Asia.

When it came to consumer excess, Sheikh Mo led from the front. His shopping list around the world included the *QE2* – complete with Tilbury and Southampton docks; Barneys, the upmarket department store in New York; a share of Standard Chartered Bank; half of the Las Vegas Strip; and Australia's leading thoroughbred stud operation, to add to his stud farms in the UAE, Britain and Ireland. Not to be outdone, Sheikh Khalifa, has invested in Warner Brothers and in an unlikely English Premiership football club, Manchester City, with instructions to spend whatever it takes to make it the biggest club in the world. Most of the sheikhs' buying is done by aides who run private equity-style investment houses; but it is they who stump up the cash.

Sovereign Wealth Funds achieved their true money in the UAE. The wealth became truly sovereign. The biggest of the thirty or so funds is the Abu Dhabi Investment Authority (ADIA). Throughout the period of global growth, as the oil price soared, the funds looked for institutions into which to invest. The assumption was of steady returns. The Kuwait Investment Authority paid $3 billion for a stake in Citigroup and invested $2 billion in Merrill Lynch; ADIA had already bought a 4.9 per cent stake in Citigroup for $7.5 billion.

Funds from Qatar and Dubai took hold of a third of the London Stock Exchange.

Initially, the concern was expressed only in one direction. Western politicians complained at how funds owned by authoritarian regimes and run as secretively as any hedge fund or private equity firm were taking over strategic assets. One of Germany's leading politicians, Franz Müntefering, who went on to become Vice Chancellor, described them as "locusts". That term became widely used as protectionist impulses increased.

The wake-up call for the UAE came in 2006. The British company P&O, which owned six US ports in its global portfolio, including New York's, agreed to a takeover by Dubai Ports World. The acquisition was referred to Congress and to the Bush administration, which gave it the nod. The White House was keen to keep Sheikhs Khalifa and Mo happy, to show appreciation for the discreet cooperation of past years. When the deal became public, however, popular opposition led to the House Appropriations Committee voting an astonishing 62–2 to stop the takeover. That humiliation hurt in the UAE, amid allegations of dirty dealings on all sides. Bush was furious. Politicians and business leaders on both sides were chastened, and vowed to prevent a recurrence. Key to that was a public relations campaign extolling not just the financial virtues of the Emirates, but its atmosphere as an easy place to do business and relax. All outward manifestations of "fundamentalism" were played down. Religion, too, played its part in the pact.

Sheikhs Mo and Khalifa have long balanced the competing requirements of Western influence with religious traditions that forbid alcohol, unmarried sex and homosexuality. Most of the time the authorities turn a blind eye, particularly in Dubai: alcohol is freely on sale in all hotels and restaurants, even during the holy month of Ramadan. They have sought to assuage increasing indignation at home and in other Muslim countries about Western decadence by announcing regular crackdowns (accompanied by the odd person being made an example of, before business returns to normal) and exuberant assertions of allegiance to Islam. On the outskirts of Abu Dhabi, they have been building the Sheikh Zayed Mosque, an architectural feat containing a Persian carpet said to be the biggest in the world. Inevitably, Sheikh Khalifa wanted it to be the world's largest mosque, in honour of his father, but neighbouring Saudi Arabia complained, insisting that it should not usurp Islam's two holiest sites – Mecca's Grand Mosque and the Prophet's Mosque in Medina.

Dubai's hedonistic image was proving increasingly problematical. One Dubai government official described a particular class of Westerner to me as the "the tattoo and sunburn brigade". The lowest point was reached in 2008 with the arrest, and conviction, of two Britons on charges of having sex in a public place. The "bonking on the beach" story became a cause célèbre back in the UK. Newspapers sent teams of reporters over to write vivid articles about both their antics, but also about the "brutality" of the host country. This was one of those classic cases of a smattering of racism with a hint of colonialism, not a little xenophobia, and a simplistic view about social customs. The couple concerned had done what hundreds of expatriates do on the main day of prayer for Muslims, and gone to one of the city's hotels for the now traditional Friday all-you-can-drink champagne brunches. They emerged, inebriated, and were discovered by a police officer on Jumeirah beach having sex on the sand. He let them off with a caution, but ordered the couple to leave. They ignored the warning and were arrested when the officer returned to the scene. According to police sources, the woman launched a tirade at the policeman after being disturbed for a second time. She is alleged to have hurled abuse and tried to hit him with one of her high-heeled shoes (as George Bush was later to find out in Baghdad, a particularly insulting act) before being restrained and taken to a cell. In October 2008, they were found guilty by Dubai's Court of First Instance of unmarried sex and public indecency and were given three-month jail terms. That was later suspended on appeal, and the two were allowed to leave the country.

Theirs was an egregious breaking of the pact – a combination of booze, rudeness, violence and religious insult. Rather than being a symbol of repression, it could be argued that the treatment of the couple was lenient. I can imagine many countries, including some described as "democracies", where they would have been treated more harshly. On Dubai's lively expat websites, most foreigners expressed anger at their actions, which would make it harder for them to enjoy themselves in future. Westerners had been allowed to get on with whatever they wanted to do, as long as they did not flaunt it in public. For as long as the money was flowing, it seemed an easy compromise for most to make.

The balancing act extends beyond cultural sensitivities into geo-politics. The UAE has been used a number of times in recent years as a discreet venue for sensitive Middle East negotiations, such as over Lebanon, Libya and Pakistan. The host government can assure the various parties, with confidence, that their cover will not be blown. The unwritten pact ensures that, particularly after a word in an editor's ear, certain subjects will remain off limits. Abu Dhabi and Dubai have been likened to Vienna during the Cold War – a meeting place for East and West. A less flattering comparison could be Switzerland during the Second World War, a country that played one side off against the other, providing a financial bolt hole for anyone, and asking no questions about what they were getting up to.

A modern-day version of this deal is made with the Americans, who have much invested in the UAE, militarily and politically. Although it does not have a permanent base, as it does in Singapore, the US Navy puts more sailors ashore for more days a year at Jebel Ali than at any other foreign port. The US Defense Department supplies the Emirates with billions of dollars of the latest sophisticated weaponry, most significantly the recent sale of Patriot missiles. Having a loyal and well-armed ally so close to Iran serves US interests well. At the same time, the Americans turn a blind eye to the UAE sending daily shipments of Western goods to Iran. This trade, on which Iran is utterly dependent, violates sanctions designed by America to punish Tehran for its long-standing defiance.

Then there is the terrorism pact. It has long been a curiosity as to why the UAE has avoided a bombing spectacular, given the country's geography, the ethnic mix and the number of signature buildings that would prove tempting for al-Qaeda and affiliated groups. Such a strike would prove a spectacular publicity coup for militant Islamists. It would lead to mayhem, capital flight and a collapse in confidence. The Americans know that two of the nineteen men who staged the 9/11 attacks were UAE nationals. It was said that half of the attacks' $500,000 budget was wired to the US from Dubai. Yet the Americans directed their ire at Afghanistan and later at Pakistan, but not at the UAE, as they could easily have done. They saw that relationship as too important to jeopardise.

Local and Western security services keep a close eye on who is doing what in Dubai and Abu Dhabi. Residents say that some people who have got into trouble for petty crime are quietly offered immunity in return for reporting on colleagues. Other inducements are offered, as one businessman tells me: "People are given residency in return for spooking. Others who get into trouble are told they won't be thrown out of the country as long as they cooperate. Everyone assumes there are spooks in every office." He adds, in an intriguing example of the deal on offer: "I rather like the fact that if I caused trouble here I'd be caught within a couple of days." The pact, it seems, has a variety of uses.

The number of threats monitored by Western embassies has increased steadily in recent years; but until now they have remained only threats. Perhaps the most compelling reason for the absence of terrorism is the role the UAE plays in laundering the money of some of those deemed responsible for 9/11 through local banks and businesses set up in elaborate chains. It is, say some, a "gentleman's agreement" – you can use the territory for rest, recreation and wealth creation, as long as you keep your military activities offshore. It is not just al-Qaeda that has benefited. The father of Pakistan's nuclear programme, A. Q. Khan, admitted heading a clandestine group that, with the help of a Dubai company, supplied Pakistani nuclear technology to Iran, Libya and North Korea.

The role of the UAE is not dissimilar to the role played by London, which offered militant Islamists a place to make and save their money in the pre-9/11 era (Londonistan), just as it became a haven for oligarchs of dubious repute after that (Londongrad). Members of a lower-grade form of Russian mafia have also made Dubai their home. It is said that at any given time a half of all the rooms in the top hotels are occupied by Russians. From time to time shoot-outs occur, most famously in the luxury Burj al Arab hotel in 2006 when a Syrian diamond seller was shot dead. The industries in precious metals, drugs and prostitution are controlled largely by the Russian underworld. Most of the escorts and call girls are flown in quietly through Al Ain airport, ending up in brothels masquerading as nightclubs. The most infamous of these is Cyclone, where girls are said to be valued according to their nationality, with Russians usually commanding the highest prices. Globalisation meets market meets demand. Expat websites gossip endlessly about places such as these, but they are not talked about in polite society or in the official media. From time to time they are raided and shut down. They then reopen after "renovation" or re-emerge in different premises. This is the sleazy side of the pact.

"We want to provide moral integrity," says Nicholas Labuschagne. A South African, he is one of a number of foreign consultants who have been brought in to advise the ruling family. Dubai is keen, he says, to shed its reputation for low taste and amorality. Education, healthcare and efficient governance provide the key. He points to a new Academic City, with thousands of new places in university and technical colleges. His message is similar to that of several people I spoke to in Abu Dhabi. It is a far cry from Western concepts of liberal democracy, but it is also far removed from other countries in the region. Is this, I ask him, an attempt to provide a cloak of respectability, or does it signify something more?

"We are genuinely seeking to develop a positive model of development for the rest of the region to follow," Labuschagne tells me. "This is not just about money."

My last visit to the region took place the week after the collapse of Lehmann Brothers in New York. Most of the financiers, real estate and tourism bosses I met in Dubai and Abu Dhabi were cautiously confident that they would escape the sudden economic collapse being experienced in the West. One CEO, while acknowledging the potential dangers, told me his biggest problem at that time was dealing with the plaintive requests for a job, any job, from people he knew back home in Britain who had either lost theirs or feared they would imminently. "I'm getting inundated by emails with people offering their CVs," he said. Most people I spoke to then were reasonably confident that Dubai, even with its exposure to property, would get away with a "soft landing". They convinced themselves that the UAE was de-coupled from the economies of the West, and that their wealth pact was more durable than that of the "old countries".

The speed and the depth of the economic collapse shook the royal family. Sheikhs Khalifa and Mohammed had, in their different ways, seen their city states as beacons of this new consumerist world, but more than that, too. They saw them as an example for others to follow, particularly those in the Middle East, a melting pot of different cultures brought together by the allure of prosperity. With thousands bailing out of town, the government announced an expansionary budget to stimulate the economy; an extra $50 billion would be pumped in for infrastructure projects, to add to the $200 billion already earmarked. Such measures were easier to perform in a country where the politically powerful had a stake in every major corporation. The source of the money was the older family member, Khalifa, coming to the rescue of the younger, profligate, Mo. Desperate and indebted Dubai was helped by oil-rich and demure Abu Dhabi.

There was another bail-out story, too, one which the authorities were even more desperate to keep secret. From the autumn of 2008, the US and other Western nations secretly cajoled and coerced the UAE to help them out in these times of need. Old favours, such as America's discreet security guarantee to the sheikhs and its preparedness to turn a blind eye to their dealings with some around al-Qaeda, were being called in.

Henry Paulson, Bush's Treasury Secretary, had several unpublicised meetings with Gulf leaders and ministers, urging them to inject money into the desperate American car industry and other parts of the economy. The Sovereign Wealth Funds had already taken a large hit, thanks to investment in that very same American economy, but there were still tens of billions ready to be invested. President Bush feted several members of the Emirati royal families at Camp David, including a number of figures in senior positions at the ultra-secretive ADIA wealth fund. It seemed at that moment that the only place in the world with spare cash was Abu Dhabi. It was time, he told them, to repay an old friendship. Another intriguing meeting came at the start of November 2008 when Gordon Brown, the British Prime Minister, made a two-day visit to the UAE. The trip aroused little attention back home, as it coincided with the dramatic results of the US presidential elections. The Prime Minister urged China and the Gulf to use their wealth funds to boost the IMF's coffers after it had been forced to dig into reserves to provide emergency loans to European countries in danger of going bust, such as Iceland, Hungary and Ukraine. He framed his appeal in somewhat narrow terms. The problem was considerably broader. The West was broke. The so-called democratic world was going, cap in hand, to its new paymasters.

All problems were relative in these new dramatic times. Dubai had flaunted itself on easy money and – in the eyes of its Arab neighbour – easy living. It had indulged in the economics of a housing boom, excessive credit and other irresponsible financial practices. Dubai is in many ways a brand more than a country, dependent on its reputation for money and luxury, and with little else to fall back on if the glitz comes off. It would suffer in the short term. But, thanks to Abu Dhabi, it would not collapse, and should prepare itself to start afresh.

For those who had not been forced to sell up and leave (mostly those who had bought property early, when prices were low), life would remain relatively unchanged. The White Tribe of Arabia could continue to shop in the same shops they had back home; they could continue to work in environments similar to home. They could top up their tans, play tennis, and they could drink, indoors, whenever they wanted. Nothing was required of them except to make and spend money. This was the most undemanding of pacts, and for many people it was an attractive one. This was the money pact, in its purest form. Everyone, from the British office worker, to the Lebanese entrepreneur, to the Iranian importer, to the American government had made the appropriate compromises to enjoy what it had to offer.

5

INDIA: POPULOUS
ALTERNATIVE

*"The myth of tolerance remains strong . . . we must
surely be one of the cruellest free societies in the world"* –
Tarun Tejpal

TWO ARMED GUARDS LURK BEHIND THE LOWERED GATE OF
Teesta Setalvad's home. They slouch rather than stand alert as I
approach. I have come to see one of India's bravest campaigners for
civil liberties, the granddaughter of a former Attorney General, a
woman who decided to step out of the mainstream in order to
expose state abuses and collusion in what is supposed to be the
world's largest democracy.

A journalist by trade, Setalvad edits a monthly magazine called
Communalism Combat. She set it up because she was alarmed that
the national media had given up reporting on the more unpleasant
side of life, concerned rather to portray India as being on a shining
path to modernity and prosperity. In particular, they had stopped
investigating the role of politicians and security forces in the many
incidents of communal strife that India has endured over the years.
"The media are silent on brutality and caste," she tells me, as we sit
on a bench in the courtyard that divides her home from her

ramshackle office. "The relationship between reader and papers has been commodified. Today protests and real politics don't make news," she says.

I ask her why she needs all the protection around her home. She tells me she receives several threatening telephone calls every week. The Central Industrial Security Force, one of India's security agencies, has given her round-the-clock protection, particularly in the Mumbai area and whenever she travels within her native state of Gujarat. That provides some reassurance, but not much. Bodyguards provided by the Indian state are not among the most feared in the world. Her security men try their hardest but have failed to prevent at least six attacks on her car so far. Setalvad is regarded by many in power as a troublemaker. A number of newsagents no longer stock her magazine. It is, they are warned, not worth the consequences.

Having toured countries that fall into the supposed authoritarian camp, I want to test the pact in a democracy – and not just any democracy. India's constitutional achievement over sixty years of independence is remarkable. This country of more than one billion people, with two thousand ethnic groups and two hundred languages, has, for all but one brief period, doggedly pursued a path of multi-party democracy, a separation of powers, independent judiciary and free expression. In theory, it ticks just about every democratic box. But beyond the ritual of the vote, what freedoms exactly does it deliver, and for whom? Does it, as some in China suggested to me, deliver real freedom for people to determine the way they lead their lives?

Setalvad began *Communalism Combat* after a series of religious riots in the early 1990s involving Hindus and Muslims. Her journalists looked not just at the causes of the violence, but at the response by the security forces that followed. In one of her first issues she pointed out how in areas run by Hindu nationalist groups the police were encouraged to target Muslims and other minorities. "In its callous disregard for civil liberties and gross violation of human rights, the police in India have been thoroughly non-discriminatory in the past," she wrote. "With growing com-munalisation of politicians and the police, Muslims have been selectively targeted for detention, ill treatment and torture in a number of states since 1990."

She and her team have spent years investigating one of the most brutal episodes in the history of independent India. In February 2002, just outside the town of Godhra in the western state of Gujarat, fifty-eight Hindus, many of them women and children, were burnt alive as mobs set fire to their train. They had been returning from the town of Ayodhya, the centre of a dispute between Muslims and Hindus over the building of a temple on the site of a demolished Mughal mosque. Dozens of Muslims were arrested and charged; they pleaded that they had been taunted by the Hindus. The Chief Minister of Gujarat, Narendra Modi, decreed a day of mourning so that funerals could take place in the state's largest city, Ahmedabad. Crowds of people, many wearing the saffron scarves and khaki shorts that are the uniform of Hindu nationalism, and armed with swords, explosives and gas cylinders, rampaged in search of vengeance. They poured kerosene down the throats of men, women and children, before setting them alight. As many subse-quent investigations have shown, police chiefs and politicians from the ruling Bharatiya Janata Party (BJP) either stood by or helped them in their task, providing them with computer printouts of addresses. More than a thousand people, most of them Muslims, were killed. About 230 mosques and shrines were razed to the ground. When asked to condemn the violence, Modi instead quoted Isaac Newton's third law: "Every action has an equal and opposite reaction." Modi has neither apologised nor expressed regret for what happened.

Setalvad has many enemies, but Modi in particular does not appreciate her endeavours to pursue justice. He is not one of those colourful local warlords of a failed or failing state. He is one of the country's most talked-about politicians, and he is seen – for better or for worse – as a face of modern India. Only months after the Gujarat riots, Modi was re-elected Chief Minister. In 2007 he won again, for an unprecedented third time. A man who dresses modestly, is seen as a paragon of fiscal rectitude and possessing an alluring gift of oratory, he is already a key player on the national scene. Many observers say it is only a matter of time before he becomes Prime Minister. He is feted by India's corporate elite, the heads of the giants like Tata, Reliance, Airtel and Infosys. These men, the types that over the years have graced the covers of *Forbes* and *Fortune* magazines, point to Modi's role in fostering Gujarat's consistently high growth rates, fiscal probity, efficiency and entrepreneurial spirit. Gujarat is known as the pioneer state, the beacon for the rest of the country to follow, India's version of Singapore. Western entrepreneurs queue at Modi's door. His state has more internal investment than any other. The saying goes that, unlike the rest of India, the trains really do run on time in Gujarat.

Yet, for several years, Modi has been refused a visa to visit the United States on human rights grounds, a decision that India's business elite see as humiliating and undeserved. They have been lobbying Washington to reverse its decision, confident that it will. Money, they insist, will eventually talk. In the years straight after independence the elite had a great sense of responsibility for the development of the country as a whole. Now all it wants to do is make money and live well. I am from the self-same privileged elite. But if we're not able to take on people like Modi, then what's the point of our democracy?" Setalvad asks.

Why is this one individual, this one incident of violence among so many in India, and this one state so important? Everyone I talk to has an impassioned view about Modi. He is alternately a saviour or dictator (in some cases both). Many ordinary voters, not just in Gujarat, and many international and local business leaders, appear willing to overlook whatever misdeeds took place because they identify in him a chance for India to advance. They see him as providing a hospitable business environment, an oasis of entrepreneurship in a country whose long-term aspirations are impeded by a large and

mainly poor and uneducated population, bad and decaying infrastructure and a chaotic political system. This was a similar thought
process to the one that greeted Vladimir Putin in Russia and has sustained the Communist Party in China. Chaos is the word many
Russians used to describe the Gorbachev–Yeltsin years and the
Chinese used to warn about what would have happened if the
Tiananmen protests had been allowed to succeed.

Modi is the latest politician on whom India's business elite
have pinned their hopes over the past two decades. The country has
moved a long way from the vision of its founding father, Mahatma
Gandhi, another Gujarati, the man who made the spinning wheel
the symbol of the freedom movement. Gandhi sought an India in
which poverty alleviation, religious pluralism and the protection of
minorities against the Hindu majority would be the abiding priorities. The governments of Jawaharlal Nehru and his daughter Indira
Gandhi expanded the role of the state, nationalising the banks and
introducing land reform. Although the economy did grow, the gap
between India and developed countries increased. A series of financial crises led to a sudden about-turn in 1991, and the adoption of
economic liberalisation under the Congress government of
Narasimha Rao and his Finance Minister, Manmohan Singh. Rao
announced to India that out of economic malaise came the opportunity to "sweep the cobwebs of the past and usher in change". Red
tape was cut, capital markets were partly deregulated, labour markets were opened up, and credit became the order of the day. In his
authoritative study of the economic changes, Gurcharan Das likens
financial deregulation in India to Deng Xiaoping's opening up of
China. Das argues that Rao's revolution was, if anything, more
important than Nehru's political revolution of 1947.

Modern India was born in 1991, or at least that is what the free
market proselytisers subsequently argued. It joined the ranks of
globalised states, offering a new and potentially attractive pact to its
people, or rather those who would be able to join it. Under its terms,
tens of millions of people would be left alone to make money. The

state would not stand in their way, turning a blind eye to tax avoidance and other excesses. The new wealthy would be free to become involved in politics if they wished – this, after all, was a democracy – but they would be wasting their energies if they did. Instead, they disengaged from politics and from state activity, safe in the knowledge that, once elected, politicians at all levels would look after their interests, as long as they looked after the politicians' interests. That meant their wallets.

From that point on, material spending was elevated into a national pastime. Economic growth was seen as a symbol of national virility. Between 1999 and 2008, India's economy trebled in size. In July 2006, the US magazine *Foreign Affairs* declared India a "roaring capitalist success story", throwing off its shackles on a one-way path to prosperity. The Indian dream became an attractive mix of the old "spirituality", coupled with a romanticised view of its democracy and now the ability for foreigners to find a Starbucks on many a street corner. Back home, the *Times of India* carried daily reports of takeovers and business deals under banner headlines such as "India Poised" and "Global Indian Takeover". The BJP benefited most, with its alluring slogan "India Shining". The "market wallahs", as they were dubbed, the IT whizz-kids, the new aspiring call centre worker in Bangalore and Hyderabad, were all part of a single linear narrative – we are making it, we are joining the world club.

The Gandhian ideal of national self-sufficiency gave way to full exposure to global markets and alliance with the West. Many of the global questions of human rights and social justice – from Burma, to Tibet, to Palestine – were no longer treated with the same priority by Indian governments. Non-aligned status was abandoned, and in return the Bush administration succeeded in persuading US Congress to wave through a deal in July 2005 allowing India to become a nuclear power. India received a special dispensation. Assisting the economic and military rise of a democratic India, Bush believed, would help reinforce the shift of the global balance of power in favour of "freedom". As with Singapore, the UAE and

China, India came to a deal with America: all would march to a similar economic tune, in return for discreet cooperation and a willingness on all sides to turn a blind eye to the more unsavoury actions of the state.

The enthusiastic portrayal of India in foreign media as the coming nation, in competition with China, fed a new-found patriotism. It also loosened the inter-communal cohesion that had been a feature of the early years of independence. The BJP was in pole position to harness both of these trends, and to convert *Hindutva*, a sense of Hindu belonging, into the abiding national cause.

In the twenty years of liberalisation, the poor, the 75 per cent of the population living on less than $2 a day, have lived a parallel existence. Their plight is as acute now as it has ever been, inextricably twinned with malnourishment and illiteracy. The grinding routine of India's downtrodden, and the humiliations they endure, has been documented in trenchant critiques by Pankaj Mishra, Arundhati Roy and others. Books and films have described the deals between the slumlords, the police and the politicians, the extortion and protection rackets, the beatings, the constant threats of relocation and demolition, the particular misery the monsoons bring. Research academies provide a welter of statistics, charting levels of inequality. For all the economic growth, less than 1 per cent of the budget goes on public health. Child malnutrition levels remain higher than much of sub-Saharan Africa. UNICEF studies have shown that more than half of all women and three-quarters of all children below the age of three in India are anaemic. The problem is not a lack of information or transparency, but a lack of will.

Amartya Sen once asked how India could ever thrive being half Californian Silicon Valley and half sub-Saharan Africa. But it has done – and with consummate ease. In cities like Mumbai, the proximity of the haves to the have-nots is an inconvenience that the wealthy do all they can to avoid. City slums, from Juhu to Dharavi, are within view of the passengers in their SUVs, nestled close to airports, railway tracks and main highways. Air-conditioned shopping malls have helped to shut out the people that shoppers might otherwise encounter in the bazaars on the street. One of the more popular malls for Mumbai's middle class is Atria, which opened in the Worli district in 2006, offering India's first Rolls-Royce showroom, Apple computer outlet and food mall. It is situated just a few yards from corrugated sheds, a sewage treatment plant and other manifestations of slum dwelling.

There was nothing unusual about the spending patterns of India's wealthy and aspiring wealthy over these years. They fell into the same pattern as their counterparts from Singapore to Moscow to Shanghai, from London to Milan. Consumer tastes were globalised and homogenised. Perhaps the only difference is the Indians' sense of discomfort at having to endure unsavoury sights of the poor on the way to their hermetically sealed pleasures.

The author Pavan Varma has studied the development of the middle class during the two decades of economic reform. He divides this group into four segments: the Very Rich, comprising around six million people, the Consuming Class (the equivalent of the developed country's middle class), then the Climbers (with a certain amount of disposable income, but a strong intention to acquire it), and the Aspirants (who do not have very much but think their children one day might). It is the first two groups that are most important politically and economically, while the latter two reinforce them in their certitudes.

The paradox for India is that all these groups see themselves as hostages to forces beyond their control. In theory they are. They are subject to a democratic process without precedent in the world, in which hundreds of millions of illiterate or barely literate people determine the outcome of elections. Which other country boasts a system of universal franchise for national, regional and local governments on such a vast scale? Vote-buying and rigging takes place, as before, but even the harshest critics concede that the electoral process tends to reflect the popular will. And that means the will of the hundreds of millions of the poor. Is it any wonder that the middle classes have adopted a siege mentality? Turnout among the wealthier has long been lower than among the poorer, so much so that the newspapers have taken to exhorting the middle classes to vote. The *Times of India*'s most recent campaign was entitled "Wake Up India". What it really meant was wake up, you wealthy; don't put your fate in the hands of others.

Setalvad's mini-fortress is close to the beach in Juhu, the district in northern Mumbai that is synonymous with Bollywood. Set back from the main roads are long lines of whitewashed villas, many with their own security guards. The Marriott Hotel is the favourite venue for actors, producers and financiers to discuss deals. I am there discussing democracy with one of Hollywood's – not Bollywood's – chosen number, the director Shekhar Kapur. His latest project is a film about water shortages, a far cry from his previous more glamorous ventures. "Economic prosperity is the defining power here. Only the wealthy and the powerful have real freedom in India," he says. "Here the systems are subverted. For example, the judicial system works on a high level, but not for the poor." How come India has such a loquacious intelligentsia and such a poor body politic, I ask him? "The only way to get ahead in politics is to be corrupt. Politicians think they have a sense of entitlement after investing so much time in getting elected." Coalition building is a lucrative business. At national level, ministries such as telecommunications and transport provide the best opportunities to cream off contracts. A similar system applies at each rung of the ladder.

    Sometimes the odd individual breaks the mould. One of the more attractive features of election campaigns in a number of democratic countries is their ability to produce mavericks. Adolf D'Souza is one. When I call for directions he tells me that his constituency office is next door to a temple in "garage number one". Surrounded by plastic chairs, crates, a water cooler and mounds of paper, he tells me of his miniature political experiment. An activist

in Juhu's Catholic Church since his teens, he set up his own neighbourhood group, the Aware Citizens Platform, in 2002, which would
monitor the performance of candidates for Mumbai's council, the
Municipal Corporation. The ratings among voters were so low that
they decided to offer their own next time around, which is where he
came in. At the 2007 local elections, D'Souza defeated the candidate
from the Congress Party by six hundred votes to become the representative of Ward 63. His team spent only 57,000 rupees (roughly
£800) on the campaign; he estimates his opponents spent massively
more.

"I didn't make specific promises on the campaign. I simply
told people that if they want to make a difference they had not just
to vote but to participate," D'Souza says. His ward committee meets
twice a month to make collective decisions that he has to abide by.
Most of his time, however, is devoted to the immediate problems of
the district – bad roads, garbage that is not cleared, dodgy sewerage
and dirty water. The problem is that, to get anything done, to hurry
things along, contractors invariably require payment, and unless
you stick to the code you are likely to be frustrated. "Here you can
pay your way out of anything. There is an unspoken language."

D'Souza lives with his father and travels around the area in
rickshaws. He is paid 10,000 rupees a month (around £140), which
would be a comfortable sum for most people, but is derisory for
politicians. Estimates vary for the extent of the corruption of India's
three layers of politicians. The assumption is that the vast majority,
no matter what their professionalism at the job itself, use their
tenure, particularly at local and state level, to make money. People
point to the odd individual – Manmohan Singh is one – whom they
would call "clean". On the polite dinner party circuit, where politics
is treated with a mix of intrigue, disdain and apathy, such questions
raise hackles.

For many potential candidates, politics provides a route out of
poverty – their own poverty. "Thousands of men have emerged from
among the general mass of deprived people and taken positions in

parliaments," says the writer Pankaj Mishra. "They have no special training, sometimes not even basic literacy. A large number are criminals." Even if they are not criminals, they enjoy the trappings. Politicians are dubbed "go-to people". If you want anything done, the local MP or councillor can help fix it, at a price. The sight of petitioners outside their offices is evidence that they have moved above their peers. They can enjoy a car and can afford foreign travel. D'Souza says he refuses to take bribes. "My colleagues in the council think I am naive, but I don't care if I'm the only person swimming upstream." I ask him what he could have made in bribes so far. "Fifty lakhs" is his response, which corresponds to £70,000. "I could have made in these five years what it will otherwise take me a lifetime. You could look at it as an opportunity lost."

My meetings with Setalvad, Kapur and D'Souza – all within a mile of each other, but yet all inhabiting different worlds – remind me of an encounter I had the last time I was in Juhu, two years before. Then the China miracle was running at full pelt. I remember meeting a group of young entrepreneurs, men in their early thirties who were living in Silicon Valley and earning fortunes spearheading India's software revolution. They pointed to Mumbai's decrepit airport and the slums of Juhu and Santa Cruz nearby. Why, oh why, they declared, could India not just adopt the same practices as the Chinese? Why could they not simply remove these eyesores and impediments to progress? Give these locals some compensation, if you have to, relocate them if you really must, but why should India put up with all this grubbiness? The problem was that these slums contained voters, members of parliament keen to get re-elected and a planning process that is one of the world's most cumbersome. Democracy as impediment to growth was a fashionable theory. "Can we afford democracy in this highly competitive world?" was the question frequently put. I heard the same in China itself, from young entrepreneurs who had been to India and disparaged this same "chaos". More recently, the argument has been aired in the sporting arena. Indians marvelled at the speed and efficiency of China's

Olympics. They contrast that with the hapless attempts at building new stadia for the much more low-key Commonwealth Games in Delhi. Some commentators even suggested inviting the Chinese over to help.

So, is the impediment to such progress not so much the existence of democracy as a political mechanism, but the *quality* of that democracy as a vehicle for delivery? Is the failure of past governments to improve infrastructure and public services the result of having the vote, or the fact that the vote did not translate into pressure for action? Pallavi Aiyar, Beijing correspondent for the *Hindu* newspaper, has made a study of the two countries' systems. She offers this neat comparison: "While in China the Communist Party derived its legitimacy from delivering growth, in India a government derived its legitimacy simply from having been voted in," she writes. "The legitimacy of democracy in many ways absolved Indian governments from the necessity of performing. The Chinese Communist Party could afford no such luxury." If elections are not seen as the ultimate performance indicator, as they are in Singapore, are they then denuded of purpose?

In India's case, perhaps elections are there simply to provide a single reference point for the whole population, for rich and poor, for Muslim and Hindu. It is hard to deny the sheer exuberance of election campaigns. As the 2009 general election was called, the media went into overdrive about the runners and riders and the prospects for the two main parties, the Congress and the BJP, and the various coalition-building machinations. From Sonia Gandhi, the Italian-born scion of the great dynasty, to Modi, to several other only marginally less controversial Chief Ministers, Indian politics is not short of characters. Another candidate who excites passions is the leader of Uttar Pradesh. Mayawati, as she is known, invariably raises snorts of derision from the aspirant middle classes. She is a Dalit, a member of what used to be known as the Untouchables. She is openly ambitious; she appeals to caste allegiance, which remains strong in determining voting patterns. The middle classes see her as unashamedly gauche. One of

those perennial jibes made about her at not-so-polite dinner parties is
that Mayawati once complained that one of the many posters of her
in the state capital Lucknow did not show the Gucci label on her
handbag. They laugh at one of her campaign slogans: "I'm low caste,
I'm unmarried; I'm yours." They disparage her promise to her people
that when she eventually makes it to the Prime Minister's residence in
Delhi, they will be able to live like her. Her critics may not be wrong
in denouncing her penchant for bling, but they are deliberately sin-
gling her out for opprobrium. The elite fear her because she is
unpredictable. They have not yet managed to co-opt her into the
club, but they are confident that they eventually will.

In the end Mayawati flattered to deceive. Her performance in
the May 2009 elections was poor, as was that of other groupings
based around caste. The BJP, led by the octogenarian LK Advani
also disappointed, leaving the field open to the great party of the
Gandhi dynasty, Congress, to secure re-election, with its strongest
showing for twenty years. Many pundits hailed the result as a victory
for moderation and a "historic moment" for India's democracy.
Congress would now have no excuse for failure. Its ability to deliver
an improved economy and greater social justice would be put to the
test, as would the mandate for a more centrist politics. The BJP had
taken a hit, but its target consumerist-nationalist target audience was
continuing to grow.

Turnout on election day has traditionally been high in India,
no matter how great the graft or how low the performance of parliamentarians – the Lok Sabha, the lower house, met for only
forty-six days in 2008. Historians such as Ramachandra Guha attrib-
ute this to the power of democracy itself. They go further and argue
that democracy is what holds India together, a feat of wonder in a
country of dozens of disparate languages and nationalities, of such
geographical variety and such a stark wealth divide. Without democracy, why would there be an India at all, Guha asks? Its survival is
certainly remarkable, in the face of inter-communal tension, seces-
sionist movements and hostile neighbours. Democracy is, for most

Indians, their own version of the American dream, the unifying power of the constitutional settlement of the nation that shook off its colonial past. Just as China would, according to many I spoke to, fall apart if the grip of the Communist Party loosened, so India would lose its *raison d'être* if democracy was dispensed with.

"The idea of India is stronger than Indians," the commentator M. J. Akbar puts it. He cites three freedoms that hold the country together – democracy, secular rights and gender equality (this last category is highly debatable). He compares India with the other countries in the region that took up where the British left off, particularly Pakistan, where a tiny and shrinking elite lives alongside increasingly radicalised masses. India's success, Akbar insists, can be put down to more than the fact that Nehru survived long after 1947 and Jinnah did not.

Yet whereas Pakistan is dubbed a failed state and one of the most dangerous places on earth, the death toll from terrorist attacks in India exceeds Pakistan's. This is rarely mentioned in India or in the West, because it does not conform to the narrative of a successful democracy. According to figures from the National Counterterrorism Center in Washington, nearly four thousand people died in India from bombings and shootings between 2004 and 2007, three times higher than in Pakistan And that did not include Jammu and Kashmir. The total put India as the second most dangerous place in the world, after Iraq. From Bihar and Orissa in the east to Punjab in the west and Karnataka and Tamil Nadu in the south, almost every state has at some point been affected. Most of the time, however, the elite in Delhi and Mumbai have been able to shrug off the violence, safe in the knowledge that, as long as they take precautions, they will remain unaffected. The same applied even to a terrorist attack on parliament in 2001, in which nine people were killed. That was attributed to specific security failings and did not intrude into the national consciousness.

The events of 26 November 2008 changed that equation. That was the night when militant Islamist fighters stormed the Taj and

Oberoi hotels, the central railway station and a Jewish cultural centre, killing 172 people in an audaciously coordinated shooting spree. What mattered was not the *number* of people who died – several other terrorist attacks had been larger – but the *kind* of people who died. The Taj Mahal Palace and Tower, on the seafront next to the city's famous monument, the Gateway of India, was not just Mumbai's most opulent hotel, but it was the place to be seen for dinner or drinks by the courtyard pool. It was where important business meetings were held; it was the perfect marketing tool for India's elite to project power and style to the world. That was why India's television stations rushed their outside broadcast vans to that particular site, even though more people, ordinary people, actually died at the railway station.

For three days Indian viewers were glued to their TV sets. The country has five twenty-four-hour English-language news channels. Such is the nature of rolling news that the temptation is to broadcast information before it can be verified. This was done ceaselessly during the frenzy of coverage, and a number of journalists have subsequently been blamed not just for sensationalising but for putting lives at risk, even for causing the deaths of guests by inadvertently identifying on air where they might be located in the hotel. One of those blamed was Barkha Dutt, the face of NDTV. She flew down from headquarters in Delhi and alternated her reports from the two hotels. "There wasn't a single briefing; there was no coordinated point of information," she told me. During these three days the state collapsed. Journalists ran around looking for anyone with a quote. "Everyone was briefing – the navy, politicians, the police – and yet I got a sense that nobody knew what they were briefing about," says Dutt, who is also a senior editor at the station.

The Indian channels focused on public outrage, not just at the terrorists themselves, but at the incompetence of the authorities' response. It took six hours for the main commando unit to arrive from Delhi because its plane had been sent to the Punjab on a regular mission, and nobody had the foresight to call it back. The regular police were woefully inadequately armed, and did not carry even basic radios. "We showed that terrorism is a great leveller," says Dutt. "We showed that the country was completely uncontrolled. We wouldn't even know what it would be like to have proper surveillance." She draws a broader conclusion: "People are at the end of their tether in terms of sloppiness. But the danger is that people translate this into a rage over the political process as a whole." Only when Dutt returned to her station did she realise the extent to which she had become the brunt of bitter criticism. "The internet venom was startling," she says. "I was made the fall guy for what everyone was doing."

Strange as it may seem, NDTV is more restrained than most. Two other stations, Times Now and Headlines News, which are owned by the media groups of the *Times of India* and *India Today*, are an assault on the senses. They do not separate news from comment. They are modelled on the Fox News concept of patriotism first, complexity second.

Although the various channels pursued their own, often mistaken, lines of investigation during their coverage of the gripping and terrifying siege, they all alighted immediately on the central conclusion: this must have been the work of a foreign hand, namely Pakistan. Pundits vied to outdo each other in the vehemence of their condemnations of Pakistan, and in the darkness of their calls for India to strike militarily at its neighbour. Rarely was it put to these armchair generals that both countries are heavily armed with nuclear weapons. The government's response was more measured than most of the media's. Ministers chose their words carefully, aware that inflammatory language could lead to anti-Muslim pogroms. Muslim leaders in India helped calm frayed nerves by condemning the terrorists.

But the siege of Mumbai was a watershed for India's prosperous classes. It prompted many of those who live in their own private Indias, insulated from the country's dysfunction, to demand a vital public service: safety. A public interest lawsuit was filed in the city's highest court accusing the government of failing to fulfil its constitutional duty to protect citizens' right to life. Such suits have been an important mechanism for defending the rights of the downtrodden. The supporters of this one included investment bankers, corporate lawyers and the Bombay Chamber of Commerce and Industry. It was the first time it had lent its name to litigation in the public interest.

The night after the carnage in Mumbai, thousands of protesters gathered at the Gateway monument for a candlelit march, where they vented their fury at their elected leaders. Similar protests took place in Delhi, Bangalore and Hyderabad. All were organised spontaneously, with word spreading via text message, email and Facebook. I discussed the events of those few days with Kalpana Sharma, a journalist and writer who specialises in the problems of the poor and of other vulnerable groups. We were sitting in the Leopold Bar, just around the corner from the Taj. The Leopold was where the gunmen had begun their operation that November night, calmly finishing up their dinner and paying their bill, before opening fire on customers and staff, killing six people. The manager has refused to cover over the bullet holes, in memory of the events. Sharma recalls her surprise at seeing the well-to-do on the streets rather than in their cars. Their chants included a call for a ban on criminals from running for political office; their placards bore demands such as "No Security, No Votes" and "No Security, No Taxes". Sharma said she approached one man carrying one of these placards and said: "You don't pay taxes, and you probably don't vote anyway." Given the rich's previous disengagement from the state, Sharma's observation was probably correct.

When Shobhaa De, a writer of steamy novels and India's version of Jackie Collins, declared on NDTV that "enough is enough" she was reflecting a public yearning that something had to be done. The trouble was that nobody knew quite what. De was accused by some of inciting violence against Pakistan, or against Muslims in India. She vigorously denied such charges, arguing that she was about no longer tolerating state incompetence. I was intrigued to meet her. "We are in an intellectual, emotional and moral crisis," she told me in her opulent apartment in Cuffe Parade, overlooking the

Arabian Sea, a home befitting one of the star turns on Mumbai's celebrity circuit. "Icons, movie stars, business leaders: none of them spoke out properly against the terror attacks. The first thing they did was to urge their government to ensure the safety of themselves, their projects and their factories." De said that the elite had become "immunised, institutionalised against corruption" to get anything done. "It's too deep-rooted now."

The fury of wealthy Indians at the Mumbai bombings arose from the realisation that their pact had been broken. They had enjoyed a comfortable relationship with politicians and the state. They would finance political parties and line the pockets of their elected representatives. They would privately connive in corruption, while berating its existence in public. They would demand little from the state and receive little in return, except the right to avoid taxation. They would not have to rely on lamentable public services. Their air-conditioned 4x4s would glide over the uneven roads; their diesel-fed generators would smooth over the cracks in the energy supply (in some cities power can go off for up to twelve hours at a time); their private tanks would ensure a constant supply of clean water. The elite had seceded from active politics and had been happy to do so. They never asked questions of the security forces when violence was meted out to the less fortunate. But what they did not expect, or take kindly to, was that their lives would be put at risk by incompetents at the Home Ministry, police department, army or intelligence services.

Heads did roll, quite a break with tradition in which officials are rarely forced out for wrongdoing. In the major cities security was stepped up. Airports, railway and bus stations, hotels and government buildings were sealed off. Random road blocks were mounted. But the armed officers often look as if they are going through the motions. It would not be difficult for terrorists to mount further attacks. The fear now among the well-to-do is not about a security clampdown, but the lack of it. They want their cocoon to be restored.

The media reflected those fears, and played on them, too. In the course of the 1990s, as they sought profitability and increased circulation, most of the mainstream English-language newspapers and magazines – the ones catering to the aspiring middle classes – jazzed up and dumbed down. "Negative" stories all but disappeared from the pages. Rural coverage is rare, as the wealthy are concentrated in a dozen or so urban areas. Major scandals such as the suicides of tens of thousands of indebted farmers are barely touched, nor are the long-standing conflicts in Kashmir and the north-eastern states. What coverage there remains is often simplified and sensationalised. None of this was the result of direct censorship – least of all from politicians – but, rather, of commercial requirements. The *Times of India* went the furthest in blurring the lines in 2003 by introducing a service called "Medianet". This allowed companies to buy space in the paper, not for advertisements but for a certain amount of column inches in sections of the paper casting them, naturally, in a good light. Readers seemed either not to notice or not to care. The *Times* then came up with the idea of "Private Treaties", in which it would take stakes in companies in return for advertisements. In its official marketing, the paper described this as "a product of a progressive school of thought that believes and endorses the fact that every brand was once an idea and every idea can be a brand". Overall sales of the newspaper continued to increase, and others rushed to copy the examples it was setting. The most popular editorial section was the so-called "page three", a constant diet of gossip and glamorous photographs of India's celebrity circuit – a mix of Bollywood stars, beauty queens, cricketers and industrialists. They provided the right images for the new, confident and assertive India.

Once in a while, the media do pursue injustice, but usually on behalf of a certain type of victim. The sad story of Jessica Lall was one such case. Lall was a model and actress who, one evening in April 1999, agreed to act as a celebrity barmaid at a party. Late that night a young man, Manu Sharma, and his friends approached her and asked for a drink. She refused, saying the drink had run out. They tried slipping her some money; she refused to accept it. Sharma then shot her dead. The men slipped away in the ensuing panic. Sharma was eventually arrested. The case finally came to court seven years later, when he was acquitted in spite of all the evidence. The reason? He was the son of a wealthy Congress politician. A public campaign for a retrial, Justice for Jessica, was led by NDTV. Ten months later, under a fast-track procedure, Delhi's high court overturned the verdict and sentenced Sharma to life imprisonment. On one level, this was a laudable case of justice being done and being seen to be done, but would any of this have come to pass if Lall had not been well-connected and middle class? Such a question in India would be deemed rhetorical. "Everyone was delighted about the outcome," says Meenakshy Ganguly of Human Rights Watch. "But this was a classic case of the one rule for the blessed, another for the teeming masses."

One of the many curiosities of public life in India is that the English-speaking intelligentsia – an impressive array of authors, commentators and public intellectuals – have rarely been more vocal, and yet it has rarely had so little impact on political and economic outcomes. Outright censorship does exist, but it is rare and often subject to successful legal challenge. It is most frequently applied by state, rather than federal, authorities, and mostly against the film industry. The Central Board of Film Certification has the power to ban anything it deems offensive – sex or nudity or violence – anything it regards as inflammatory to religious sensitivities, or anything it regards as politically subversive. Its actions are invariably challenged in the courts, and more often than not it is forced either to compromise or back down completely. One such case was a 2002 film called *War and Peace*, which referred to nuclear weapons and to 9/11. The director won his appeal in court after the censors had demanded twenty-one cuts to his movie. The most recent high-profile example was the banning of *The Final Solution*, a film by the director Rakesh Sharma, on the Gujarat riots of 2002. The courts

said its showing could trigger communal violence. That decision
was overturned after a sustained campaign.

The biggest challenge to free expression comes from laws, some
old, some new, on so-called "hate speech". It is a problem that other
multicultural states, including the UK, have had to get to grips with.
India's constitution guarantees freedom of speech, but it qualifies
that right by imposing "reasonable restrictions", notably a requirement not to harm relations between religious groups. Given the
combustibility of communal relations, some form of protection
could be seen as understandable. But a number of recent examples
suggest that, as in other countries, Indian courts are interpreting
more widely than before the notion of "offence". In February 2009,
the editor and publisher of the *Statesman* in Kolkata, one of India's
oldest papers with an honourable tradition of standing up for free
speech, were arrested after reprinting a comment piece from a
British paper, the *Independent*. The article, which had praised secu-
larism and denounced religious intolerance, particularly from Islam,
led to angry protests from Muslim groups. The newspaper, which
over the years had led the way in the pursuit of free expression,
issued a swift apology. Many saw the climbdown as a symbol of a
wider problem – mob protest influencing government action and
instilling in public life a new mood of self-censorship. Why cause
trouble?

One person who has seldom, if ever, posed that question is
Tarun Tejpal. He left mainstream journalism in 2000 to start an
investigative website called *Tehelka*. Within weeks he had embroiled
himself in controversy and turned himself into a national name.
The *Tehelka* team devised a sting operation, entitled Operation West
End, producing tapes that showed several top government ministers
and members of the military top brass taking large bribes for
approving defence contracts. Many commentators reacted to the
scoop by asking what was new. Such was the level of cynicism
among the public it was assumed that this kind of thing went on all
the time, so why the fuss? Those with something to hide were less

blasé. Tejpal narrowly escaped assassination in April 2001. Meanwhile, the government mounted a sustained campaign to discredit his investigation. The Defence Minister resigned after the tapes were made public, only later to be reinstated. In 2004, Tejpal turned his operation into a magazine as well, employing up to forty journalists. Three years later, his team caught on camera a number of politicians, businessmen and policemen proudly boasting about how they had overseen the murder and rape of Muslims in Gujarat in 2002, the same bloodshed that Teesta Setalvad's magazine had also probed.

Tejpal's security detail is even tighter than Setalvad's. His office in the south of Delhi is guarded around the clock, and he has armed police with him, operating in shifts, day and night. In the height of the arms revelations, his office and home were sandbagged. His operation is frequently on the brink of closure. "It's a miracle that we're still around, in more ways than one," he says. Two weeks after he published his Gujarat story, two promised funders pulled out, although he says he never ceases to be pleasantly surprised by the number of wealthy individuals who want to help him. "People know a free press is vital to democracy and they want this information out in the public domain. But they don't really want their lifestyles to be disturbed either. That is a trade-off the middle class is happy to make."

He points to a gulf between the constitutional functions of India's democracy and the liberties it provides. "People abroad have been bowled a Gandhian googly," he says, using the inevitable cricketing analogy. "The myth of tolerance remains strong. In fact, through our treatment of caste, gender, children and class we must surely be one of the cruellest free societies in the world." The poor, he points out, have been living with the fear of terrorism, crime, intercommunal violence and state violence for years. "When you are skirting life and death you have less to lose from sudden outbreaks of violence, and so you tend to make less of a fuss when they happen."

"Police encounters" is a term used to explain the death of someone at the hands of the police. Each time, an official version is put out claiming that the people killed were militants or "subjects of interest", who were gunned down just before they were about to open fire themselves. These encounters are often staged, with weapons planted on the corpse at the scene. Attempts to hold the police to account have achieved little success. In the state of Andra Pradesh, a lower court ruled that police killings should be treated as murder. This was promptly overturned by the state's Supreme Court. Former police chiefs have explained that these execution squads are necessary to protect the public from criminals who will not be punished in the courts, because of their judicial or political connections. In other words, the police are aiding the democratic process. Controversy arises only when a clearly innocent person is killed. For nearly thirty years these shoot-to-kill encounters have become a regular occurrence in the major cities, and are, according to opinion polls, highly popular with the public. Journalists and television reporters are regularly invited to the scene to film the aftermath. Or they are sent elaborate press releases describing the drama which they faithfully reproduce, emphasising the heroic actions of the officers concerned. These cases are almost never investigated.

Shortly after the Mumbai attacks, parliament voted overwhelmingly to toughen anti-terrorism legislation. The most controversial of the changes was to endorse the right of the courts to accept evidence extracted by the police from confessions, and the right to hold suspects without charge for up to six months. Over the years, human rights groups have highlighted thousands of cases of the death and maltreatment of people held in custody, but few have taken any notice. The security forces have acquired almost untrammelled powers to engage in counter-insurgency across the country. The border dispute with Pakistan over Kashmir and the long-running insurgency campaigns by the Communist-led Naxalite movement in Bihar and other states to the east have provided the pretext for a wide array of security legislation. This includes the Armed Forces Special Powers Act, which allows for shoot-to-kill and searches without warrants; the National Security Act, which permits the suspension of rights to legal representation and access to courts; and the Terrorist and Disruptive Activities (Prevention) Act of 1987, which has led to widespread instances of unrecorded detentions and torture, and the arresting of relatives as hostages when a person wanted by the police absconds. Politicians argue that these measures are necessary in order to defend India's democracy from those seeking to destroy it. Their point is undermined by the almost complete lack of transparency and accountability.

Lawyers and human rights activists argue that the security forces have long targeted the poor, the vulnerable and minorities, with or without legislation as cover. They provide considerable evidence pointing to what is called a "saffron" bias among the police, particularly in cities run by the BJP or its affiliated groups. They mean discrimination on behalf of Hindu nationalists against minorities. The problem goes far beyond demographics. Civil rights groups estimate that up to 80 per cent of crimes reported by members of the public are not investigated by the police. The assumption is that the officers, or their commanders, have been paid off by criminal gangs. Conversely, a similar proportion of charges that are made have been trumped up, or achieved under duress. Governments of all parties have shown little interest in tackling the problem, in spite of efforts by NGOs and others to persuade them. Meenakshy Ganguly recounts one example of her own, an audience she was granted with a senior government minister. "There he was, sitting behind an empty desk," she tells me. "I talk, giving him several specific examples of problems and abuses by the police and security forces. Nothing would be written down by him or his officials. At the end he would stand up and say 'I will look into it' and then leave."

J. K. Galbraith once called India a "functioning anarchy". The Mumbai bombings showed how apposite his description was. I wonder, given the frustrations about police competence, how far people were now prepared to go to impose greater order. Some columnists have begun to speak the unspeakable: "I am beginning to hear the same kind of middle-class murmurs and whines about the ineffectual nature of democracy and the need for authoritarian government," argued one pundit, Vir Sanghvi. He was referring to the seminal moment in India's post-independence history, the imposition by Indira Gandhi in June 1975 of a state of emergency. Some one thousand dissidents were rounded up and jailed. Two dozen political groups were banned. The media were ordered not to publish any "unauthorised, irresponsible or demoralising news items". This included cartoons and advertisements. The clampdown on virtually all human rights conformed with India's constitution, as Gandhi justified it by claiming that she needed to thwart "a deep-rooted conspiracy" that would have "led to economic chaos and collapse", making India "vulnerable to fissiparous tendencies and external danger". Democracy, she declared, "has given too much freedom to people". The most vivid memory for many Indians of that era was the forced sterilisation of millions of people who had already had two children or more – or who were politically troublesome. A birth-control programme that had previously been based on cooperation was turned into an instrument of state repression. In a number of villages and towns, demonstrations against the policy were put down violently by the security forces.

And yet the wealthy and the comfortable responded, as ever, with equanimity. The world's most populous democracy had been suspended with consummate ease. L. K. Advani, the Minister for Information and Broadcasting at the time, who went on to become leader of the BJP, recalled how easy it was to corral the media. He told a group of journalists shortly after the emergency that some "resisted these draconian measures to suppress dissent, and paid the price for it". As for the rest, "when you were only asked to bend, many of you chose to crawl".

Most historians and present-day commentators prefer to dwell on the plus side: the fact that the emergency was withdrawn after twenty months, that Gandhi went straight to the electorate, assuming an endorsement for her firm hand, only to lose, surprisingly, and stand down peacefully. No matter how flawed it may be, India's democracy showed its credentials during that extreme situation.

Indira Gandhi has had a significant historical rehabilitation in recent years. Opinion polls regularly rate her as the most popular politician of the modern Indian era. "People remember her as being strong," explains Swapan Dasgupta, a prominent columnist. "She took no nonsense from hostile forces within the country, and she took no nonsense from Pakistan." According to this theory, India has since then been lumbered with a succession of prime ministers lacking the personal drive or the votes in parliament to push through radical agendas. Most have been ejected after one term. Dasgupta and many like him see in Narendra Modi the only member of the current crop of politicians capable of exercising strong leadership and following in Indira's footsteps. I ask Dasgupta if he has any foreign models in mind. He mentions Lee Kuan Yew of Singapore. It is worth recalling that during the Emergency Indira's son and close adviser, Sanjay Gandhi, frequently cited Singapore's authoritarianism as the model for India to follow. For many Indians of that period, Singapore was the first foreign country they had visited. They admired Lee's success in keeping a lid on inter-communal tensions, the professionalism of Singapore's civil service, the cleanliness of the streets and the combination of pro-market economics and strong public services. He then dwells on another possible mentor, Russia's Vladimir Putin. "Putin inherited a collapsed superpower and restored its honour and pride. He pulled Russia back up by the bootstraps. Yes, there are distortions, the mafia, for example, and intolerance of dissent. You could call him autocratic, but he is not a dictator and he does have a popular mandate. Most important of all, he has made it a top-notch country again."

"India Shining" and the other slogans of the past two globalised decades were designed with the very aim in mind of portraying India as a top-notch country. Middle-class India is

intoxicated by superpower talk. The writer Pankaj Mishra says that
for this ambition to be realised in a country of such woeful poverty
and inequality, the elite has to create a parallel universe. This is the
world of Bangalore call centres, IT giants, Bollywood and the international acquisitive zeal of industrial giants such as Tata. This world
lives alongside the slums, the fetid sewers, the disease and malnu-
trition, but is able to keep these manifestations of the old India at
arm's length. Mishra agrees with Sangupta about the comparison
with Russia. The business and political elites in both countries have
framed their modernisation projects in reference to the West. This
sets them apart from China. It also, argues Mishra, provides fertile
ground for frustrations to grow. "The fascistic undertones are
unsettling," he says. "But this is also what Indira Gandhi helped
create: a widely shared mood among the Indian middle class compounded equally by fear, aggressiveness, contempt and apathy; a
climate of opinion in which India's various encircling cruelties feel
far away."

Yet, for all the dark warnings, nobody I spoke to, from a wide
range of political affiliations, saw any serious prospect of a return to
the Emergency. The modern, global side of India – the India outside
the slums and the poor villages – is proud of its raucous public discourse and its flamboyant democracy. Indeed, some NGOs and
others working on community projects suggest that there may be
cause for cautious optimism. They point to an increasing representation for lower castes and for women in village communes,
panchayats, and in urban local councils. They point to an increasing
sophistication among voters, including the technically illiterate.
They cite as evidence the impossibility of predicting the outcome of
elections in the country. Back in 2004, the experts forecast a BJP victory and got it hopelessly wrong. They suggest, further, that voting
habits and motivations are changing. Identity politics through caste
or religion, although still very strong, may in some cases be giving
way to a different process that bases itself more on accountability.
The city of Delhi has twice re-elected the same administration, in

recognition of infrastructure improvements. None of this, they say, is coming from the top, but from a bottom-up process.

The problem in India is not the lack of formal democratic institutions, but of governance, the inability to deliver social and economic freedoms for the vast majority of its people. After an initial period of state-steered socialism during the early years of independence, politicians and businessmen latched on to globalisation, using power as a means of enrichment. The comfortable classes, the people over the past twenty years who could have used the country's new wealth to engineer improvements, either turned a blind eye to society's failings or knowingly played a part in them. They could have been active in the public realm. Unlike in authoritarian states, they would not have been punished for causing trouble. Instead, they chose not to. The level of complicity, therefore, is surely higher.

6

ITALY: ONE-MAN SHOW

*"The lowering of the quality of democracy is embodied
by a politics that doesn't ask for the mobilisation or
participation of citizens. It simply needs a good
vibration"* – Ezio Mauro

IN APRIL 2008, WITHIN DAYS OF SECURING A STUNNING
electoral victory, Silvio Berlusconi invited his best friend in global politics to be the first to celebrate with him. Vladimir Putin was happy to
accept. "I haven't seen him for a long time. I missed him," the Russian
President declared as he arrived at the Berlusconis' holiday home on
Sardinia's Costa Smeralda. The twenty-seven-room "villa", La Certosa,
offered VIPs and family friends (one and the same thing) a botanical
garden, an artificial lake with remote-controlled waterfalls, a four-
hundred-seat Greek amphitheatre and, just in case, a nuclear bunker.

The Putins were regular visitors. One summer a few years earlier their two teenage daughters had been house guests. One of the
Berlusconi daughters had flown back from Australia to join them,
enjoying the sea and the night life at the millionaires' clubs in Porto
Cervo and Porto Rotondo – under the careful watch of their bodyguards.

Vladimir and Silvio had a natural affinity and similar mind-
sets – they enjoyed money, beautiful women and faithful wives;

they had no time for judges or journalists or anyone else who asked too many questions. The night before they had watched a show featuring scantily clad dancing girls; then the two men stayed up until 4.00 a.m. discussing the woes of the world. So it was with some trepidation and no little courage that Natalia Melikova, a correspondent of the Russian daily *Nezavisimaya Gazeta*, stood up at a press conference held later that morning by the Italian host to ask Putin to comment on three rumours that had been swirling around Moscow. Was it true that one of his daughters had moved to Munich? Was it true that he was on the point of divorcing his wife, Lyudmila? And what of those reports of his close friendship and impending nuptials to Alina Kabayeva, a glamorous twenty-four-year former gymnast voted the most desirable woman in Russia by readers of one magazine and now member of parliament for the pro-Kremlin United Russia party?

As a furious Putin pursed his lips and pondered his response, Berlusconi exclaimed: "Oh! Is that true?" Putin, who had once suggested to a French journalist who had asked a question about Chechnya that he "have himself circumcised", told Melikova: "You have uttered not a single word of truth." He decided to try to make light of it and to reinforce his credentials as a lady's man. "You mentioned an article in one of the Russian tabloids featuring the Olympic Champion in rhythmic gymnastics, Alina Kabayeva, and your colleague, the anchorwoman, Yekaterina Andreyeva. Other articles sometimes feature other beautiful and successful women. I think that nobody will be surprised if I say that I like them all, just as I like all Russian women." He paused to accept the applause of Italian journalists and a few elderly local residents who had been allowed in to see their idols. "I think that nobody will be offended if I say that I personally believe that our Russian women are the most talented and most beautiful. The only women who can compare with them in this regard are Italian women. *Grazie*."

Putin then adopted a more serious demeanour: "I have always reacted negatively to those who, with their snotty noses and erotic fantasies, meddle in other people's lives." Berlusconi followed this up by pretending, mockingly, to mow down the offending reporter with a machine gun. He then joked about swapping the Russian press with the Italian. Melikova was visibly upset. Others laughed nervously. Later, a spokesman tried to play down the incident: "It was just a gesture, a playful gesture; in fact, it was appreciated, as it helped give the technical time needed for a long Russian translation." "I saw Berlusconi's gesture and I know he has a reputation as being a joker," Melikova said. "I hope there are no consequences." There had already been consequences for the tabloid, *Moskovsky Korrespondent*, which had published the original stories about Putin and Kabayeva. Its website was immediately blocked. The paper, which had only been in existence for a few months, specialising in celebrity and gossip, was part of the growing media empire of Yevgeny Lebedev, a former KGB operative turned billionaire businessman. (He would later make the spectacular purchase of London's evening newspaper, the *Evening Standard*.) The head of Lebedev's publishing house denied any link with the controversy, saying the website had been suspended because it had overspent its budget. But the ramifications were clear when the paper issued a front-page retraction, expressing deep regret for the "insults". It added: "We apologise to all those who consider that this story has caused them emotional suffering."

Once they had dealt with the annoyance, Berlusconi and Putin privately resumed their business – and business had for some time been booming between the two countries. Italy was Europe's second largest recipient of Russian gas, and, along with Germany, was its main economic champion in the EU. The Italian company Eni and Russia's Gazprom were closely linked. Aeroflot was in complex discussions with Alitalia about a possible takeover of the struggling Italian airline. In this respect, these two leaders were merely following a pattern established by Boris Yeltsin and a succession of Italian prime ministers. Even during Soviet times, business contacts were strong.

The friendship of Berlusconi and Putin dates back to 2001. Berlusconi had just won his second election victory; Putin was a year into establishing his hegemony over Russia. Berlusconi would see Putin in an average year more frequently than he would various EU counterparts, let alone President Bush. He would consistently defend the Russian President against international concerns about human rights and authoritarianism. Everything is easier when there is "esteem, trust, respect and friendship," Berlusconi declared. "It is a deep friendship, which, as in all things in life, helps better understanding and making decisions for the best – in this case in the interest not only of our countries but of the global community."

Putin's disdain for free expression, and the dangers faced by troublesome Russian journalists, had long been clear. But is the bar not set higher for supposed democracies? It is easy to belittle the assault on Italy's liberties by focusing on the buffoonery of Berlusconi. With his penchant for vulgarity (*brutta figura*, as Italians call it), he enjoys playing to the caricature. This is a man so vain that he has had a facelift and hides his hair transplants with a bandanna; a man who seeks to ingratiate himself with anyone rich or powerful, from Putin to his other "best friend", Tony Blair, and, yet, a man who offends just about anyone, too, from Queen Elizabeth II, to Angela Merkel, the German Chancellor, to Barack Obama, whom he described as "handsome, young and suntanned".

The Berlusconi story is about more than the rise of a prankster. All electorates can, from time to time, take leave of their senses and opt for incompetents or demagogues. A properly functioning system of checks and balances should expose their failings or their excesses. But Italians have voted for Berlusconi three times, most recently in 2008, giving him a landslide majority. This is a man who encourages Italians to indulge in their national pastime of making money on the side, and who has used parliament to debilitate the two forces that can stand in the way of power – the judiciary and the media. The Italian version of the pact is mutual myopia. So low is the voters' view of the state's ability to improve their lives that all they want it to do is to turn a blind eye to what they get up to; in return they pledge not to trouble their leaders too much either. This country at the heart of the European Union, NATO, the G8 and other international institutions is, by most barometers of constitutional and political theory, a failed state. And yet it continues to function quite happily, just as it has always done. Berlusconi's rise to the top in politics and business, and his continued hold on power, speak volumes for the concerns and priorities of Italian voters. It also has lessons for the rest of Europe and for nations further afield.

"We have lived with him for twenty years. He's not an accident." Ferruccio de Bortoli is the editor of *Il Sole 24 Ore*, Italy's main business newspaper, a man who has tracked and tormented Berlusconi throughout his career. De Bortoli points to Italians' ambivalent approach to democracy itself. "Berlusconi is the Italian social success model. He personifies what people would like to be. They would love to have made that kind of money without being caught." With more than five million small firms employing fewer than ten people, the small businessman holds a particular locus in Italian society. Berlusconi is the expression of the bourgeoisie. He thinks like them. He acts like them. He does, almost instinctively, what they do. He has the same tastes, the same sense of humour. And the people at the top whom they respect – entrepreneurs and others who have made money – tend to regard checks and balances as inimical to wealth creation. "Business and the establishment consider democracy as a cost, not an advantage," de Bortoli tells me. "Many entrepreneurs and managers complain about how they have to talk to journalists, to open themselves up to scrutiny. They say things to me and to my journalists such as 'Why can't you do something for your country?' or 'Why do you wish to ruin my relationship with the market?'" These people want the state to protect them, but also to leave them alone to do their business, and – with tax evasion said to be five times higher than the

European average – to make money and keep it. That function had been performed, to general satisfaction, by the Christian Democrats. Now they entrust their faith in Berlusconi, which is why he does so little to reduce red tape and clamp down on restrictive practices or corruption. "We live in a country of thousands of conflicts of interests, but one always prevails," de Bortoli says. He should know.

In May 2003 de Bortoli was sacked as editor of *Corriere della Serra*. His offence was to have riled Berlusconi by publishing a series of derogatory commentaries and cartoons. Founded in 1876, *Corriere* is the giant of Italian newspapers, with daily sales of more than 700,000 – a highbrow, liberal and somewhat fusty daily with some of the strongest news values in the country. A paper of the Turin and Milan bourgeoisie, it has long played a central role in national life. De Bortoli ensured that the paper maintained its independence; it opposed Italy's participation in the Iraq war and has consistently tried to uncover political corruption. Its front-page cartoonist, Giannelli, would regularly depict Berlusconi as a grinning dwarf in shiny bowler hat and built-up shoes. The last straw for the bosses was a column that lambasted a line in a speech by Berlusconi, in which he said: "It will not be permitted for anyone who has been a communist to come to power." One of the newspaper's writers noted: "Mussolini used to say the same words. He [Berlusconi] has no reason to be afraid. But I have." After all, Fini, his coalition partner, once described Mussolini as "the greatest statesman of the century".

The son of a Milanese bank official, Berlusconi created his own small building firm in his mid-twenties. His rise from this point to becoming Italy's richest man, with an estimated fortune of $10 billion, is a story of business prowess, dodgy dealings and no little mystery. Just who or what financed him at different points of his career remains unknown. Berlusconi came to national prominence in the 1970s, as he built up his empire first through property in Milan, then in the media, taking his Mediaset company, and its holding company Fininvest, from virtually nothing to control of the three largest private television stations – Canale 5, Retequattro and Italia 1 – thus ensuring a virtual monopoly of the non-state TV sector. These channels proved hugely popular, offering a diet of low-grade game shows, soap operas and sexually titillating broadcasts. In both his political and business endeavours, he was hugely assisted by Bettino Craxi, long-time leader of the Socialist Party. Personal allegiances count for far more than political ones in Italy, and each man contributed to the other's success. Berlusconi's TV stations were funded by banks controlled by the socialists. Once his media empire was established, he used his channels to fund Craxi's political machine and to promote the image of its leader on the news. Craxi, in turn, fashioned a media law made to measure for Berlusconi's needs. He became godfather to Berlusconi's daughter at a secret baptism (she was born outside marriage); he was then best man for Berlusconi's subsequent second wedding.

From the end of the Second World War until shortly after the collapse of the Soviet Union, Italy was ruled by coalitions dominated by the centre-right Christian Democrats, who saw their main task as keeping the Communists at bay. Governments collapsed almost as soon as they were formed, but real power stayed in the same hands. A system of state larceny was established. The collapse of the Cold War order broke that sense of invulnerability and impunity. Along with Giulio Andreotti, the head of the Christian Democrats, Craxi was one of the main figures who symbolised *Tangentopoli*, the network of bribes and corruption that characterised post-war Italian politics. Craxi managed to avoid Italian justice by fleeing to Tunisia, where he died in exile. Andreotti, nicknamed variously the Prince of Darkness or Beelzebub, is an even more dubious figure. He was put on trial charged with ordering the murder in 1979 of Mino Pecorelli, a journalist who had linked Andreotti to the mafia and to the kidnapping of the then Prime Minister, Aldo Moro. A court acquitted Andreotti in 1999, but he was convicted on appeal in November 2002 and sentenced to twenty-four years in jail. He was immediately released, due to his age of eighty-three, and the following year he was acquitted again.

Craxi and Andreotti personified the First Republic, Berlusconi the Second. The constitutional apparatus around the two could not have been more different; the end result was the same – a politics denuded of respectability and credibility, and rotted to the core by corruption.

Between 1992 and 1994, Italy seemed to be reborn. For a fleeting moment voters began to wonder whether their state institutions might be worthy of respect. The courts finally began to tackle a web of corruption so ingrained that every party and almost every senior politician was implicated. Dozens of civil servants and businessmen were arrested and imprisoned during the *Mani Pulite* (clean hands) investigation. Others committed suicide. The political landscape was transformed, with the extinction of all the old parties, the creation of new ones and the establishment of a constitution designed to bring stability – two blocs in a straight left–right split – and end decades of sordid deal-making. Into this void stepped Berlusconi. He established a very different political party from any that had gone before. Forza Italia was run like a corporation, headed by his friends and contacts, and funded largely by Fininvest. In 1994, a mere three months after it was established, Forza won its first election. Berlusconi formed a coalition with the far-right party of Gianfranco Fini, which until that point had been confined to pariah status. Then he made a deal with Umberto Bossi's Northern League. Ironically, *Mani Pulite* had thereby helped to the pinnacle of the Italian state a man whose rise, like no other, was a result of the corrupt old system. The business of Italian government was his business. That victory could have been seen as a one-off, and indeed his first administration did not last long. Many voters in democratic states have opted for a maverick, only to regret their decision, and to reverse it at the first available opportunity. But Berlusconi was different. It did not take long for voters to come back for more.

Berlusconi made his big push in 2001. The centre-left "Olive Tree" government had expended its energies on adapting Italy's economy to the strictures of the European Monetary Union. Berlusconi offered voters an easier ride, tempted by tax cuts. In fact, he achieved little of note in his second term, devoting his efforts to protect himself from prosecution, as a number of corruption cases were grinding through the courts. Three successive laws were speeded through parliament: to block evidence of illegal transactions abroad, to decriminalise the falsification of accounts, and to enable defendants in a trial to change judges by shifting the case to another jurisdiction. When the first and third were ruled unconstitutional by the courts, Berlusconi responded with an even more drastic law. This was to grant himself immunity from prosecution. He gave his measure a constitutional imprimatur, stipulating that it should apply to the holders of the five top jobs in the land – president, prime minister, the speakers of the two houses of parliament and the head of the Constitutional Court. He then went about protecting his media empire. Legislation was rushed through allowing Mediaset to retain its channels, but also granting it a huge subsidy to pursue its digital ambitions.

Berlusconi's dominance of politics was matched by dominance of the media. He combined ownership of the major private stations with increasing control over state broadcasting. He ensured that recalcitrant editors or managers were removed, usually through a word in the ear of board members. He ensured that programmes he did not like were taken off air. The most famous example came in November 2003 when Rai Tre, the third channel, was forced to take off air a late-night political satire show called *Raiot*, after it lampooned the Prime Minister. The director and writer, Sabina Guzzanti, who also appeared in the show, was then sued by Mediaset for "lies and insinuations". She turned the saga into a film, *Viva Zapatero!*, which became an art house favourite around Europe.

The print press mattered less, but Berlusconi again did what he could to stifle criticism. The history of *la Repubblica* is shorter and less illustrious than *Corriere*, but, under its editor, Ezio Mauro, it has been just as assiduous in highlighting Berlusconi's assault on what is left of his country's democracy. The offices of newspapers such as these are heavily guarded. The security outside *la Repubblica*'s Rome headquarters is elaborate – armed guards, permits and individual scanning booths.

I knew Mauro during our time together as correspondents in Moscow in the early 1990s. He is keen to discuss the trade-off between liberty, security and prosperity, and Berlusconi's important place in it. I ask him about the role of free expression. Italy, after all, has a thriving public intelligentsia. Whatever the pressures and setbacks, many newspapers produce successful investigations and trenchant commentaries. We talk about the internet, and Mauro provides me with an intriguing analysis that, he says, applies not just to Italy. The online revolution, far from enhancing participation, has actually set it back. "With the internet we have no walls or boundaries. Everywhere is here. We are not bound by history, but we disconnect ourselves from the public discourse," Mauro tells me. "If you want to call it democracy, then it'd be better to call it democratic solitude. The citizen feels alone, feels disconnected from information and thinks he can go it alone. Once there was the possibility of interpreting personal feelings and values within a general framework of common interest. Now the citizen no longer believes in the effectiveness of publicly organised action. The citizen becomes the spectator. Politics is just a big event. The structures of power say to the citizenry: 'You feel alone, you look after your life; you delegate the rest to me. Public affairs are my business.'"

His is the closest corroboration of the Singapore pact that I have heard to date on my journeys. Yet, although the trade-off may be similar, Berlusconi is a far less impressive figure than Singapore's long-time leader, Lee Kuan Yew. Whatever one's reservations about the state of free expression and democracy in Singapore – and, as I have described, mine are copious – its founder had a coherent political philosophy and a set of principles upon which to be judged. Yet, one is regarded as an authoritarian; the other belongs to the family of democracies. This is another example of blurred dividing lines, of labels masking reality. For Berlusconi, as with Putin, political power and economic power form the same nexus.

Another spiritual soulmate of Berlusconi is Thailand's Thaksin Shinawatra. Billionaire populist, demagogue and Prime Minister, Thaksin was the darling of the middle classes, who believed that, without a strong state and a strong leader, they would not have made the money they had. After more than five years in power, he was ousted in a military coup in September 2006, accused of corruption and abuse of power.

In each of these cases rulers have used elections and the veneer of constitutionalism in order to consolidate a rule that straddles democracy and authoritarianism. Mauro suggests that history offers a telling guide. He refers me to the story of Italo Balbo, a confidant of, and heir apparent to, Benito Mussolini and one of the most ruthless leaders of the Blackshirts. Balbo was also a pioneering aviator, who led two trailblazing flights across the Atlantic. When his fleet of twenty-four planes reached the US, he was greeted by adoring crowds, ticker-tape parades, and even lunch with President Franklin Roosevelt. To many people, Balbo embodied nobility and a dashing style; that was more important to them than his politics. Italy, Mauro suggests to me, faces a similar problem now. Yet he warns off the more direct and simplistic Berlusconi–Mussolini comparisons. The contemporary phenomenon, he says, is more subtle. "People think of Berlusconi as 'old Italian', quirky, amusing. He's actually very modern and very European. There is little understanding in Europe about this new kind of leadership."

Mauro also cites Norberto Bobbio, a philosopher. A strong advocate of the rule of law, the separation of powers and the limitation of powers, Bobbio was a liberal socialist opposed to the authoritarian tenets of Marxism. The gravest danger, pointed out by Bobbio, is that "politicians are always looking for a way out of a tangle. Populism offers them a short-term solution; it provides the appearance of a sword-like cut through difficult problems", Mauro says. He calls it "modern populism" or "demagogic democracy". It is not, he says, represented by "Le Pen or Haider, or such extremes. I see some elements of Sarkozy, and before him Blair. The lowering of the quality of democracy is embodied by a politics that doesn't ask for the mobilisation or participation of citizens. It simply needs a good vibration. The degradation of democracy has taken place imperceptibly across Europe, and not just in Italy. We are at a tipping point."

Mauro's is an important warning. It is easy to identify the dangers posed by people like Berlusconi. They do not hide their ambitions or their disdain for the institutions that seek to hold them in check. France does not have a chapter of its own in this book, as it combines manifestations of both the Italian and British approaches, but Nicolas Sarkozy has adopted much of the personal bombast and quixotic use of power employed in Italy, with the more methodical move towards a surveillance state in Britain.

Sarkozy stands accused of capitalising on the mood of insecurity by introducing an array of measures ranging from surveillance to preventative arrest of individuals the state deems to be a danger. In November 2008, anti-terrorist police arrested twenty people in the small village of Tarnac, in the centre of France. Little evidence was presented against them, but central to the prosecution was their alleged authorship of a book, *The Coming Insurrection*, and their association with what the government has termed the "ultra-Left". The opposition Socialists, which had made few complaints previously, unveiled a "black book" of "attacks on public liberty" since Sarkozy became President in 2007.

One of the most controversial new measures is the EDVIGE database. Created in June 2008, it might sound like a girl's name but stands for the more sinister *Exploitation documentaire et valorisation de l'information générale.* Its purpose is to file data on groups, organisations and individuals who, by their individual or collective activity, are deemed to endanger public order, passing on that information to the police and intelligence services. Anyone not just suspected of a crime, but being vaguely associated with anti-social elements, will be included. Categories to be recorded include occupation, marriage status and family history; addresses past and present, phone numbers and email details; physical characteristics, photographs and behaviour; identity papers; car number plates; tax records and legal history. Gay organisations have protested after hearing that it will also keep data relating to sexual orientation and health, in particular information relating to HIV. France's magistrates' union has denounced it as undemocratic, saying that it will "inform the government on politically active people". The normally restrained *Le Monde* newspaper attacked the notion of a pre-emptive database. "A state governed by the rule of law cannot accept the penalisation of supposed intentions," it declared.

Much of the focus, the government says, will be on France's gang crime in the suburbs of the major cities. In an attempt to justify the collection of data on children as young as thirteen, the Interior Minister, Michèle Alliot-Marie, said: "We have observed an increase in child delinquency." Alliot-Marie had the dubious distinction of winning the tenth annual Big Brother Awards. The judges cited her overall contribution to privacy violations and her "immoderate taste for putting French citizens on file" and her love of video surveillance. Another instrument of government with a deceptive acronym is ELSA, *Engins légers de surveillance aérienne.* Tests have been conducted on drones that will be able, thanks to day–night vision, to track potential criminality and anti-social behaviour from the skies. Many local officials have argued that a simpler, more effective and less instrusive approach would be to increase the number of neighbourhood police officers.

If, in the security agenda, Sarkozy's approach is more in keeping with that of Tony Blair and Gordon Brown, it is in his attitude to media independence that he most resembles Berlusconi. Even before Sarkozy became President, during his term as Interior Minister troublesome editors either fell into line or were sacked. Patrick Poivre d'Arvor, the country's most familiar face on prime-time news, was dumped by the main private station TF1 after once describing Sarko as looking at a G8 summit "like a little boy in the big boys' club". The owner of TF1 is a long-standing friend of his. Another career to come to an abrupt end was that of Alain Genestar, editor-in-chief of *Paris Match*. In 2005 the glossy magazine published photographs of Cécilia Sarkozy in New York with the man who would become her next husband. Sarkozy rang Genestar to berate him and later bragged to journalists that he had been handed the editor's head. Two years later, *Le Journal du Dimanche* withdrew a story at the last moment about Cécilia refusing to vote during the presidential election. When Sarkozy heard about the story he ensured that it was "killed" and that the editor was told off. After that, the coverage became suitably pliant, with pictures of the leader and his new wife, Carla Bruni, under the headline "The Star Couple". Two-thirds of all France's newspapers and magazines are owned by Dassault and Lagardère, the leading arms manufacturers in the country, with close links to the Elysée Palace.

As with Berlusconi, Sarkozy has recognised the importance of television and presided over the merging of politics with business interests, media coverage and the cult of celebrity. In January 2009, parliament approved legislation strengthening governmental control over public stations. Under the law, commercial advertising would be phased out and the shortfall would be made up by state funding, thus making the channels dependent on the goodwill of the President. To consolidate that position even further, the Chief Executive of *France Télévisions* would no longer be nominated by the broadcast regulator but by the President, who could also sever that contract at any point. Sarkozy earned the nickname the *Télépresident*, for orchestrating politics as if it were a reality show.

"France has produced a new model of media control, somewhere between Berlusconi and Putin," commented *Le Monde*, a paper that remains beyond the President's grasp. "Sarkozy does not need to emulate Berlusconi in actually owning the titles: his friends will do that for him."

The studio of Paolo Flores d'Arcais is crammed with watercolours and oils. Painter, philosopher, journalist and man of letters, d'Arcais is also one of the best-known critics of the Berlusconi regime. In 2002 he was one of the founders of the *girotondi*, a series of rolling demonstrations, given the name of the Italian equivalent of ring-a-ring o'roses. He is looking a little tired as he welcomes me into his elegant Rome apartment. He immediately beckons me to his window and points out the vibrant street market below, with a variety of meat, fish, fruit and vegetables on sale. It strikes me as one of those quintessential scenes of bourgeois Italian contentment. My host explains what really goes on. Early each trading day the same traffic policeman drives up in a van, greets the stallholders, has an earnest look over their produce and tells them he is checking hygiene standards. Within minutes, the back of his van is miraculously filled with gifts and he goes away. Everyone is content with the outcome. What is needed, d'Arcais says, is zero tolerance against all forms of criminality, from the bottom to the top. But where does one start, particularly when so very many benefit from the status quo?

The evening before we met, d'Arcais had addressed about 50,000 people in the Piazza Navona. The numbers have fallen sharply since the protests of previous years, when at one rally they reached one million. Newspaper coverage that morning was largely derogatory, pointing out that most of the speakers had spent most of the time attacking each other. D'Arcais is despondent about the state of the opposition. Italy's Left, he says, has had no meaningful purpose or ideology and only a passing interest in democracy. "Has there ever been a centre-left administration in Italy that is moral and courageous?" He laughs and answers his own question dismissively. Craxi was no aberration. The socialists had connived in Berlusconi's assault on the media. "That generation of the Left grew up in a Stalinist milieu. For them liberal powers and free journalism and the independence of prosecutors is not part of their anthropology. They have helped Berlusconi consistently." D'Arcais points to constitutional reforms introduced in the late 1990s by a socialist-led government designed to produce stronger and more stable government. "At that point Berlusconi was on the ropes, politically, financially and judicially. These reforms got him off the hook. These politicians are all in it together."

Once he had secured a stranglehold in the media, Berlusconi moved on to the judiciary, or at least that part that was still offering some resistance. He set out to trim the powers of the judges, to get them off his back. D'Arcais offers up one striking statistic: Berlusconi has escaped conviction in twelve major cases; he has never been convicted. He has been put on trial six times, accused of embezzlement, tax fraud and false accounting, and attempting to bribe a judge. In some cases he has been acquitted. In others, he has been convicted, but the verdict was overturned on appeal. In others still, the statute of limitations – which limits the amount of time an individual can be under suspicion – has expired before the case could reach its conclusion.

Those who might seem perturbed by all this, such as members of the political opposition, instead seem strikingly relaxed. D'Arcais recalls a private dinner he had with Massimo d'Alema, a leading figure of the Left, in 1996. Their meeting took place just as Berlusconi's first term was coming to an end. D'Alema had publicly projected an image of a man keen to break with the past, to help clean up Italian public life, but d'Arcais says he realised then that he possessed the same instincts. "He was furious with the judges. I understood that for the Left, the independence of the judiciary was something they too couldn't accept." Two years later, in 1998, d'Alema became Prime Minister. The new constitution of the

Second Republic had produced a new type of political rotation, but the old instincts of the political class defending its privileges, irrespective of ideological hue, had been preserved.

The sense of resignation or despair is palpable among the few members of the judiciary who have sought change. As chief prosecutor in Milan, Gherardo Colombo was one of the key figures in *Mani Pulite*, prosecuting officials for corruption. He retired in 2007. He now spends his time travelling the country teaching about the rule of law, from universities to primary schools. "There is a plaque in every Italian court, saying everyone is equal before the law," he tells me. "Now they are trying to affirm the principle that Berlusconi is anointed and untouchable." He says root-and-branch reform of the judiciary is overdue, but adds that the problem goes deeper, to the heart of the public's priorities: "We have a genuine problem with justice. People see it as ineffective." He traces it back to the 1970s when hundreds of people died during the period of the Red Brigades' terrorism. Most cases went unresolved, due to fear, bribery or sheer incompetence. "Many Italians lost confidence in the judiciary then."

Berlusconi has dressed up his assault on the judiciary as part of a necessary set of "reforms" to a moribund system. In that respect he is not wrong, although his record suggests a much narrower motive. The average trial lasts up to twelve years. One bankruptcy case of a small firm in the south started in 1962 and lasted forty-six years. The longer a case can be drawn out, the more the defence can claim that the passage of time has weakened the charges. The statute of limitations has brought up to a fifth of all cases to a premature close, with the political and business classes being the main beneficiaries. As in India and other countries that are notional democracies, the legal system is skewed towards the wealthy and influential. The vast majority of people convicted for white-collar crime are acquitted. Those who do receive punishment are rarely sent to jail for more than a token period of days or weeks. Conversely, poor Albanians or Africans caught shoplifting or pick-pocketing tend to see the full weight of the law applied to them.

In April 2006, Berlusconi was forced out after serving a five-year term of unprecedented constitutional stability. In that time he achieved precious little in terms of economic or social reform. Italy's finances had been in trouble for over a decade, falling down the EU league table for just about every economic indicator. Italy's manufacturing system – the production of machine tools, shoes, handbags, tiles, cheap furniture, ready-made clothes – was gradually being wiped out by more cost-effective goods from developing countries, particularly China. Few serious measures were taken to counter the trend. Between 2001 and 2006, under Berlusconi's leadership, Italy dropped from 14th to 53rd place in the global competitiveness index. Spending on education continued to fall, as it has done for the past twenty years, down to less than 5 per cent of GDP. Only half the population has post-compulsory schooling, one of the lowest levels in Europe, with only a fifth of young people entering further education, of whom a majority drop out before graduation. The availability of healthcare and the standards of that care are low.

Berlusconi attributed the result to allegations of corruption that he said had been dredged up to undermine him. Still, given his poor performance, the narrowness of his election defeat, by a margin of only 25,000 votes, was widely seen as a consolation victory. It ensured that his long-time rival, Romano Prodi, would struggle to survive. In the two years that followed, Prodi abided by many strictures of fiscal orthodoxy set out by the European Central Bank and other economic institutions. He cut the size of Italy's national debt, abolished a host of bureaucratic restrictions and took decisive measures to counter tax evasion. He earned plaudits from the IMF and EU but drew dismay from Italy's taxpayers, who suffered for his efforts. Given the priorities of Italy's core votes, this was more of a kamikaze run than an attempt at political longevity.

Prodi's administration did, however, maintain the tradition of political self-help. Under the guise of clearing the hopelessly overcrowded prisons, it declared a sweeping amnesty, which also benefited those charged with corruption. The Left's leading lights – Prodi, d'Alema and Walter Veltroni, the Mayor of Rome – presided over another period marked by stagnation and widespread disillusionment over the standards of Italian politics. The most vivid symbol of the state's decrepitude was the garbage crisis in Naples, where a strike by mafia-controlled trash collectors led to huge piles of rotting refuse spread over a vast area.

The Left's gradual demise during the Second Republic left a gap that the Northern League filled. Portraying itself as the outsider, it played to a number of resentments felt equally by working-class voters and the millions of small shopkeepers and traders that determine Italy's electoral politics. The top two concerns were the large fiscal transfers from the rich north to the poorer south and, inevitably, immigration. Berlusconi's victory in April 2008 was stunning. His coalition obtained almost 47 per cent of the vote, the highest share for decades, with the Northern League the most important partner. He triumphed throughout Italy, with the exception of the centre of the country, the Left's last redoubt. Restored as Prime Minister, he set the tone for his new administration, appointing a former topless model, Mara Carfagna, as minister for equal opportunities. He suggested other countries should learn from Italy's approach to women in public life. He chided Spain's Prime Minister, José Luis Rodríguez Zapatero, for choosing a cabinet that was the first in Europe to have a majority of women. The Spanish government was now "too pink", Berlusconi suggested, adding: "Now he's asked for it. He'll have problems leading them." Such remarks might have played well with much of his constituency. They might have played well with friends such as Vladimir Putin. They seemed to represent part of the prevailing mood.

One of the most alarming sides to Berlusconi's third term

was the increasing hostility towards immigrants and others who threatened the "Italian way of life". Voters expressed considerable fear about the arrival of African asylum seekers via the island of Lampedusa, and Roma who were using the accession of Romania into the EU in 2007 to use Italy as their point of entry to the West. Berlusconi played to these feelings, describing these various incomers as "an army of evil". Several laws were passed in quick succession, packaged as anti-crime measures. These speeded up the repatriation of illegal immigrants, imposed far stiffer jail sentences for those breaking the law and allowed for checks making it a requirement for foreigners, including EU citizens, to show they had jobs and adequate living conditions. Citizens' patrols were extended across the country, allowing local groups to patrol their neighbourhoods. Italian democracy was reinforcing a very particular type of vigilante justice. In one southern town, Foggia, a special bus service was established only for immigrants, to keep them away from working-class districts. This prompted inevitable comparisons with American segregation in the 1950s and apartheid South Africa. Then, in February 2009, parliament passed a bill compelling medical staff to contact police if they suspected the patient they were treating did not have a valid visa or work permit. Critics pointed out not only the ethical repercussions – doctors turning informers of the kind last seen under Mussolini – but the fear that asylum seekers would avoid seeking medical help, even if they had contagious diseases. These complaints were to no avail. Berlusconi was tapping into the popular mood, making his own personal pact with the people – to keep them safe from "foreigners".

Berlusconi's main concern remained his own fate. With a huge majority in parliament's two chambers, he moved quickly to ensure that the judiciary would never hound him out again. He set the tone within weeks of returning to office, devoting most of a speech before the Shopkeepers Association, a constituency close to his heart, to a tirade against the judiciary, calling it a "cancerous growth" on Italian life. Referring to himself in the third person, he insisted that from 1994 to 2006 "789 prosecutors and magistrates took an interest in the politician Berlusconi with the aim of subverting the votes of the Italian people". He quickly introduced a number of legal reforms. The first was aimed at restricting telephone tapping in criminal investigations, a bizarre reversal of roles with other European countries that were seeking to expand them. In Berlusconi's case, as ever, the motive was self-preservation as prosecutors had for a long time relied on wire taps instead of the more conventional collection of evidence, particularly in fraud cases. He then sought to reintroduce the plan for a top people's amnesty that he had first proposed in 2003, which had been thrown out by the Constitutional Court. This time he was far more confident of success.

He did not stop there. He made a spectacular announcement that 100,000 criminal trials would be frozen for twelve months. The law would cover any cases that had begun before June 2002 and for which conviction would carry a sentence of less than ten years in jail. The offences ranged from manslaughter to theft, kidnapping, grievous bodily harm, extortion, fraud and corruption. The government said the law would help judges focus on "more serious crimes" and that a suspension of "lesser trials" would help clear the backlog. One of the cases halted was the trial of police officers who launched a night-time raid on a school in Genoa during the 2001 G8 summit that was being used as sleeping quarters for protesters, doctors and journalists. More than sixty people had been injured. Another involved three people who allegedly paid bribes to Iraq in return for more than a million barrels of oil. One of the most colourful trials involved a British lawyer, David Mills, the estranged husband of Tessa Jowell, a government minister. Mills was sentenced in February 2009 to four years in jail for accepting a £500,000 bribe from Berlusconi in return for giving false evidence in two legal cases against him in the late 1990s. The wheels of justice, it might be argued, did actually turn in this instance, except that Mills was confident all the way through that he would not have to serve any of his term. By the time he had exhausted all his appeals, the statute of limitations would come into effect.

Liberal Italy, that small pocket which continued to attend *girotondi* marches, was in uproar about Berlusconi's latest legal sleights of hand. The twelve-month amnesty was dubbed the "Salva-premier", or "Save the Prime Minister", an interpretation he did little to deny. "My lawyers have informed me that this law may be applied to one of the many fanciful trials that the extreme left-wing judges have targeted me with for political ends," he declared. His Justice Minister, Angelino Alfano, was even more candid in his defence of the bill. "Having brilliantly won the elections, Silvio Berlusconi deserves to be able to calmly govern this government. And this country needs to be governed," he declared. Much of the country regarded it either with resignation or equanimity, or believed it to be his just reward. The pact was in full swing.

It is hard to gainsay Berlusconi's popularity. Two days after the Senate, the upper house, had approved the amnesty legislation, I was walking along the Piazza Venezia with Sergio Rizzo, one of Italy's most prominent writers. Rizzo pointed me in the direction of a small crowd that had gathered outside the driveway of a large building. The group comprised mainly women and older folk, but seemed to be a reasonable cross-section of the electorate. These were ordinary voters seeking a glimpse of their hero, Berlusconi, as he left his official residence for work. "You have to understand what motivates these people if you want to understand the trade-off here," Rizzo told me.

Rizzo is the author of a book that took Italy by storm in 2007. *The Caste: How Italian Politicians Have Become Untouchable* was reprinted twenty-three times in its original Italian edition in just six months, a remarkable achievement for a book of political analysis. To date, it has sold more than a million copies, in a country where sales of 20,000 are considered a bestseller, and made Rizzo and his fellow author, Gian Antonio Stella, national names. The book describes how "a greedy and self-reverential political class became a caste and invaded Italian society". That class is "becoming increasingly indifferent to the common good and the notion of sound administration in order to nourish itself". The details are eye-opening; everyone at all levels of society is at it, making the rules, twisting the rules or breaking the rules in order to give themselves privileges and money. The book shows how towns and villages cook the books in order to maximise subsidies and minimise the tax they must hand back to the centre. It lists the number of state organisations that start-up companies must deal with – approximately seventy. That is seventy sets of individuals to bribe.

"Berlusconi represents the stomach of Italians. Everyone wants to win the lottery," Rizzo says. "He ensures that he gets what he wants by looking after those around him." The President, a figurehead in Italy but notionally in overall charge, has at his disposal a staff of nine hundred. The book lists the privileges of the nearly one thousand members of the two chambers of parliament, of whom an astonishing seven hundred have escort and armed protection. It describes how tiny fringe parties refuse to merge with larger ones because every group in parliament receives copious funding. Italian deputies have raised their salaries almost sixfold since 1948, earning about double their UK, French and German counterparts. A governing class of 180,000 elected representatives around the country has at its disposal 574,215 official cars, *auto blu*. Berlusconi has thirteen cars in his cavalcade and eighty-one security agents, second only in the global pecking order to the American President.

It would be understandable if Italians disowned their political system, if they withdrew into their cocoon, as I had found to be the case with wealthier Indians also faced with institutional corruption of such an unfathomable scale. Rizzo points out, however, that turnout in Italian general elections is around 80 per cent, well above the European average. Italians are just as gripped by the drama of election campaigns as other countries even if, as with

India, voters conclude that, once elected, governments are under little pressure to deliver. So if this is not anti-politics, what exactly is it? Many of those I spoke to see a longer-term trend – the yearning for a strong leader, or at least, as in the case of Berlusconi, the perception of one. "Authoritarianism is gradually seeping into many countries, even within the EU; power is being handed over voluntarily," Rizzo says. "Here it simply takes a more obvious form." None of Italy's institutions appears able or willing to confront the danger.

One of those institutions is the Vatican. Around a third of Italy's voters profess to be practising Catholics, and polls suggest that an overwhelming majority ally themselves with Berlusconi or with his right-wing coalition partners. Berlusconi's pact with the Holy See is clearly delineated, although it has not been without its fissures, particular on questions of personal morality. In spite of his entreaties, he was not allowed to take communion after divorcing his first wife in 1985 in favour of a former showgirl. His continued liaisons with numerous other attractive young women led one of Italy's biggest selling Catholic magazines, *Famiglia Cristiana*, to complain of his "shifting morals". Even his second wife, Veronica Lario, finally declared, in May 2009, that she had had enough of a man "who consorts with minors", and was filing for divorce.

At the top of the Vatican, the understanding was that Berlusconi would ensure that its doctrinal messages were applied in law. In return, it would not complain about his assault on the constitution or democracy – just as it had not done under Mussolini or during the post-war *Tangentopoli*. This arrangement, dubbed "a clerical dictatorship" by one former parliamentarian, was brought to the fore during the case of a certain Eluana Englaro. She had lived in a persistent vegetative state since a car accident in 1992, and her story became a battleground over euthanasia. Her father finally succeeded in securing support from the Supreme Court for the family's wish to stop feeding her and letting her die. Under Vatican pressure, Berlusconi passed an emergency decree forbidding doctors from withholding food. In a rare show of defiance, the President, Giorgio Napolitano, refused to sign it, calling it unconstitutional. Berlusconi said he would ask parliament to force the President's resignation. Englaro died three days later, but MPs ensured there would be no repetition of this case. The furore confirmed in Berlusconi's mind that there was only one solution. He should simply become President himself.

Not only did Berlusconi enjoy a large majority, but the opposition was in disarray. Veltroni's newly created Democratic Party was paralysed by timidity. The "party of good people", as it was dubbed, appeared reluctant to criticise the ruling coalition. This led to the establishment of a new party, Italy of Values, under a former *Mani Pulite* magistrate, Antonio Di Pietro. In January 2009, Di Pietro presented to Italy's highest court a petition of one million votes protesting against the immunity law for top state officials. This was twice the amount needed by law to force a referendum. Yet across the country a number of opposition figures had been embroiled in a further series of local government scandals, while Di Pietro's credibility was damaged after his son was caught up in a Naples sleaze inquiry. After years of being accused of corruption, Berlusconi could barely conceal his glee. He even took to talking about the "issue of morality" in politics. He signalled that one of his main tasks was to accelerate his "reforms" of the judiciary.

The more the global financial crisis took hold, the more relaxed he appeared. Perhaps it was the fact that the Italian economy, having grown much more slowly than others in Europe, had less far to fall. Perhaps it was the opportunity presented by the crisis. He exploited the emergency to project himself as the strong man needed for occasions such as this. After a meeting with European leaders on global finances he danced until dawn at a disco. "If I sleep for three hours, I still have enough energy to make love for another three," *La Repubblica* quoted him as telling the young crowd. "I hope that when you hit seventy, you're in as good shape as I am." Only the state, he insisted, could be trusted to help the country out of its predicament. In March 2009, he consolidated his power yet further by incorporating Fini's National Alliance into his own party. Berlusconi named the grouping the People of Freedom. He was star of the show at its founding convention. As he entered the hall, the six thousand delegates sprang to their feet to give him an ovation, while loudspeakers blared out Beethoven's Ode to Joy followed by his campaign song, "Thank Goodness for Silvio". He declared to the jubilant crowd: "We are the party of the Italian people. We are the party of Italians who love freedom and who want to remain free." And in many respects he was right. It depends on one's definition of freedom. In Berlusconi's case it was freedom for individuals to make a living, by whatever means, and away from the prying eyes of the state. As ever, the opposition was not a match. The leader of the Democratic Party, now the only other force in politics, said the foundation of the new party was "positive for democracy".

By absorbing his allies, Berlusconi served notice that he did not want parliament to frustrate his ambition. With the judiciary and media already tamed, he now had his hands well and truly on all the levers of power. His next venture: creating an executive presidency, tailor-made for his needs, following in the footsteps of his good friend Vladimir Putin.

It is all too easy to lay the blame for Italy's democratic recession on one man. If democracy is narrowly defined as the will of the majority, expressed in free and fair elections, then Italians might be forgiven for wondering what the problem was all about. If democracy is meant to be about something more, about public participation, scrutiny and accountability, then Italy could be seen as not so different from the so-called authoritarian states I had visited. The institutions that should be acting as a check on politicians have been equally culpable. "Forget television: that was lost long ago. Even Italian newspapers are very close to power. They cannot be watchdogs. We criticise our politicians, but we want the same privileges," Rizzo told me. "Systemic corruption is so deep and all-pervasive that it no longer matters whether a particular politician takes money on the side, although most of them do." The *Mani Pulite* period of the early 1990s offered a chance of a break with the past. "Fifteen years ago we had the chance to revitalise our politics. We didn't take it."

7

BRITAIN: SURVEILLANCE STATE

"Britain used to export textiles, iron, steel and pop music; now it exports Orwellian methods for monitoring the masses" – Brendan O'Neill

"THE BRITISH PEOPLE'S COMMITMENT TO HUMAN RIGHTS IS born from a sense of our history, of rights forged out of shared struggles, and on the belief that free societies offer the best prospects for long-term stability and growth." It was March 2009. I was sitting in the second row of an ornate hall in Lancaster House, the venue for many triumphant and not-so-triumphant moments in past diplomacy. I was listening to David Miliband, the Foreign Secretary, launching his department's annual human rights report. I suppressed a howl of disbelief as he explained how the UK was setting the example for others to follow. I have known Miliband for years and have seen how, like other of his colleagues, he had searched his conscience about a number of the actions of his government. Scarcely an hour after Miliband's address, the Attorney General announced that she had ordered a police investigation into whether MI5 agents had been complicit in the Americans' torture of detainees at Guantánamo Bay. The lawyer for Binyam Mohamed, a former inmate who made the initial allegation, said the trail could lead back to Miliband's department.

This was all a far cry from twelve years earlier. The country was gearing up for the arrival of Tony Blair and his New Labour Camelot with almost childlike enthusiasm. I had just returned to Britain after reporting on the downfall of dictatorships. I had joined that most British of institutions, the "lobby", the inner sanctum of political journalists at Westminster, in the hope that I might be galvanised by the democratic processes being played out before me. Even before the 1997 election I had seen enough of the behaviour of those around Blair, and the journalists who were supposed to be holding them to account, to caution me to scepticism about any brave, new and more liberal world.

The record of the Conservatives had been appalling. From internment, the absurd attempts to gag Sinn Fein leaders on television and shoot-to-kill policies in Northern Ireland, to the politicisation of the police in breaking up strikes, to the use of the Official Secrets Act and other measures to bully journalists and stifle investigation, the governments of Margaret Thatcher and John Major had shown a classically high-handed approach to those they regarded as undermining the "British way of life".

Labour vowed to be different. It came to power promising to restore public faith in democracy. It would do this by rebuilding "trust" and introducing radical constitutional changes that would modernise Westminster and Whitehall and make them both more transparent and accountable. Power was devolved, in Scotland, Wales and London. A Freedom of Information Act was passed, albeit after a considerable delay and heavily diluted from the original plans. Most important of all, the European Convention on Human Rights was incorporated into UK law, enshrining basic rights into Britain's unwritten constitution. So how did it happen that the administrations of Blair and Gordon Brown would go down as being two of the most illiberal in modern British history?

There is no single answer, but there are many clues. Some are

narrowly political. Blair had inherited the package of reform measures from his predecessor, but his heart was clearly not in them. Why
disperse power when you have suddenly acquired so much of it? The
large parliamentary majorities secured in 1997 and 2001 engendered
in the Prime Minister and those around him a hubris that would be
their undoing – manifested most famously in the Iraq war, but also in
domestic preoccupations. That hubris was accompanied by a less
perceptible but equally damaging under-confidence. Blair believed
essentially that Britain was both a Conservative and conservative
country and that he would achieve little if he did not acquiesce to the
tastes of the majority view as represented to him by pollsters and
selected newspaper magnates and editors. The terrorist attacks of 11
September 2001 allowed him to elide his instincts with theirs, but his
journey towards an authoritarian mindset had begun before then.
Throw in technological advances, such as biometric data collection,
and the mix became potent.

By the time Blair left office in 2007, he had bequeathed to his
successor a surveillance state unrivalled anywhere in the democratic
world. Parliament passed forty-five criminal justice laws – more
than the total for the whole of the previous century – creating more
than three thousand new criminal offences. That corresponded to
two new offences for each day parliament sat during Blair's premiership. The scope was extensive: police and security forces were
given greater powers of arrest and detention; all institutions of state
were granted increased rights to snoop; individuals were required to
hand over unprecedented forms of data. Abroad, the government
colluded with the transport of terrorist suspects by the US government to secret prisons around the world, giving landing rights at
British airports for these so-called "rendition" flights. At home, new
crimes were created, such as glorifying terrorism or inciting religious
hatred. Control orders were imposed on people deemed a security
threat, but who the government said could not be prosecuted
because the evidence that had been gathered by bugging or other
means would not be admissible in courts. Anti-Social Behaviour

Orders (ASBOs) were imposed on people for actions that were not illegal in themselves (such as visiting a part of town deemed out of bounds or talking to certain people deemed dangerous), and for which the burden of proof was considerably lower. In 2005 double jeopardy was removed for serious offences, meaning that people could be tried for a second time even after being acquitted. The government also tried to cut back the scope of trial by jury, suggesting some cases, such as serious fraud, were too complex for ordinary people to understand.

The more the state intruded into the lives of individuals, the harder it became to convince people it was making them safer. Whenever figures registered a rise in crime, particularly violent crime, newspapers indulged in a bout of moral panic. Whenever figures suggested crime rates had fallen, newspapers insinuated that ministers had massaged the figures. Yet even though the public doubted the effectiveness of many of these laws, most opinion polls suggested either support or acquiescence for the general idea of being tough – particularly when the specific measures were not explained to them. Civil liberties groups secured one or two notable victories in curbing ministerial zeal, but they felt they were battling against a popular tide.

I have never denied the important role of the state, at national and local level, in helping to provide more equitable social outcomes or to secure safer streets. Several spells of living in continental Europe have made me appreciate the more communitarian spirit alive in a number of countries. The social responsibility of the Germany of the 1980s where I lived compared well to the more mean-spirited atmosphere of Britain, in which Margaret Thatcher had famously said there was "no such thing as society". In the mid-1990s, as Labour prepared for office, I, like many, welcomed a recalibration away from selfish individualism. I believed then that there was no problem in individuals handing over more of their information to the state. I carried an identity card in Germany and in Spain, and neither I nor my friends even thought of questioning it. But a few years of life under Blair and a succession of Home Secretaries with a thirst for authoritarianism led me to change my mind.

A number of incidents symbolised the zeal for control and use of arbitrary power. One of the most powerful was the arrest of peace protesters for reading out the names of British soldiers killed in Iraq at the Cenotaph in Whitehall. This violated a no-go area for demonstrations around the Houses of Parliament. Then there was the arrest of a fifteen-year-old boy for using the word "cult" to describe the Church of Scientology in a demonstration outside the church's London headquarters. The police subsequently issued a public warning that "insulting" Scientology would now be treated as a crime. The most excruciating example, which I remember watching open-mouthed, came during the 2005 Labour Party conference when an eighty-two-year-old man, Walter Wolfgang, was manhandled and bundled out of the hall for shouting "nonsense" during a speech by the then Foreign Secretary, Jack Straw. Police justified their actions under a notorious clause in the Terrorism Act which gives them power to search any individual in areas designated as being vulnerable to terrorist attack. Wolfgang, a member of the Stop the War Coalition, had escaped Nazi Germany in 1937.

But one episode alerted me more than any other to the scale of the shift that had taken place in British society. As editor of the *New Statesman* magazine, I had defined my job as doing everything I could to hold power to account. I described it as "rattling cages", and wanted to focus on investigative journalism, a dying art in much of British journalism. In September 2006, I asked a journalist, Brendan O'Neill, to report on the use of closed-circuit television around the UK and to try to get into one of the watching stations. It was a subject about which many people speculated, but I had not read a definitive account of how it worked and how widespread the practice was. What O'Neill came up with startled me.

I published the piece as the cover story of the magazine, under the headline "Watching You, Watching Me". In his article, O'Neill describes how the CCTV control centre for Westminster is happy to invite him in. He is met by an official escort, entering a "dark and dank warehouse" and into a lift which takes him two floors below ground. "There, we walk through subterranean concrete corridors, past industrial-sized dustbins emitting odours of rotting food, towards a pristine wooden door that seems out of place in this sewer-like setting. My escort taps in a code, and we walk through. There's another door. We wait for the first one to lock behind us and then walk through the second. I can barely believe what I see next. I am inside what can only be described as a bunker of spies. Deep beneath the Trocadero – where unsuspecting tourists are poring over maps of the city over coffee at Starbucks and bored teens are playing beat-'em-up arcade games – there is a state-of-the-art CCTV facility where men and women in suits watch the streets of London live on vast tele-screens."

This particular watching station controls 160 cameras, 24 hours a day, 365 days a year. "Since becoming operational in 2002, the control room has recorded 24,000 'incidents', ranging from 'low-level' graffiti, fly-tipping and public urinating to 'high-level' robbery, drug dealing and prostitution. It has also had 5,000 visitors from more than 30 countries whose governments or police forces are looking to adopt similar systems," O'Neill writes. "Britain used to export textiles, iron, steel and pop music; now it exports Orwellian methods for monitoring the masses." The author is given a set of instructions for how to monitor people. He hits a button marked Leicester Square. "Suddenly I have a perfect, bird's-eye view of the square and its strolling, love-struck couples and rushing pedestrians." The camera zooms in. "I get a remarkable high-resolution close-up of a young man and woman in intimate conversation – students, perhaps, or young French tourists, maybe, she wearing a trendy red vest and he a white shirt. It feels wrong to be watching them from this underground bunker a few streets away."

The article ends with the following statistic: there are an estimated five million CCTV cameras in the UK; that is one for every twelve citizens, or 20 per cent of the total on the whole planet, which, considering that Britain occupies a tiny 0.2 per cent of the inhabitable global land mass, is quite an achievement. The average Londoner going about his or her business may be monitored by three hundred cameras a day. In other major city centres, such as Manchester and Edinburgh, residents can expect to be sighted on between roughly fifty and a hundred cameras a day. The technology and scope have advanced since then.

Rereading that piece several years later, I am struck by how dated the tone feels. Perhaps I was a little naive. If so, I no longer am. In the intervening period of time, Britons have become thoroughly reconciled to cameras, even dependent on them. Several arguments are put by the advocates of surveillance. One says: poor people are more likely to be victims of street crime, so if you believe in social justice, you should have no objection. Another is more general and goes along the lines of: "You want your daughters to come home safely from school, don't you?" Well, yes, but does that mean we need this? Apparently it does. Time and again, Labour ministers cited opinion polls and private research that showed not just public support but public impetus for greater surveillance.

Two sets of images changed the relationship in Britain between liberty, surveillance and security. Recorded at 15.39 on 12 February 1993, and later broadcast nationwide, a grainy CCTV picture showed a trusting toddler taking a stranger by the hand and being led out of a Liverpool shopping centre. Days later, two-year-old James Bulger was found bludgeoned to death on a railway track. On 7 July 2005, at 07.21, camera number 14 at Luton railway station captured four young bombers appearing chillingly calm as they prepared for their mission to blow themselves up, taking fifty Londoners with them.

In the first instance, the camera did not prevent the crime, but its imperfect images helped the police find the two eleven-year-old boys who were later convicted of his murder (and who, on their eventual release from custody, had to change their identities for fear of mob revenge). In the second case, the pictures made absolutely no difference to the crime. But their wide dissemination afterwards was seen by the government as important for spreading the message that it would stop at nothing in its battle against terrorism. "Let no one be in any doubt, the rules of the game are changing," proclaimed Tony Blair.

Britain has become, as the *Washington Post* observed, "the world's premier surveillance society". CCTV was first used in shops in the UK, but during the 1970s gradually moved into public space, particularly the London Underground, trains and buses. Cameras, fixed and mobile, have long been used to monitor protests and trouble spots such as football games. The technology has been getting ever smarter. Most cameras now come with automatic number-plate recognition, facial recognition and even suspicious behaviour recognition. In 2003, software called Intelligence Pedestrian Surveillance was introduced. This analyses clusters and movements of pixels in CCTV footage in search of unusual activity. British scientists, backed by the Ministry of Defence and a £500,000 government grant, have been developing cameras with "gait recognition". The aim is to recognise whether people are walking suspiciously or strangely, and alert a human operator.

In September 2006, Middlesbrough became the first town to launch "speaking" CCTV. Cameras were fitted with loudspeakers, monitored round the clock by council officials based in control rooms. These cameras bark orders if they capture anyone dropping litter or behaving in other anti-social ways. If they obey, the operator is supposed to say "thank you". If they do not, the police can be alerted and the evidence used against the offender in court. So pleased was the government with the pilot scheme, as part of its "respect" agenda, that the follow year the project was extended to twenty more towns. Not to be outdone, in May 2007 Merseyside Police launched their latest tool to combat anti-social behaviour, the Microdrone, a small battery-powered, radio-controlled helicopter that comes with a camera and a loudspeaker. It is so quiet that it can operate from a height of 100 metres without being noticed.

According to its manufacturers, it is robust and can return to base even if it loses two of its four rotor blades. One unusual feature is a speaker that allows the police to give instructions to those on the ground. In George Orwell's *Nineteen Eighty-Four* what so tormented Winston Smith about the omnipresent telescreen was that not only did it watch, but it spoke, too.

An important early measure taken by the government was the 2000 Regulation of Investigatory Powers Act. This snoopers' charter, like several of the government's assaults on liberty, predated the terrorist attacks of 9/11. Designed to equip the police and security services for the fight against crime and terrorism, it was so widely drafted that hundreds of public bodies were brought into its remit, and encouraged to avail themselves of the powers. By 2008, more than a thousand interception operations a day were taking place and more than six hundred public bodies had been given permission to monitor intercepted communications data – over three-quarters of which are local councils.

The annual report of the Interception of Communications Commissioner for 2006 was chillingly matter-of-fact. I cited it at length in a leader article I wrote in the *New Statesman*. The report noted that, in only nine months, more than 250,000 applications were made to intercept private communications; most were approved. Not only did government departments – such as the Foreign Office, Home Office, Ministry of Defence and Scotland's First Minister – enjoy the right to snoop, but so did bodies such as HM Revenue & Customs, the intelligence agencies, all fifty-two police forces and even the fire service. The tone adopted by the commissioner, Sir Paul Kennedy, was largely sympathetic to the prying needs of the state. He hailed the "quality, dedication and enthusiasm" of the army of people listening into telephone calls and tapping into computers, although he noted that more than a thousand of that year's bugging operations had been flawed. He put this down mostly to administrative errors. One can only speculate on the kinds of fascinating conversations some of these council investigators uncovered. Kennedy gave a clue, saying that the suspected criminals tracked included "rogue traders, fly-tippers and fraudsters". The commissioner was adamant that these powers were also successful in preventing murders, and in tackling drugs gangs, people-smuggling, serious violent crime and "terrorist and extremist organisations". Add to this the following statistic: more than 10,000 permits were granted during this period allowing state inspectors to enter people's homes. A government review found there were 1,043 state powers of entry, including the right to check that illegal hypnotism was not taking place or that hedges were not too high.

By this point, even professionals at the heart of the security system were beginning to express reservations. The government-appointed Information Commissioner, Richard Thomas, warned that the profusion of data in the hands of the state was in danger of becoming a "toxic liability". In his report for 2008, Thomas said: "Just as terrorism and other threats to our national security remind us that privacy and data protection cannot be absolute rights, so the fight against these evils must not run roughshod over our liberties. Sometimes the best-intentioned plans bring the most insidious threats, where freedoms are not appreciated until it is too late to turn the clock back." Thomas dismissed out of hand plans to create a government database to hold details of telephone and email communications of the entire population, by means of a "live" tap. "Do we really want the police, security services and other organs of the state to have access to more and more aspects of our private lives? Any such scheme would require the fullest public debate to establish whether, whatever the benefits, it amounted to excessive surveillance as a step too far for the British way of life." The project was being masterminded by MI6 and GCHQ, the government's listening station in Cheltenham, and called the Interception Modernisation Programme. The budget they were seeking and the scale of the project were staggering. In 2007 alone, fifty-seven billion text messages were sent in the UK (one thousand per member of the population), up from one billion in 1999. The number of broadband internet connections grew from 330,000 in 2001 to eighteen million. Each day some three billion emails are sent, corresponding to 35,000 per second.

Thomas said he was not aware of such a database in any other country. Until that point police and intelligence agencies could ask telecommunications providers for information on phone calls made, texts sent and internet sites visited. The provider could query the request, which might then go to the interception commissioner and another watchdog – but under the new proposals that right would be removed. "We do have to stand up and say these are our fundamental liberties and our freedoms and lines have to be drawn somewhere, and there should be a full democratic debate about where exactly the lines should be drawn." After more than six years of fighting against the tide, Thomas went into retirement.

By stealth and with little discussion, the UK amassed the largest known national DNA database in the world, with the most modern technology. By early 2009 it was said to contain the records of more than five million of its sixty million citizens, including a third of all black men in the country. Records are now kept of everyone who is arrested, meaning that many on the system have never been charged with any crime. New profiles are being added at a rate of one every 45 seconds, 2,000 a day, or 700,000 a year. Ministers, egged on by the police, suggested the scheme should become universal, taking the records of everyone. Dissatisfied by the rate of increase, they then proposed to allow police to take the DNA of anyone stopped, including speeding motorists, litterbugs and people not wearing seat belts. In December 2008, the European Court of Human Rights ruled that the British government had violated the right to privacy by storing the genetic details of people who were not convicted criminals. Ministers responded by saying they would remove such profiles from the database, but keep the original DNA samples. The inventor of genetic fingerprinting said he had been left "almost speechless" by the government's attitude. "I have significant concerns there," Sir Alec Jeffreys said. "My genome is my property; it is not the state's. I will allow the state access to that genome under very strict circumstances. It is an issue of my personal genetic privacy."

Another database, called Contact Point, was created to store the details of every child in England and Wales, his or her exam results, difficulties within and outside the family – just about anything relevant to their lives. By the time these children all reach adulthood, the databases will have merged to give the state complete access to their most personal information. The idea was to allow all professionals working with under-eighteens to find out who else had been in touch with them. The files – accessible to 330,000 vetted users, including police and doctors – would include each child's name, date of birth, address, school, doctor, and any social worker or probation officer who was looking after them, as well as their parents' names and addresses. As was often the case, the concerns that had driven the change were genuine. The public had been horrified by several high-profile cases of young children abused by their guardians, particularly the murder of Victoria Climbié, a girl who had arrived in the UK from the Ivory Coast.

The problem for the government was that the public sent out mixed signals. The problem for the public was that the media sent out mixed signals. On the one hand, newspapers fed on fear, implying that Britons had never felt so unsafe; on the other, they warned of a police state, forever telling people what to do and punishing them if they did not. The problem for ministers was not confusion, but dogma. They reduced the debate on the relationship between state and individual to a simple matrix, a zero-sum in which you could either be a naive libertarian who worried only about individual rights or you could be a responsible citizen, ever on the alert for threats. Historically, this has not been a Left–Right issue, but, after a decade of Blair–Brown rule, the Labour Party had all but abandoned a credible human rights agenda. For me, and others like me, that was one of the most dispiriting aspects of the age.

Within weeks of the 9/11 terrorist attacks, David Blunkett,

then Home Secretary, proposed the idea of a national identity card scheme. In truth, Labour had been toying with the idea ever since taking power in 1997, and was merely looking for the right opportunity. Blunkett, perhaps the most illiberal in a series of illiberal incumbents, declared that they be called "entitlement cards" and that individuals should pay for the privilege of carrying one. He did so without irony. The idea took some time to materialise into policy, but in 2003, amid some fanfare, the government announced plans to introduce an identity card scheme of perhaps greater sophistication than possessed in any other country. The chip inside the cards would contain up to fifty categories of personal information on each citizen. The legislation gave the Home Secretary powers to add to that total, without seeking a vote in parliament. In the first few years, public support for ID cards appeared strong, but opinion polls showed support ebbing away amid growing concern over data losses and estimates of costs increasing from £6 billion to up to £20 billion. Ministers adapted their arguments to suit the moment. First they would be used to tackle benefit fraud, then illegal immigration (when that was high), then terrorism. Charles Clarke, Blunkett's successor, described the bill as a "profoundly civil libertarian measure because it promotes the most fundamental civil liberty in our society, which is the right to live free from crime and fear". In spite of robust opposition in the House of Lords, the legislation was eventually passed in March 2006, with planned full introduction in 2010. The Conservatives vowed that if they took power they would stop the plans, although many doubted they actually would.

The ID-card debate was a manifestation of a broader problem. I was continually struck by the gulf between politicians' regard for Britain's democratic credentials and the reality. MPs referred to the UK as the mother of parliaments. Rarely would debates go by without references to Magna Carta, the Glorious Revolution or other great moments in history. Eurosceptics would marvel at Britain's doughty individualism, compared to the herd instincts of those continentals. Yet it is hard to find a nation in the self-declared democratic world where more power is concentrated in the hands of individuals with such a weak mandate. The depth of the disconnection was set out by an independent panel, the Power Inquiry. This was established by a group of eminent public figures in 2004 to recommend ways of increasing public participation in politics and improving the quality of democracy. When it published its findings two years later, its analysis was stark: the legitimacy of government was being undermined by the voting system, turnout and much else besides.

The 2005 general election demonstrated the depth of the malaise. Once again, one of the main parties, Labour, had been given untrammelled power, but with the endorsement of only 22 per cent of the total electorate. Only half of all voters had bothered to cast their ballot. In local elections that figure was consistently worse. The inquiry suggested descriptions of the British system as "executive democracy" were inaccurate. A better title might be "elective dictatorship". The chairwoman of the inquiry, the lawyer Baroness Helena Kennedy, said the pool from which Britain's political leaders are chosen had shrunk to a puddle. Britain's elected representatives had ceased to be representative. "Politics and government are increasingly in the hands of privileged elites, as if democracy has run out of steam," she declared. "Too often, citizens are being evicted from decision-making, rarely asked to get involved and rarely listened to." As a result, people were turning away from voting and formal politics in favour of direct action and single-issue campaigns. The commission's final report, which it declared was designed to "save British democracy from meltdown", made thirty key recommendations. It was welcomed by the government; it spurred considerable but brief debate. It was quietly laid to rest.

Low turnout and limited mandates are compounded by a lack of checks and balances. Parliament is seldom able to exercise more than cursory oversight. Once in a while, a government is defeated on a major vote, debates are virtually ignored by the public and press, while select committees – so powerful in the United States – are institutionally and intellectually more of an embarrassment in the

UK. Parliament's jurisdiction over other organs of the state, notably the security services, is lamentably weak. Ironically, over the past few decades Britain's two least democratic institutions have been the two most important guardians of its liberties – the judiciary and the unelected House of Lords.

In truth, there has never been a "golden age" of freedom in the UK. Governments of all colours have trodden similar paths, prime ministers in awe of the daily security briefings they receive. Blair and his ministers followed in the footsteps of the Conservatives in setting as their default position a disdain for a liberal "dinner party set" that obsessed about human rights. Their pollsters told them that the British public would put up with just about anything, from cameras, to cards, to pre-emptive custody, to stop and search, in order to feel safer. They bought the line that only those with something to hide had something to fear. If you kept out of trouble, you would not get into trouble. Where had I heard that before? The Singapore model has been exported far and wide.

Every country has its pact between liberty, security and prosperity. Blair expressed his approach with the eminently reasonable notion of "a society with rules but without prejudices". If one looks back at this era and asks to point out the area where Blair might have made the biggest difference for the better, one might say in the social sphere. Britain became, at least on paper, more tolerant. Laws were enforced recognising "civil partnership" for gay couples, and increasing penalties for discrimination on the basis of race, religion, gender, sexuality and age. Blair was marking the divide between public freedoms, which were negotiable, and private freedoms, which were sacrosanct. In the private realm, Britons had never been freer to lead their lives in the way they chose. In the public realm, from their behaviour in the local park, to their utterances in the media and in demonstrations, Britons were given ever narrower boundaries in which to operate. Overstep them, and the state would be given unbridled powers to hunt you down. Blair summed it up like this: "I believe in live and let live, except where your behaviour harms the freedoms of others." But who and what determines harm? Unfortunately, it was a parliament denuded of power, a government with scant popular mandate, and security services accountable to almost no one.

The idea of "choice" was interpreted more widely than simply social mores. Like others who spent their formative years during the Thatcher hegemony, Blair also saw as a fundamental right the ability of people to "choose" their public services. A state that did not allow individuals to choose their own school or hospital was, he believed, embarking on another form of coercion. This was one area where the state should intervene as little as possible. He believed that if people felt "free" to determine more of these day-to-day decisions, they would be more prepared to hand the authorities greater jurisdiction over their lives, such as security. Blair made a small amount of headway on this front during his tenure, but his successor did not see "choice" as a panacea, taking a more traditionally centre-left view of the benign role for the state in the provision of public services.

As he angled for Blair's job, Gordon Brown hinted that he would take a less cavalier approach to Britain's constitutional norms and civil liberties. He pledged to do away with his predecessor's "sofa" style of government, a clique of officials making decisions out of sight of parliament and cabinet. To a small degree, he did change procedures. But in the fundamental relationship between state and individual he continued where Blair had left off. Brown might not have sounded as zealous as his predecessor. Indeed, he laid down a different approach in his first forty-eight hours in office when he dealt with a series of attempted terrorist attacks on London and Glasgow with calm restraint. Yet, as time went on, whenever he was faced with a choice of curbing state excess or demonstrating that he was being "tough" on crime, he opted for the latter. Blair had bequeathed him a security apparatus in Whitehall that knew how to play ministers. The problem had worsened with the splitting of the criminal justice and terrorism remits between the old-style Home Office and a new Justice Ministry. Many of the more level-headed figures moved to the latter, leaving the inexperienced but ambitious new Home Secretary, Jacqui Smith, effectively a prisoner of hard-liners, many of whom had been seconded to her department directly from the security services. The Home Office, rarely a bastion of liberalism, began to resemble a ministry for public security. Smith knew it was not in her political interests to gainsay these apparent experts. She was happy to admit that, saying that in her job "you see some scary documents". She spoke of the possibility of terrorist groups gaining access to chemical, biological or nuclear materials, the so-called "dirty bombs". The first freedom, Smith declared, was "the freedom that comes from security". All other freedoms, by definition, were subservient to that.

In October 2007, four months after taking over, Brown set out his approach to human rights in a speech on "liberty". He turned criticisms about Labour's authoritarianism on their head, saying new state powers were guarantors of liberty, not threats to it. Brown framed the issue of liberty through a "distinctly British interpretation", one, he said, that "asserts the importance of freedom from prejudice, of rights to privacy, and of limits to the scope of arbitrary state power, but one that also rejects the selfishness of extreme libertarianism and demands that the realm of individual freedom encompasses not just some but all of us". He added: "In my view, the key to making these hard choices in a way that is compatible with our traditions of liberty is to, at all times, apply the liberty test, respecting fundamental rights and freedoms, and wherever action is needed by government, it never subjects the citizen to arbitrary treatment, is transparent and proportionate in its measures and at all times also requires proper scrutiny by, and accountability to, Parliament and the people." That was a classic red herring. Such checks and balances, such scrutiny, might apply if parliament had shown itself a guardian of liberties. The problem was that some of the major changes had been brought about by ministerial order, circumventing MPs; on other occasions, Labour members were ordered to vote according to party lines, rather than on the merits of the case.

The only time Labour MPs had shown their mettle was in November 2005 when they inflicted on Blair his only parliamentary defeat, refusing to endorse plans to increase pre-trial custody to three months. In stages, the government had shifted the ancient law of habeas corpus from twenty-four hours to fourteen days, but it insisted on the extension because of what it said was the increased dangers posed after 9/11 and 7/7 and the greater access by terrorists to new technology.

Brown initially seemed uninterested in pursuing the battle. But, as with Blair, he was guided by two imperatives – the perennial warning by security chiefs that the situation "out there" was "more dangerous", and the perennial advice of pollsters to "talk tough". He was advised to seek an increase in pre-trial custody, but to portray it as a compromise. So, instead of the wished-for ninety days, and the present twenty-eight, forty-two was the number his officials randomly chose. In spite of lobbying for the change, police chiefs could not point to a single instance so far where they had needed the extra time. But that was not the point. They based their justification on the precautionary principle, on the basis that they *might*, one day, need it, thereby reinterpreting criminal justice law on the basis of an undefined possible future threat. This was a variant on the "if only you knew what I know" line adopted by Blair in reference to the elusive weapons of mass destruction in Iraq – and, as it later transpired, he used that information deficit to mislead parliament and the public.

The government was reinterpreting its task not to minimise risk, calibrating security needs against liberty, but to set itself up as the guardian of all risk. Figures showed that the number of victims of terrorism among the British public was actually lower than before. In the decade of the Labour government terrorists had killed around 150 people in the UK (87 in Northern Ireland and almost all the rest on 7/7). This marked a decline of 88 per cent on the 1980s. Yet, security experts and ministers countered, that did not take into account the number of attacks that *might* have happened, that were foiled. Some of the cases came into the public domain, with terrorist cells broken and suspects convicted. But in many other cases, the information was not brought to light, for fear of jeopardising future intelligence operations. This debate came down ultimately to the public being asked to trust the politicians and the security services when they warned of dangers, and asked for extra measures to counter them. After Iraq, that commodity, however, was in dangerously short supply.

A succession of senior figures in criminal justice, including the former head of M15, Eliza Manningham-Buller, and the then Director of Public Prosecutions, Sir Ken Macdonald, lined up to oppose the forty-two-day plan, and to dismiss the thinking behind it. Theirs was a dogged campaign, marking perhaps the first clear sign that the mood among the public might be changing. Eventually, in October 2008, it was reluctantly dropped by ministers. The successful derailing of the legislation sent out a strong signal that law should not be made on the basis of undisclosed fears about an uncertain future. One single line in the sand had been drawn.

The government may be cavalier about others' privacy, but it is zealous in protecting its own. In my last months as editor of the *New Statesman* I came face to face with one such incident. The Official Secrets Act is the most draconian of all the various laws circumscribing legitimate inquiry. The issue is not the existence of such a law – few would disagree that one is necessary to protect vital national security interests – but the way it has been framed, used and abused over decades. The law was created a century ago, but in 1989 under Thatcher it was tightened, making it harder to cite a public interest defence. This is a law that governments of all hues have exploited in order to save them from political embarrassment, as much as to preserve security.

In early 2006, Derek Pasquill, a Foreign Office official, provided, in a series of leaks to the *New Statesman*, information about the government's approach to militant Islam. I didn't necessarily

agree with Pasquill's concerns, but I was convinced that the debate
he was opening up was in the public interest. I had no hesitation in
publishing. Pasquill was charged under the Official Secrets Act and
for a year he was harassed and interrogated. I refused a polite but
menacing letter from the Foreign Office to provide them with documents. I pointed out that ministers had already changed policy to
address those points raised by Pasquill. Therefore he had no case to
answer and the prosecution was designed to save the skins of man-
darins and ministers, notably Jack Straw, who had been Foreign
Secretary and who by this point was Justice Minister. We decided to
defend Pasquill to the hilt. Throughout the case I had the impression
that the government had become so arrogant and vengeful against
anyone trying to coax out the truth that ministers would invoke all
arms of the law to do their bidding. Faced with bullying, we tried a
spot of it ourselves. I went for a one-to-one meeting with my old
friend Miliband. Sitting on our own in his opulent office (a room I
had known well since my dealings with Robin Cook a decade earlier), I suggested to Miliband that he might want to look into the
problem. I warned him that when the trial began, we would bring
forward evidence that would embarrass senior figures in and around
government, particularly Straw. It was no idle threat. We had that
information. On the first day of the trial, at the Old Bailey in January
2008, the case was abandoned. "This is a spectacular and astonishing
victory for freedom of the press in the United Kingdom," I said at the
time. "This was a misguided and malicious prosecution, particularly
given that a number of Government ministers privately acknowledged from the outset that the information provided to us by Derek
Pasquill had been in the public interest and was responsible in large
part for changing Government policy for the good in terms of
extraordinary rendition and policy towards radical Islam." Legal
experts said the result would make similar prosecutions more difficult in the future. We shall see.

   In 2008, I took over as Chief Executive of Index on Censorship,
the UK's leading free expression organisation. This was another cru-

cial area in which the Labour record had been found seriously wanting. Three pieces of legislation had important consequences – the
Terrorism Act 2000, Terrorism Act 2006 and the Racial and Religious
Hatred Act 2006. These laws tightened the notion of speech crime
and created the notion of thought crime. They made it an offence
under UK law to advocate any form of violent activity, even in
another country, even an effort to change an illegal or undemocratic regime. While the first two laws were designed to deal with
Islamic extremism, the latter was aimed at soothing the frayed
nerves of the Muslim community, by providing Islam (and
Christianity) the same defence in law as long enjoyed by mono-
ethnic groups such as Jews and Sikhs. In so doing, the government
entered a minefield, promoting itself, the police and the courts as the
arbiters of taste and offence on anything from newspaper cartoons
to theatrical performances to parliamentary appearances. In
February 2009, a Dutch MP, Geert Wilders, was refused entry to the
UK. He had intended to show his anti-Islamic film, *Fitna*, at the
invitation of a member of the House of Lords. Wilders was declared
a "threat to public policy, public security and public health". The
government's decision was widely derided as providing the leader of
the small far-right Freedom Party with more publicity than he could
have dreamt of. It transpired that a visit he had made to London
only a few weeks earlier had passed virtually unnoticed. Shortly
after, ministers published a list of sixteen "undesirables" who would
be prevented from entering the country.

The public was also encouraged to complain whenever it felt
offended. In February 2009, a senior official at the Foreign Office,
Rowan Laxton, was arrested after he was heard shouting expletives
about Israel as he watched a television news report while running on
the treadmill at the London Business School gym. He had been
asked by other members of the gym to stop his tirade and, when he
did not, they subsequently alerted police, who charged him with
inciting religious hatred.

Not all the erosions in civil liberties could be attributable purely to government or state action. I had become increasingly mindful of the extent to which public organisations were self-censoring, not just in the media, but more broadly in cultural life. Public bodies across the land were tiptoeing away from areas of controversy. When chairing a round-table discussion organised by the Arts Council, I was startled to hear theatre directors and art gallery curators admitting that they avoided tackling issues of race or religion. Some cited police advice about potential unrest; others cited concern from funders or local authorities. Others took a more fundamental view, accepting the right of communities to be protected from offence. This right appears in the minds of some cultural figures to have taken precedence over the right to free speech. "The reality is that news editors, nervous members of the university computer department, radio talk shows and producers . . . are thinking there is a law that stops me doing 'this', but they are vague and anxious about what the 'this' is that they refuse to do," wrote the human rights academic Conor Gearty. His remarks provide another reference point with Singapore, where the line is drawn so as to be deliberately vague, leaving journalists and others in limbo, relying on the natural human impulse to keep out of trouble.

The longer-term threat to free expression in the UK comes from its libel laws, which are among the most restrictive in the world. English libel law is founded on an archaic premise: the assumption of a gentleman's good reputation. This burden of proof (the reverse of the usual presumption of innocence), along with the very high costs of libel actions, have made British libel laws singularly attractive to claimants and singularly pernicious to journalists and writers. The rich and powerful look for any mention of them in publications in the UK, either online or in hard copy. They then sue for libel in British courts, knowing that they have every likelihood of winning by default. The cost of litigation is so high that few are able to defend themselves. The plaintiffs string the case along for as many months as possible, ensuring that the defendants run out of money and then attempt to settle out of court, even when they know that theirs is a cast-iron case. The UK has become the global centre of what has come to be called "libel tourism". One senior editor of a national newspaper has said that he has been advised by his management board to avoid upsetting Russian oligarchs or anyone else with the power to disrupt their finances.

The increased use of libel has had a chilling effect on free speech and investigative journalism; it has also hindered the work of NGOs that have long relied on confidential informants in reporting on tyrannical regimes around the world. They now spend large parts of their budget trying to shield themselves from litigation. English libel law was singled out for particular criticism in a UN Human Rights Committee report, which noted that it served to discourage critical media reporting on matters of serious public interest and adversely affected the ability of scholars and journalists to publish their work. Following a libel action brought by a Saudi businessman, Khalid Bin Mahfouz, against the American writer Rachel Ehrenfeld for allegations in her book *Funding Evil*, the issue began to be seen within the US as a threat to the First Amendment, which guarantees free expression. New York State passed the Libel Terrorism Protection Act (known as "Rachel's Law") to defend its citizens from any future suits in the UK. Illinois did the same, while other states considered similar legislation. In Washington, a group of Congressmen tabled a law, the Free Speech Protection Act, seeking to provide similar protection in federal courts. The saga damaged the reputation of the British legal system among US judges and politicians.

In late 2008, the first signs emerged of a concerted effort to tackle the problem. Three backbench MPs, from the three main parties, joined a group of eminent lawyers to take up the battle against libel tourism. In a debate in parliament, Denis MacShane, a Labour MP, described Britain's libel laws as "an international scandal" and "a major assault on freedom of information". Lawyers and courts, he said, were "conspiring to shut down the cold light of independent

thinking and writing about what some of the richest and most powerful people in the world are up to". He cited, among others, cases
heard in London where a Tunisian had sued a Dubai-based television
channel and an Icelandic bank had sued a Danish newspaper. But
overall, the British government and parliamentarians are unsympa-
thetic to the cause. Instead, they are far more exercised by the many
incidents of press intrusion into people's private lives, confusing,
deliberately or otherwise, the crucial role of investigative reporting
with salacious, low-grade, celebrity journalism.

With such weak parliamentary scrutiny, much of the burden of
holding the government to account has fallen to Britain's media.
The results have been mixed. I was struck by the herd mentality of
parliamentary journalists to follow each other and to think only of
the next day's headline. Issues such as the state of democracy were
derided by reporters just as much as they were by politicians.
Around the turn of the millennium, I had a chat with a colleague
who had just quit working for a newspaper to become a government information officer. It was one of those periods when Fleet
Street was taking potshots at Blair, and I asked my friend, the
poacher-turned-gamekeeper, how it felt to be part of an embattled
government. He laughed: he had been shocked to discover how
little reporters – never mind the public – knew what was going on in
Whitehall. "I reckon on any given day you'll be lucky to find out
1 per cent."

In one of his last speeches as premier, Blair described parts of
the media as "feral beasts". He and his advisers took the view that the
problem was an excess of criticism, and a lack of accuracy and
accountability. He had a strong argument for the last two points, but
the first was off the mark. British journalism was adept at shouting
and screaming, but, whenever tested, such as in the run-up to the
Iraq war, print and broadcast media all too often fell for the government line. The "spin" culture produced by New Labour's chief
practitioners, Alastair Campbell and Peter Mandelson, was born out
of fear and loathing of the media. It succeeded in the short term,

producing more pliant coverage, but in the long term it caused untold damage to free expression in the UK. Yet I always had more sympathy with government officials than I did with journalists complaining about being bullied or hoodwinked. Spin doctors could only succeed in manipulating information if they were allowed to get away with it. The problem was that editors and their underlings enjoyed the access to top figures in government that came only when they did their work for them. That was another manifestation of the unseemly trade-off in British public life.

Campbell's vicious crusade against the BBC over Iraq not only caused the resignation of the corporation's Director General and Chairman; it produced a new atmosphere of timidity in its journalism. In 2005, I wrote a cover piece in the *New Statesman* describing how the BBC had lost its nerve and had begun to buckle in the face of authority. For the title, I played on the organisation's acronym, calling it "Broken, Beaten, Cowed". So enraged was the BBC's Director General, Mark Thompson, that he sent an email to its tens of thousands of staff denouncing the piece. He produced no evidence to counter it, though, and I received dozens of messages of support from managers and staff. In the years that followed, this genuflecting in the face of authority intensified. I felt more saddened than vindicated, as the BBC had been one of the great symbols of a robust public life.

The crisis in the British media is now acute. The internet has produced a new outlet for instant opinion, and the occasional piece of instant reporting. It has democratised the dissemination of information, without necessarily improving its quality. Twenty-four-hour instant communication requires politicians and others in public life to produce instant responses to breaking stories, rendering them accountable in the short term for a pithy response; but soon the agenda moves on, and so the attention span of the inquisitors wavers. Investigative journalism takes time and money, and, as a result of the financial crisis and the changing priorities of the media, it has suffered the most. One can count on the fingers of perhaps two hands the serious practitioners, many of whom rely on whistle-blowers.

Such is the requirement of secrecy in the British civil service that those who do break ranks, as Derek Pasquill found in his dealings with me, are invariably confronted with the full weight of the law. One development, in November 2008, was even more alarming. A team from the Metropolitan Police's "special operations directorate" barged into the office and home of a senior Conservative politician, Damian Green, the party's spokesman on immigration. They took him off to the cells and stripped his office of computers and files. Green was arrested under an arcane eighteenth-century law designed to outlaw "misconduct in a public office". It later transpired that officers had warned him he could be sent to prison for life. His offence was to have obtained information from inside government and made it public. The police said the operation had been requested by the top civil servant at the Home Office desperate to stem a series of politically embarrassing leaks. Issues of national security played no part. As the Prime Minister defended the actions, the paradox of his position was acute – Brown had made his name during the early 1990s publicising similar leaks to the detriment of the ruling Tories.

Five months after Green's arrest, the prosecuting authorities all but admitted that the police action had been designed merely to save ministers' skins. The Director of Public Prosecutions, Keir Starmer, said that no charges would be brought against Green. His reasons were scathing: "I have concluded that the information leaked was not secret information or information affecting national security," he said. "Nor, in many respects, was it highly confidential. Moreover, some of the information leaked undoubtedly touched on matters of legitimate public interest, which were reported in the press." The Labour government had humiliatingly lost this particular battle. But ministers privately concluded that, in spite of the setback, it had in the longer term been worthwhile. The whistleblower concerned was sacked from his job at the Home Office, even though no charges were brought. More than ever, civil servants will fear putting misdeeds into the public realm.

The threat to robust inquiry is perhaps greater now than ever before in our system. Newspapers vent their spleen, but they uncover little of what is being done. Much of British journalism has become supine in the face of intimidation from state organs and from libel and other laws. For some time reporters have complained that editors and proprietors are shying away from difficult stories for fear of "getting into trouble": in so doing, Britain's once fearless press is merely following a global trend.

On 28 February 2009, more than a thousand people attended an extraordinary gathering of civil libertarians. Delegates at the Convention on Modern Liberty dwelt not just on the erosions that had already taken place, but on legislation on the point of being taken through parliament. The government's latest gambit was the Coroners and Justice Bill. This would allow ministers to use data-sharing orders to overturn strict rules that required information to be used only for the purpose for which it was taken. It would place no limit on the information that could eventually be shared between public bodies, potentially allowing vast amounts of personal data to be shared by officials across Whitehall departments or other public bodies. It was the assembling and aggregating of data that was so potent, and dangerous.

Whenever such concerns were raised, ministers countered criticism by saying that the public had already proven by its actions that it was not bothered. After all, individuals readily handed all manner of information to supermarkets, internet service providers, social networking sites, airlines and others. They seemed quite prepared to have their streets mapped by Google. The boundaries between public and private were being redrawn, with government and citizens merely following. Rarely, though, did the government see its role as helping society to navigate a sensible way through the difficult issues of privacy and confidentiality. Instead, it used the private sector as a smokescreen for taking the debate to its logical conclusion.

One of the most revealing insights was provided by a state official pivotal to this process. Sir David Omand, Whitehall's intelligence
and security coordinator, wrote in a paper for a think-tank about the
increasing need for the authorities to carry out "data mining". This
entails looking at the private and personal data of anyone in the
country – their telephone records, emails, shop transactions, and
personal movements tracked on car number-plate recognition cameras and CCTV. These are then fed into giant computer banks to be
analysed for "suspicious" activity. Omand said "application of
modern data mining and processing techniques does involve exam-
ination of the innocent as well as the suspect to identify patterns of
interest for further investigation. Finding out other people's secrets
is going to involve breaking everyday moral rules." His candour was
commendable. For the first time a serious figure in authority
pointed out that, in order to deliver the kind of "pre-emptive" security to minimise risks from terrorism and other threats, the public
would have to understand and accept that, as Blair originally warned
in 2005, the rules of the game had changed. Everybody's movements, everybody's conversations, almost everybody's thinking
patterns (provided by internet searches and other clues) were a legitimate source of inquiry by the authorities.

The ethical issues surrounding these new mega-databases were
only part of the problem. What about the professionalism of those
running them? A string of embarrassing cases came to light of government departments and agencies losing confidential information.
These included Revenue & Customs, which managed to lose computer sticks containing twenty-five million child benefit records,
and the Ministry of Defence, which misappropriated 600,000 service
records. A survey by one respected NGO, the Joseph Rowntree
Reform Trust, concluded that of the fifty main government databases, fewer than ten were "effective, proportionate or necessary",
while a further ten actually broke privacy law.

The government eventually relented on its data-sharing plans
after a sustained campaign that had brought together groups as

diverse as the Licensed Taxi Drivers' Association, the Royal College of Psychiatrists and the British Medical Association. Civil liberties groups celebrated the fact that, as with the forty-two-day detention plan, the government's authoritarian tendencies could occasionally be curbed. But individual successes were minor compared to the broader trend.

From ID cards and CCTV, to a universal DNA database, to long periods of detention without charge, to restrictions on protest and publication, the government has rewritten the relationship between state and the individual. In doing so, it has drawn on technological advances. It has met little popular resistance. The issue in the UK has always divided the Left and Right equally, but what was noticeable at the Convention on Modern Liberty was how few people affiliated to the Labour Party were present. This epitomised the crisis of liberalism in the British Left. In 1997, the incoming government included several prominent individuals, cabinet ministers such as Robin Cook and Mo Mowlam, who cared about these issues. Their views were quickly sidelined, and replaced by machine politicians who saw the "delivery" of outcomes as the most important marker of success. Civil liberties became reduced to a lobby, instead of a core part of the political project.

Labour ministers saw only benefits in the role of the interventionist state in changing behaviour for the common good. The philosophical underpinnings for increased state power lie in the ideas of the social reformer Jeremy Bentham. His utilitarian notion of the greatest happiness for the greatest number was recast by the British government as the greatest security for the greatest number – the "do whatever it takes" line of thinking. The Right took hold of the argument and reframed it in patriotic, libertarian tones, claiming as one of its own John Stuart Mill, who wrote: "The only purpose for which power can be rightfully exercised over any member of a civilised community, against his will, is to prevent harm to others. His own good, either physical or moral, is not a sufficient warrant."

The doyenne of the liberal commentariat, the *Guardian*'s Polly

Toynbee, put it like this: "There is a moral blindness in pouring out so much righteous indignation over potential minor infractions against liberty while largely ignoring gross inequality. This is a middle-class obsession by those who are least likely to be surveyed. Liberty is taking priority over equality, because it can arouse pleasing middle-class angst. There are real threats to some civil liberties – imprisonment without trial, acceptance of torture – but CCTV and ID cards are not among them." Conor Gearty denounced the convention as a gathering of right-wing dilettantes. CCTV, DNA and communications interception were all justifiable methods in crime prevention and detection, he argued. The key was robust accountability of those carrying out these functions. "The idea that the state is an unwarranted assault on individual freedom is not a progressive one. This kind of libertarianism works to protect privilege by cloaking the advantages of the rich in the garb of personal autonomy, individual freedom and the 'human right' to privacy," Gearty wrote. "It is not at all surprising that the Convention on Modern Liberty is attracting strong support from those on the right of politics, politicians who hanker after a golden age of rights for the rich and responsibilities for everyone else. But the left, or at least those parts of it that believe in the progressive power of the state, need to be more careful about defining exactly where they stand when they join in this chorus of dissent."

I disagreed passionately with Gearty's analysis of the benign nature of the Labour government's surveillance practices. Yet I too felt a certain discomfort in seeing the arguments being ceded to ultra-libertarians, the kind of people who in the heyday of Margaret Thatcher celebrated the notion of getting the state "off our backs". The idea was to lower taxes and to cut back the state's role in "interfering" with people's lives. The fact that those Tory governments ended up by being at least as authoritarian as any, in terms of national security, was glossed over. Conservatives had now repackaged rights as the rights of freeborn Englishmen. What about immigrants and asylum seekers? Franklin Roosevelt's freedom from want is surely at least as important as freedom from intrusion. In any case, this is not a zero-sum game. The Labour government could have been more courageous not just on civil liberties, but also on social justice and fiscal redistribution. These concepts are not in any way mutually exclusive.

This goes beyond party politics and beyond one country. It goes to the heart of the pact. For ten years many Britons – at least the floating voters required for electoral victory – had enjoyed increasing prosperity, indulging in their favourite hobby of borrowing and spending money. The people who really mattered, the top 1 per cent, were indulged as never before. Blair and Brown resisted all attempts to tax or regulate them. Criticism about the efficacy, let alone the morality of this approach, was wafted away. Freedom from intrusion by the tax office was elevated to a sacrosanct right. Meanwhile, ministers vowed that they would stop at nothing – literally nothing – to keep them safe. This was an arrangement that suited all sides, as the polls showed. My remark about Singapore, that the state was "providing a modicum of a good life, and a quiet life, the ultimate anaesthetic for the brain", could just as easily, albeit in a somewhat different context, have applied to this decade in the UK.

The crisis of 2008–2009 was as much a political indictment as an economic one, particularly of the Anglo-Saxon model of *laissez-faire*. Jacques Monin, a French journalist based in the UK, links consumerism and political disengagement with the state of liberty. The absence of passion or strong ideology has, he writes in his book *The Shipwreck of Britain*, anaesthetised (that word again) politics. "The British don't vote very much. They don't object very much. They don't dream very much. The human has been replaced by the consumer and humanism by pragmatism. Pragmatism, in today's Britain, is all. Here, you're actively encouraged to denounce your neighbour, for not paying road tax or putting a bin out early or dishonestly claiming a benefit. Closed-circuit TV surveillance is rife. There are councils that spy on their taxpayers as if they were common criminals; others that submit benefit claimants to a lie-detector test. And while it's capable of mislaying the personal data of millions of its constituents, the home office proposes to set up a database holding information on every telephone call made, every email sent, and every website visited by every single British citizen. None of this would be possible in France; there would be rioting in the streets."

Only once in a while did Britons appear angry enough to mobilise. Over this period the police's approach had become steadily more heavy-handed, in seeking either to ban demonstrations, bribe activists for information or to use cameras to monitor people. That use of technology was, however, turned on its head during protests in April 2009 during the G20 summit in London on the economic crisis. When one man died at the hands of officers, the police's initial reaction was to distort the story to exonerate itself from blame. A different version emerged when footage taken from bystanders' mobile phones was posted on websites and then reported by the mainstream media. The footage showed specific examples of police thuggery. More importantly, it suggested that citizens were beginning to understand how technology could be used against the state, as much as it had been used by the state against them.

The tragedy for Britain is that over the past decade it has had an extraordinary opportunity to combine an emphasis on social justice with civil liberties. As the man in charge of prosecuting criminals and terrorists on behalf of the state, Ken Macdonald, the former chief prosecutor, is better equipped than most to cast judgement. He juxtaposed the state's attitude towards the bankers who had brought global finance to its knees with its attitude towards the rest of the population. "If you mug someone in the street and you are caught, the chances are that you will go to prison. In recent years mugging someone out of their savings or their pension would probably earn you a yacht," he wrote in an excoriating article for *The Times*. Britain, he said, had a business regulatory system that ignored malfeasance and a criminal justice system that was an auction of fake toughness. "So no one likes terrorists? Let's bring in lots of terror laws, the tougher the better. Let's lock up nasty people longer, and for longer before they are charged. Let's pretend that outlawing offensiveness makes the world less offensive. This frequently made useful headlines. But it didn't make our country or any other country a better or safer place to live. It didn't respect our way of life. It brought us the War on Terror and it didn't make it any easier for us to progress into the future with comfort and security."

By the end of the New Labour period, not only were civil liberties in jeopardy but democracy had rarely been held in lower repute. The public was both appalled and mesmerised by revelations about the extent to which MPs had for years been fiddling their expenses. Some of the claims, for items such as fictitious mortgages, were plain criminal; others, such as assuming the tax payer should be responsible for honourable members' floating duck islands and moats, were as quaint as they were arrogant. The scandal led to a number of parliamentarians being forced to repay their ill-gotten gains. Some were forced to announce they would stand down at the general elections. Others did so voluntarily. Amid the handwringing, Brown declared that not only would parliament change its ways, but he would be at the forefront of a new "democratic renewal". Given his track record and given his desperately low opinion poll ratings, most people regarded his new-found passion for reform with a mix of disbelief and disdain. Having consistently rejected voting reform, the Labour government was now contemplating it as a means of shoring up its vote. At the June 2009 European elections, Labour gained the active endorsement of little over 5 per cent of the population.

The overall score sheet was bleak. Yet much of the rage was synthetic. Britain had throughout this period signed up to a pact. It is hard to make the case that people were duped. Blair, Brown and their ministers had been fairly frank about their priorities. Democracy and civil liberties were flexible commodities. The role of government was to create the environment for wealth creation, and to stop in their tracks those who threatened that good.

8

USA: TAINTED DREAM

"There is a difference between two lost freedoms: those people know they have given up, and those they don't know they've given up" – Michael Kazin

IT IS EASY, PARTICULARLY FOR OUTSIDERS, TO LAMPOON THE eight years of George W. Bush. It is easy to condemn his administration for its assault on civil liberties inside its own country and far beyond. It is more important, though, to understand why so many Americans, and not just Republican core supporters, acquiesced to this assault.

The events of 11 September 2001 provide much of the answer, but not all of it, as to why the balance shifted so far so fast away from individual rights. The trade-off that was made between America's rulers and the people after the terrorist attacks was one of the purest. It might have been made in a time when a country was reeling from shock, but it was entered into voluntarily. Bush had a simple message: in order to preserve the way of life in the "land of the free", freedom had to be curtailed. It reminded me of the phrase used by Chua Beng Huat of Singapore's National University: "Understanding the limits to freedom is what makes freedom possible". The dividing lines between countries deemed to be authoritarian and countries deemed to be democracies are not as clear as people in the West believe them to be.

Many American politicians, journalists and members of the public now insist they were hoodwinked by Bush. They argue that they did not know about the extent of the deceits on the road to war with Iraq or the maladministration that followed. They only realised that corners were being cut, in the name of democratisation, when they saw the pictures of Iraqis being chained like animals in Abu Ghraib prison. Until very late in the day – and with the exception of some dogged individuals and organisations usually on the periphery of politics – few in the mainstream of public life wanted to challenge the decisions that were being taken in their name.

By pinning all the blame on Bush and his coterie of neo-Conservatives, such as Donald Rumsfeld and Dick Cheney, America's broader political class sought to absolve itself of its responsibilities. The three institutions that should have held the executive to account – Congress, the judiciary and the media – failed in their task, particularly during Bush's first term in the White House. The separation of powers and the rights of individuals, enshrined with such distinction and clarity by America's founding fathers, were cast aside with barely a murmur. How did this happen?

The 1990s saw a different kind of deal. It involved no trade-off. It provided a "win-win" situation for the people, but only within America's borders. Americans, or at least those whose votes counted, enjoyed years of material comfort and security. The collapse of Communism had reinforced the link between the righteousness of Western liberal democracy and Western free markets, both of which found their apogee in the United States. The steady growth of the Clinton years provided not so much an anaesthetic – there was no pain to dull – but a daily dose of feel-good factor, a prelapsarian state of blithe indifference. The Culture of Contentment identified by J. K. Galbraith had set in early in that decade.

The various conflicts taking place around the world did not directly affect American life, or the values underpinning it. The Democratic administration came under little domestic pressure to intervene in the Balkans and stood aside during the genocide in Rwanda until the true horrors had become impossible to avoid. Out of these episodes a new priority emerged in promoting human rights as a tool of foreign policy. It united forces on the American Right, the neo-Conservatives, with elements on the centre-left in other parts of the world. The theory was laudable: the UN declaration on human rights was universal and immutable, taking precedence over state sovereignty. Governments were under an international obligation to subject their actions – on a free press, independent judiciary, multi-party democracy, individual civil liberties and treatment of minorities – to outside scrutiny. Pressure would be applied to violators, and *in extremis* military action would be used to enforce these norms – all under the banner of humanitarian intervention, or the responsibility to protect.

When Bush took power in January 2001 the concern in foreign chancelleries was not of an excess of zeal, but a return to isolationism that he appeared to have promised during his election campaign. In his early months, he served notice that the US had no interest in intervening globally, unless its primacy was threatened. Bush tore up a number of treaty obligations, such as arms reduction, chemical and biological weapons conventions, even efforts to reduce small arms. The US boycotted some of the most important initiatives towards improvements in global governance – from the Kyoto Agreement on climate change, to reform of the United Nations. Apart from Somalia, the US was the only nation not to ratify the UN Convention on the Rights of the Child. Bush made clear the US had no interest in subjecting its actions to outside scrutiny. In this regard he was only following the lead set by Clinton, who on one of his last days in office had signed an order recognising the International Criminal Court at The Hague, but with a recommendation to Congress that it not be ratified. Bush was therefore building on a double standard – the right of America to judge others on their freedom credentials, but the refusal to be judged by them.

Unlike many other nationalities, Americans had not suffered terrorist attacks on the streets of their major cities. The audacity of the plane attacks on New York and the Pentagon and the scale of the destruction were exacerbated by the shock that it could ever have occurred in such a way on home soil. It is easy to forget how long that sense of vulnerability and fear lasted. A week after 9/11 a series of letters containing anthrax were sent to US Congress and to several media outlets, killing five people. It would take some time for the culprit and motive to be identified. That sense of "anything could happen" increased in November when an American Airlines jet plunged in the Jamaica Bay neighbourhood of Queens, New York. All 260 passengers and crew, and five people on the ground, were killed. Even though the authorities issued statements making clear they found no evidence of terrorist involvement, the crash increased an already heightened sense of panic.

In those frantic first weeks after 9/11, world leaders queued up to offer Bush assistance, with Vladimir Putin the first off the blocks. Bush's talk of the United States being at war and his promise to do whatever it took resonated with the nation, and around the world. It tends to be forgotten that, for all the powers at their disposal, the security services of the world's only superpower had been found seriously wanting. A nation had been reduced to panic and tumult by a determined cell of Islamists. America, its President and its institutions had been shown to be weak, and out of weakness came humiliation, out of humiliation defiance. Bush changed the rules of engagement. He redefined the theatre of war, declaring it be taking place within the heart of the nation, not just in foreign fields. That required the full mobilisation of a country's resources and active support of its citizenry. Limiting freedom could be justified as a legitimate act of national defence. Some of these restrictions were highly visible, such as enhanced security at airports and public buildings. Others were more insidious, going to the heart of the nation's political economy and its social structures. What was taught in schools and universities, whom one elected, what was written, could be seen through the prism of patriotism and danger. Hollywood came under strong pressure from the White House to start making patriotic films.

On 26 October 2001, the two houses of Congress passed a piece of legislation that would dramatically alter the balance between liberty and security in the US. The Patriot Act was passed with virtually no debate. Most legislators claimed afterwards they did not have the time to read the 342-page document. They almost certainly would not have changed their minds even if they had read it. Such was the clamour to be seen to be tough that the vast majority supported it with barely a murmur. The Act gave the authorities the right to unilateral and indefinite administrative detention of non-citizens. It redefined the notion of dissent, suggesting that opponents of the "war on terror" were not just helping terrorists but might be terrorists themselves. The lines were deliberately blurred between intelligence gathering, political surveillance and law enforcement.

Bush used the moment – as most politicians in his position would have done – to force through his agenda. His order of covert surveillance on American citizens was so secret that many in the CIA and FBI were left unawares. The provisions allowed all security agencies to demand personal customer records from internet service providers and financial institutions without having to be justified or approved by the courts ahead of time or by judicial oversight afterwards. A gagging order prevented anyone from revealing that such instructions had ever been issued. It took the *New York Times* three years to get the story. When it had the information, it was so worried about accusations of being anti-American that it withheld from publishing for another year.

The expansion of the security domain into all areas of society did more than curtail freedom in terms of specific civil liberties: it also empowered the forces of political repression. Opposition, in any form, was seen as undermining the "war effort"; dissenters were portrayed as either subversive or traitorous. The lead was set by

John Ashcroft, the Attorney General, who testified before the Senate that constitutional rights could be used as "weapons with which to kill Americans". Terrorists "exploit our openness", he said. "We are at war with an enemy who abuses individual rights as it abuses jet airliners: as weapons with which to kill Americans. We have responded by redefining the mission of the Department of Justice. Defending our nation and its citizens against terrorist attacks is now our first and overriding priority." All manner of nebulous groups sprung up, such as Americans for Victory over Terrorism, which took out a full-page advertisement in the *New York Times* to warn against external and internal threats. Lynne Cheney, the wife of the Vice-President, decried liberal and leftist academics as the "weak link" in the war on terror.

Only those unfazed by public opinion or immune to questions of career or preferment felt empowered to criticise the status quo. Noam Chomsky is often cited internationally as an example of the breadth of the public debate in the US. But he and others like him epitomise its weakness – a small core passionately listened to by a minority audience, but whose views are rarely aired in mainstream media. Sometimes examples are made of even the most famous. When Susan Sontag declared in the *New Yorker* less than two weeks after the attacks that they were "a consequence of specific American alliances and actions" she was condemned variously as an "America-hater", a "moral idiot" and a "traitor" who deserved to be driven into the wilderness, never more to be heard. The former Mayor of New York, Ed Koch, said Sontag would "occupy the Ninth Circle of Hell for her outrageous assaults on Israel". Such attacks are part of what, in military parlance, is called "the demonstration effect". If you cut off a head, you set the tone. Fear of causing trouble becomes all-pervasive.

The response to 9/11 affected far more than the debate on security. It circumscribed all political discourse. During the previous few years, one of the main issues galvanising politics in America had been globalisation and the role of the international institutions in forcing upon other nations ultra-neo-liberal policies – the so-called Washington Consensus. The violent protests in Seattle in 1999 and Genoa in 2001 were the more visible manifestation of a broader debate about inequality and economic models. International social forums provided the first glimpse of alternative institutions. Immediately after the terrorist strikes, such dissent was immediately treated as subversive. The magazine *New Republic* highlighted this trend, declaring that anyone taking part in protests against the IMF and World Bank – which had long been planned for later that September – had "joined the terrorists in a united front". A number of prominent NGOs pulled out of the march. In the US at least, these movements were forced to keep a lower profile.

Legislation provided the most important lever to shift the balance between security and liberty. But it could only have succeeded in the context of supportive public opinion. Journalists, legislators and judges were as caught up in the moment as anyone else. They suspended critical faculties as they were swept along by a patriotic duty. Many liberals, wittingly or otherwise, signed up to restrictions on what the press reported. Only a month after Ashcroft's testimony, Michael Kinsley produced a seminal piece on the pressure towards self-censorship after 9/11. "Almost no one is dissenting. It's hard to dissent from the core proposition that the perpetrators of a crime as monstrous as 9/11 are worthy targets of America's military and diplomatic power," he wrote. But journalism, en masse, had been replaced by an "unprecedented flood of patriotic gush and mush". He continued: "John Ashcroft can relax because people have been listening to their Inner Ashcroft. I know this for a fact because I'm one of them. As a writer and editor, I have been censoring myself and others quite a bit since September 11. By 'censoring', I mean deciding not to write or publish things for reasons other than my own judgment of their merits. What reasons? Sometimes it has been a sincere feeling that an ordinarily appropriate remark is inappropriate at this extraordinary moment. Sometimes it is genuine respect for readers who might feel that way even if I don't. But sometimes it is simple cowardice." Kinsley reminded readers of a warning issued by Bush's press secretary, Ari Fleischer. In this situation of "war", Fleischer said, Americans needed to "watch what they say". Kinsley concluded: "Opening your mouth is not an exact science, and it's harder to do well if you're looking over your shoulder at the same time."

His observations reminded me again of Singapore. American journalists who caused trouble were not thrown down stairwells, as in Russia, or imprisoned, as in China, or issued with defamation orders at the stroke of a pen, as in Singapore. But the dilemma was similar: why cause trouble when you can give yourself an easier life? Why cause trouble if, in any case, you feel you are going against the popular tide, or if you might lay yourself open to the accusation of helping terrorists?

One of the most important changes in the relationship between state and individual took place with scant comment. Indeed, it was initially hard to get information on the extent to which law enforcement was rounding up terrorist suspects. In the months immediately after 9/11, some 80,000 people were rounded up in dragnets across the country. Most were of Middle Eastern origin, many were "illegals", working in petrol stations, truck companies or corner shops. Local inhabitants were told to report anything suspicious – and they did, providing nearly 100,000 tip-offs, via the phone or websites. The notions of guilt and innocence were discarded. The overriding priority was to prevent, at all costs, the suspect from getting away. If the wrong people were locked up as a consequence, so be it. The notion of pre-emptive justice had been created without going through any democratic or political checks and balances. The dragnet led to not a single terrorism conviction.

One experienced radio producer told me of her experience. She had made a documentary for a prominent station on the difficulties Arabs and Palestinians were facing in big US cities in late 2001. She disclosed that several people were being held by the authorities without charge, and that their families were not told where they were. When she took the programme to her editors, they were deeply sceptical. Such things were not taking place, they told her. When she provided the evidence, they asked her to tone it all down. The programme was broadcast locally, but not nationally, for fear of causing offence.

The desire of reporters and editors to keep out of trouble reached its peak in the period between 9/11, the "liberation" of Afghanistan and the preparations for war with Iraq. This was not an exclusively American phenomenon, but US journalism led the way in reproducing official misinformation and failing to hold the authorities properly to account. Throughout there were many honourable exceptions. The *New Yorker* showed how to produce trenchant, fearless and well-researched journalism. The *Nation* played its part, as did the *New York Review of Books*, reporters on many websites and, sometimes, the major newspapers. As for the *New York Times*, the reporting of weapons of mass destruction by Judith Miller has been much analysed. During the winter of 2001 and throughout 2002, the Pulitzer winner produced a series of eye-catching stories about Saddam's military ambitions. It transpired that this had been based largely on discredited information provided by Ahmed Chalabi, a leading figure in the opposition Iraqi National Congress, which enjoyed close political and business links with the neo-Cons. Miller's pieces helped set the tone for much of the misreporting of the run-up to the war. The *Times* sought to redeem itself afterwards with much hand-wringing and deconstruction of what happened, but at the time Miller was only doing what others were doing: following their government in lowering the burden of proof in order to justify their country's actions.

Journalists and the broader body politic fell for the spin and the broader rationale. When the Bush administration's *National Security Strategy* document of 2002 famously declared that there was now "a single sustainable model for national success: freedom, democracy, and free enterprise", its tendentious conclusion was barely challenged. With a free hand, Bush used his State of the Union

USA: Tainted Dream 237

speech of the same year to identify his "axis of evil" – Iraq, Iran and North Korea – declaring that, just as the government had done "whatever it takes" to reinforce "liberty" on American soil, so it should do "whatever it takes" to promote "democracy" further afield. Such promotion was, naturally, confined to countries where American interests were not at risk. The human rights abuses in Saudi Arabia, for example, were seldom mentioned, nor the fact that more Saudi nationals had plotted the attacks of 9/11 than nationals of any other country. Realpolitik was alive and well but was not allowed to intrude into the public discourse. According to the Bush mantra, once "freed", by force if necessary, the peoples of these countries would embrace democracy and thank their liberators. When presented properly with the alternatives at the ballot box, voters around the world would invariably opt for the pro-Western "enlightened" one. The neo-Conservatives took American hegemony as their starting point. The collapse of the Soviet empire in 1989 was regarded as the ultimate vindication of the right-wing universalism that argued that all people did indeed desire demo-cratic, free market systems. A policy of providing moral support to anti-Soviet dissidents in Europe in the 1980s had, by 2003, trans-mogrified into a policy of exporting democracy by force of arms to the Middle East. The ideologues that came to guide Bush could not be criticised for a lack of clarity – or simplicity. The largely noble concept of humanitarian intervention had been hijacked, again with barely a murmur.

During the Iraq invasion, I came across this phenomenon of voluntary gullibility first-hand. I had spent some time in March 2003 at US Central Command, reporting on the news management of the war by the forces for a BBC television documentary entitled *War Spin*. In this hermetically sealed environment, hundreds of journalists were ensconced with their media minders in the unlikely setting of a hi-tech tent in a desert just outside Doha, the capital of Qatar. The American strategy had been to concentrate on the visuals and then to spin the message via Doha and the Pentagon. The key was to ensure the right television footage, accompanied by reports from correspondents embedded with US and UK forces inside Iraq. No matter how professional they were, these "embeds" were naturally wary of antagonising the soldiers who literally had their lives in their hands. In its overall strategy, the Pentagon had been influenced by Hollywood producers of action movies, notably Jerry Bruckheimer, the man behind *Black Hawk Down*. Bruckheimer explained the thinking in an interview in our film: "You have to have a bond with somebody. Only then will they let you in. What these guys are doing out there, these men and women, is just extraordinary. If you're a cheerleader of our point of view – that we deserve peace and that we deal with human dignity – then these guys are really going out on a limb and risking their own lives."

We discovered that this reality television was being enacted in the actual theatre of war. We revealed that one of the big "human interest" stories of the Iraq campaign, the release of the young female soldier Jessica Lynch from the clutches of malevolent Iraqis, had been largely a fake. An all-American heroine, the story of her capture by the Iraqis and her rescue by US Special Forces became one of the great patriotic moments of the conflict. "It couldn't have happened at a more crucial moment, when the talk was of coalition forces bogged down, of a victory too slow in coming. Her rescue will go down as one of the most stunning pieces of news management yet conceived. It provides a remarkable insight into the real influence of Hollywood producers on the Pentagon's media managers, and has produced a template from which America hopes to present its future wars," I wrote.

Reporters had been woken in the middle of the night to be told a story that would instantly enter American folklore. Private Lynch, a nineteen-year-old clerk from Palestine, West Virginia, was a member of the US Army's 507th Ordnance Maintenance Company that took a wrong turning near Nassiriya and was ambushed. Nine of her comrades were killed. Iraqi soldiers took Lynch to the local hospital, which was swarming with *fedayeen* militia. She was held there for eight days. That much was uncontested. The Pentagon went on to claim that Lynch had stab and bullet wounds, and that she had been slapped about on her hospital bed and interrogated. In fact, she had been cared for by the doctors, who looked after her long after the militia had fled. Two days before US Special Forces – cameras in tow – swooped on the hospital to take Lynch to "freedom", the doctors had arranged to deliver her by ambulance to a checkpoint, only for the Americans to open fire. They fled, just in time, back to the hospital. The Americans had almost killed their prize catch. None of this was mentioned, and when I confronted the Pentagon spokesman in Washington, Bryan Whitman, about this, he declined to release the full videotape of the rescue.

My film and accompanying articles on the BBC website and in the *Guardian* received wide international attention. I was intrigued, but not wholly surprised, by the tone of some of the American reporting of the controversy. During interviews on CNN and other networks, my allegations were met with incredulity. This is America, I was told. We don't manipulate the news – only for Lynch herself to confirm shortly after that the story of her "escape" had been manufactured by the Pentagon. This was the America that cheered a few weeks later when Bush triumphantly declared "mission accomplished".

Similar consternation was expressed by some in the US when I revealed later that year in my book *Blair's Wars* that, among other things, Tony Blair had agreed back in April 2002, nearly a full year before, that he would join the Americans in battle, come what may. Other journalists in the US and UK were eking out stories about what really went on before, during and after the war, long before the political mainstream finally acknowledged the extent to which it had been duped.

Yet, far from changing its ways, the US military continued its efforts to manipulate the message long after the military occupation in Iraq was clearly failing. Only a tiny proportion of the more than 4,000 US military dead in Iraq and 600 in Afghanistan were ever seen in American newspapers or on American television. The raw numbers were released on Defense Department and other official websites, but the images of flag-draped coffins or body bags were deemed too inflammatory to be shown. The administration and the Pentagon had imposed a strict blackout on media coverage of such pictures or footage. A White House spokesman, Scott McClellan, said this was in order to "show respect for those who have made the ultimate sacrifice". This was called the "Dover test", named after Dover Air Force Base in Delaware, where most casualties arrive. It was applied within the US and in the military theatre. Almost all media dutifully obeyed. Some editors and managers justified it on taste grounds. Viewers and readers did not appreciate gory imagery intruding into their daily lives, even if the dead and maimed came from their own small town. Almost nobody would admit that business considerations had swayed them: graphic images of dead Americans might upset readers and scare off advertisers. The most persuasive reason was straightforward politics, and fear. When ABC News' *Nightline* show ran names and photographs of the faces of all the US troops who had been killed in Iraq, conservative groups were enraged and accused the network of harming morale.

It would be all too easy, and wrong, to deduce from the Bush years that there was something particularly American about the self-censorship and obeisance. The post-2001 clampdown could, in similar circumstances, have happened anywhere else. It might have been most pronounced in the US, but it was practised in many other countries besides. So to what extent did this constitute a deliberate trade-off of freedom for security among the population? To what extent were people unaware of what was being done in their name? "The public has bought the line that the war on terror could last decades. People accepted regulations on their movement since 9/11 with surprising ease," says Michael Kazin of Washington's Georgetown University, an expert in social movements. "Most people don't know the provisions of the Patriot Act, such as requiring libraries to divulge their records. There is a difference between two lost freedoms: those people know they have given up, and those they don't know they've given up."

Eric Foner has written extensively on the issue of freedom in American history. He argues that its scope has been regularly circumscribed. Liberties do not apply so easily to non-citizens and do not apply so easily to people who deliberately vacate the mainstream of political action and discussion. American history is, he points out, rich with incidents of "subversives" being targeted, such as the detention of ethnic Japanese during the Second World War. Whenever such clampdowns occurred, governments received popular support. By way of anecdote, Foner tells me of a recent visit to the International Spy Museum in Washington. The museum was conducting an interactive quiz on computers dotted about the premises. The question was: does the government have the right to detain indefinitely people hostile to America? Of the 30,000 visitors who had registered their vote at that point, some 60 per cent were in favour. "There is a vigorous debate on liberty in this country, but the boundaries within this debate are strictly set," Foner says. "Teaching American history after 9/11 tells us that our devotion to freedom is not as powerful as we like to think it is." He concludes: "Of the many lessons of American history, this is surely among the most basic: our civil rights and civil liberties – freedom of expression, the right to criticise the government, equality before the law, restraints on the exercise of police powers – are not gifts from the state that can be rescinded when it desires."

Yet these liberties are rescinded, again and again, with little complaint from the vast majority of people. Their security trade-off was, in fact, not a trade-off in the original sense. This was the freedom of the few – almost always foreigners – being traded for the greater good. Values might be universal in their theory, but they could also be selective in their application. Most American voters were content with the apparent contradiction, safe in the knowledge that neither they nor anyone they knew – good God-fearing,

law-abiding folk – were likely to be affected by these measures. Those
who were affected probably deserved to be; and those who did not
deserve to be should excuse excesses in this time of war.

The war on terror was officially denoted as war. It was a war
without end, an indefinite conflict in which the enemy could be
held indefinitely. The Bush administration alighted on the uncon-
ventional and unprecedented concept of "enemy combatant", which
was not recognisable in humanitarian law. These people were picked
up anywhere, flown in the so-called "rendition" flights to secret loca-
tions, where information would be extracted by all means available.
Guantánamo became the most visible site, the interns dressed in
orange pyjamas and held in outdoor cages. All means of torture
and coercion, from "water-boarding" to more conventional techniques, were deemed admissible by commanders acting on
instructions from headquarters in Washington.

These abuses of rights were carried out deliberately, with confidence in their impunity and with the ideological fervour of
practitioners who believed that might was right, and that "bad
people" would have to suffer in order to keep America safe. Under
the banner of democracy, violence was meted out across the world –
from conventional warfare in Iraq and Afghanistan, to the illegal use
of "rendition" of terrorist suspects, to secret detention camps where
torture was regarded as a legitimate weapon. Publication in 2004 of
photographs of Iraqi prisoners hooded, naked, posed in sexually
humiliating positions and being harassed by dogs became the
emblems of the "war of terror". These abuses were deemed unfortu-
nate and isolated incidents. "Some people do bad things," declared
Douglas Feith, Under Secretary of State for Defense and one of the
administration's most trusted neo-Conservative ideologues. Many
people were shocked. Opinion polls began to show a swing against
the Iraq war. But few people were galvanised to act. Where were the
demonstrations to rival those of Vietnam?

Corey Robin, Professor of Political Science at Brooklyn College
in New York, has written a definitive account of the role of fear in

politics. He charts the various laws and actions used in America, and not just at federal level, to sow new fear or reinforce existing fears, from the Alien and Sedition Acts of 1798 to the Anarchist Act of 1918 to the Cold War. For more than half a century, police in major cities such as Chicago, New York and Los Angeles deployed special intelligence units against Communists, anarchists, civil rights activists, women's rights activists, trade unionists and other "subversives". These "red squads" used violence, intimidation and bribery of witnesses to amass information on hundreds of thousands of people. They were disbanded only in 1978.

Robin distinguishes between the "big actions" of authoritarian states – the dawn knock at the door of the dissident – and what he calls the "small coercion and petty tyranny" as intermittently practised in notional democracies. He talks of a "chilling effect", a fear that "stifles political options". He describes intriguingly the role of civil society in engendering and reinforcing that fear, rather than acting as a buffer against it. The smaller the community, the harder it is to go against the grain. Conformism is a powerful weapon: the doctor ostracised because of his atheist tendencies, the local newspaper editor forced to resign for a lack of patriotism. "One of the mistakes of the civil liberties community is to focus always on the state," Robin tells me. "It is a misunderstanding to see civil society as innocent and the state as tyrannical." America, he points out, has a rich history of the state intervening on behalf of civil liberties, dating back to the abolition of slavery. Franklin Roosevelt's New Deal sought to gain control of labour rights back from exploitative factory owners. "Most authoritarianism in the US is in the private sphere. The US therefore upends our traditional conceptions," Robin says. Often, particularly in contemporary times, "government work in creating fear is outsourced to the private sector".

That outsourcing has been exploited with most alacrity in the workplace. Many of the great constitutional guarantees applied in the state realm, not in the civic realm. The First Amendment enshrining free expression might matter when it came to government trying to censor a newspaper; but it made little difference when it came to a proprietor or editor putting pressure on a reporter, or a manager putting pressure on a worker. Even at the height of the Cold War and the McCarthy era of Congressional inquisitions, the number of people imprisoned for their political beliefs numbered fewer than two hundred. Yet its influence was more far-reaching in offices and factories across the US. Two in five employees were subject to surveillance, demotions or firings. Support for labour unions was often seen as a manifestation of non-conformity and a danger to the state.

A similar line of attack was adopted at the height of the "war on terror". Defenders of the social order claimed that any disruption – from strikers, for example – was as threatening to the war effort as opposition to the war itself. The red squads were back, if not in name. In January 2003, the office of Tom DeLay, then the House majority leader, sent out a fundraising letter to supporters of the National Right to Work Foundation, a business group seeking to rid America of unions. Claiming that the labour movement "presents a clear-and-present-danger to the security of the United States at home and the safety of our Armed Forces overseas", the letter denounced "big labour bosses" that were "willing to harm freedom-loving workers, the war effort and the economy to acquire more power". Why, in that context, would any company go against the grain?

Academic institutions faced a similar question, particularly when dependent on endowments from large private organisations, and especially on the most sensitive issue of them all: Israel. It has long been axiomatic that criticism of Israel, which would be deemed reasonable in the rest of the world, is denounced as anti-Semitic in the US. Indeed, parts of the mainstream press in Israel itself have a better track record in holding their own government to account. In the US, many journalists either instinctively accept the official Israeli point of view or are fearful of the consequences, from their editors, of speaking out of turn. Most aspiring Middle East lecturers and professors prefer to keep their powder dry. When they do not, they tend to find their career path blocked. One such individual was Juan Cole of the University of Michigan, a Middle East expert and blogger, who had been a consistent advocate of Palestinian self-determination. Cole had been in line for a faculty appointment at Yale, but the offer slipped away, without explanation, after a concerted media campaign to "expose" him as an anti-Semite.

Two academics, John Mearsheimer and Stephen Walt, from the universities of Chicago and Harvard, attempted to break the taboo. The authors were first commissioned to write a long, scholarly article on the Israel lobby by *Atlantic* magazine in 2002. They charted in depth the role of the "Israel lobby", particularly AIPAC, the American Israel Public Affairs Committee; they pointed out the extent to which American and Israeli priorities had become virtually indistinguishable over the years, accelerating under Bush. The magazine's editors sat on the manuscript for months before deciding not to publish it. The article ended up in the *London Review of Books* in March 2006, and the authors then wrote a longer version which was posted on the website of Harvard's Kennedy School of Government. It was roundly denounced. Most remarkably, one of America's top publishers dared to pay the authors an advance of $750,000 to expand on the themes in a book, *The Israel Lobby and US Foreign Policy*. Eliot Cohen, who went on to take a senior job in Condoleezza Rice's State Department, was given a prominent slot in the *Washington Post* to accuse the authors of having "obsessive and irrationally hostile beliefs about Jews". Their book opened up, for the first time in many years, a reasonably candid debate on the issues. But caution remained the watchword. Larry Wilkerson, former chief of staff to Colin Powell, revealed he had put the book on his students' curriculum at George Washington University because it contained "blinding flashes of the obvious that people whispered in corners rather than said out loud at cocktail parties where someone could hear you".

At the American Civil Liberties Union, the Director of its National Security Programme, Jameel Jaffer, takes me through the list of foreign academics denied entry to the US on ideological grounds, particularly from the Middle East. "The grounds are broad for inadmissibility. It is possible to exclude anyone for anything. You do not enjoy constitutional rights if you are a foreigner and outside the country," he says. One of the most celebrated cases of "ideological exclusion" was that of Tariq Ramadan. The Swiss-born philosopher has long been an influential voice in Europe on matters relating to Islam. That status had if anything been enhanced after 9/11. In 2003, he debated on television one-to-one with Nicolas Sarkozy. Shortly after London suffered its own bombings, on 7 July 2005, Blair appointed Ramadan to a UK government commission on tackling extremism.

In February 2004, Ramadan was given a tenured appointment as professor of religion at the University of Notre Dame in Indiana. He had rented a house, shipped his furniture there and enrolled his children in local schools when, five months later, the State Department, acting on secret information from the Department of Homeland Security, revoked the visa that it had granted him. It then took two years of repeated applications and inquiries, as well as a lawsuit by US civil liberties and academic organisations, for Ramadan to receive an official explanation. Initially they were told he had violated Section 411 of the Patriot Act, which excludes foreigners who "endorse or espouse terrorist activity". Finally, the authorities provided the details. Apparently, between 1998 and 2002, Ramadan had donated $800 to a pro-Palestinian French charity that was suspected of channelling money to Hamas, and which did not appear on the State Department's blacklist until 2003.

The authorities have interpreted the language of the Patriot Act so loosely that, according to official documents released under the Freedom of Information Act, anyone who is guilty of "irresponsible expressions of opinion" can be refused entry to the US. The ACLU filed a suit, challenging the constitutionality of the ban. It also took up the case of Adam Habib, whose visa was suddenly revoked in 2006 even though he had already spent considerable time in the

US. Habib, a Vice-Chancellor at the University of Johannesburg, had strongly attacked the war in Iraq and other US foreign policy decisions. The *Christian Science Monitor*, in a report in 2006, produced a roll call of academics and public figures who had been denied visas or had them revoked or delayed until it was too late. The list included a group of seventy-four South Korean farmers and trade unionists opposed to a free trade agreement; a Marxist Greek academic, Yoannis Milios; M.I.A, a Sri Lankan hip-hop singer, whose lyrics were deemed to be sympathetic to the Tamil Tigers and the Palestine Liberation Organisation; a Bolivian professor of Latin American history and specialist in the Aymara culture, Waskar Ari, who had been offered a position at the University of Nebraska; a Basque historian, Inaki Egana; and Dora Maria Tellez, a former Sandinista minister of health. These exclusions merely built on episodes in US history when the country was under threat, or perceived itself to be so. Those who have also fallen foul of the authorities down the years range from Graham Greene to Doris Lessing to Gabriel García Márquez. Even Pierre Trudeau was barred – prior to becoming Prime Minister of Canada.

The US administration also regarded lawyers working on behalf of the Guantánamo detainees as being on the wrong side of the "with us or against us" divide. One senior human rights figure told me that he, and representatives of five other organisations, had been summoned to a strange meeting in early 2007 with John Bellinger, the legal adviser to the Secretary of State, to talk about the Act. Bellinger told them these groups had a "megaphone in their hand" that would be heard in Europe and beyond; they therefore should be "sensible" in what they said. Such threats were not made lightly.

The anti-patriotic and potentially subversive network therefore included not just NGOs, but lawyers, journalists, trade unionists and academics. Even voters were not immune from pressure. Dick Cheney responded to the victory of an anti-war candidate in the primaries in one state, Connecticut, by declaring that the result would only embolden "the al-Qaeda types", who were "betting on the proposition that ultimately they can break the will of the American people".

"It is the policy of the United States to seek and support the growth of democratic movements and institutions in every nation and culture, with the ultimate goal of ending tyranny in our world." Bush embarked on his second term as President in January 2005 with an inauguration speech that tackled head-on the issue of liberty and security around the world. This time around he had won fair and square, albeit with a small majority, but quite enough within the context of the US electoral system. A majority of Americans had shown, through entirely fair means, that they approved of his approach. Without any sense of irony, Bush declared his conviction that "in the long run, there is no justice without freedom, and there can be no human rights without human liberty".

With no apparent qualms, here was a leader who proclaimed the virtues of liberty, while encouraging legislation and authorising executive action (torture, secret shipping of suspects, extra-legal wire-tapping) that wilfully deprived people of that liberty. Until the very end of his tenure, Bush held fast to the genuine conviction that he had been a servant of freedom. The same applied to Blair. The same applied to other world leaders. Those who threatened, or even challenged, a specific interpretation of freedom deserved to have their freedom removed or curtailed.

Yet within months of its 2004 election victory, the Bush administration had gone into a tailspin. The terms of the trade had not changed. So what had? Who better to turn to than Francis Fukuyama, the man who had, in the early 1990s, decreed the "end of history"? I had long wanted to discuss with him his assertions about the inevitable triumph of democracy, his initial support for the Iraq war, and his subsequent angry repudiation of the Bush regime. Fukuyama has been criticised in liberal circles for his political "journey", but I cannot help, as we sit in a family restaurant in one of those comfortable Virginia dormitory towns, respect a man who has rarely opted for easy assumptions.

We talk about Russia and China, states he contends are in the midst of "authoritarian modernisation", and his assertion of a statistical correlation between states of development and democracy. We talk about the "colour revolutions" in Ukraine, Georgia and elsewhere that had so cheered the advocates of democratisation. Fukuyama tells me about how he had come to teach Ukraine as a case study of political development: but not Iraq, nor other parts of the world, where the American experiment had so lamentably failed. We talk about the role of democracy. Is it an outcome in itself (free elections), or is it a vehicle for spreading liberal values? Is it the process or the outcome that matters most? Most of all, I want to talk to him about the state of liberty in America. "The entire democratic process is tainted by the instrumental use of democracy, notably in Iraq," he tells me. "It undermined the moral authority of America to stand up against authoritarian government. The paradox is the willingness to accept torture and the erosion of civil liberties by a state that promotes itself as the bastion of freedom."

Many were complicit, far beyond the inner circle of neo-Conservatives. Even when they had the power to block the excesses of the Bush regime, many so-called liberal politicians chose not to do so. When it came to performing their basic duty of providing a counterweight to executive power, Congress was throughout this period found wanting. For the first six years of Bush's presidency, Democrats complained that their hands were tied by Republican dominance. Just wait, they said, until they gained control, which they did at the end of 2006. In a defiant final act that October, the outgoing Congress passed the Military Commissions Act, which enshrined lower evidential standards for "enemy combatants". The minority Democrats, as ever, put up scant resistance. The ensuing two years, with both houses under Democrat control, saw some of the most important assaults on civil liberties of the Bush era. Time and again, when legislation was put before them, either giving an imprimatur to administration covert actions, or to extend them, the two chambers rolled over.

The most astonishing decision was to give political and judicial legitimacy to the secret eavesdropping that the *New York Times* had belatedly exposed in 2004. The FISA Amendments Act of 2008 was passed with substantial Democratic support, including the entire top level of the House Democratic leadership. With the Democratic presidential nomination safely under his belt, Barack Obama reversed the pledge he had made during the primaries and backed a beefed up version of the bill. The new measure legalised vast new categories of warrantless eavesdropping. It marked the biggest revamping of federal surveillance law in thirty years. Certainly the pressure on the Democrats had been intense. The media language of patriotism was still in full flow. Christopher "Kit" Bond, a senior Republican Senator from Missouri, teased his colleagues, telling them they had nothing to fear in the bill, "unless you have Al Qaeda on your speed dial". Even he was surprised at how easily they had got away with it. "I think the White House got a better deal than they even had hoped to get," he admitted.

On the night of Obama's election victory in November 2008, I wrote the following in the *Guardian*: "It is a sobering thought, once the afterglow of this remarkable American election wears off, as inevitably it will, to ask: what kind of health will the West actually be in? From the moment he stole the election in 2000, Bush undermined faith in everything from the electoral process, to advocacy of civil liberties, to the observance of international law. The alternative – authoritarian capitalism – has thrived over the past eight years as many around the world regarded Western rhetoric as being fundamentally at odds with practice. Now, particularly now, Obama must narrow that gap. As if his task wasn't hard enough, he will play a major part in determining the fate of Western democracy."

As the self-professed leader of the free world, US policy both at home and abroad was always subjected to particular scrutiny. The Bush administration's philosophy of pre-emption and primacy had turned America's global relationship on its head. Democracy promotion had been elevated to a major foreign policy goal without heed to the sensitivities of liberal democracies around the world.

For years, the Pew Research Center's Global Attitudes surveys have tracked international attitudes towards the US. Its findings showed that in each year after the run-up to the Iraq war resentment and anger built towards America. Majorities in 43 of 47 countries surveyed – including 63 per cent in the US itself – said that the US promoted democracy where it served its interests, rather than promoting it on principle. "The world and Americans themselves see that American democracy is in trouble at home. The president and vice president consider themselves and act as if they are above the law. Congress has failed to act as a check," it wrote. "The courts have largely been silent as basic civil liberties have been violated. The US government has secretly and without warrant collected the phone records of millions of Americans. Surveys show that only about a third of Americans now believe 'most elected officials care what people like me think.'"

The report also found that large majorities in the forty-seven countries believed that US policies had widened the gap between rich and poor around the world. Attitudes towards "American ways of doing business" were overwhelmingly negative. As Pew pointed out, the wealthiest 10 per cent of American households received almost half of the nation's total income. The top 1 per cent owned half of the top 10 per cent's money, while the top 0.1 per cent received nearly half of the share going of the top 1 per cent.

It was not just the inability to set an example in its behaviour around the world that had undermined America's idea of democracy promotion. It was a bigger failure to appreciate that the Washington Consensus, the one-size-fits-all approach linking free markets and multi-party elections, had invariably been high-handed and frequently counter-productive. In *World On Fire: How Exporting Free Market Democracy Breeds Ethnic Hatred and Global Instability*, the author Amy Chua argues that the US failed to understand the basic links between notions of freedom and ownership of wealth; it failed, too, to see how natural resources had cursed many developing countries. Chua produces this telling summary: "In the numerous countries around the world that have pervasive poverty and a market-dominant minority, democracy and markets – at least in the form in which they are currently being promoted – can proceed only in deep tension with each other. In such conditions, the combined pursuit of free markets and democratisation has repeatedly catalysed ethnic conflict in highly predictable ways. This has been the sobering lesson of globalisation in the last 20 years." Or, as Amartya Sen asked with disarming clarity: "Can the poor be free?"

Obama signalled early on that he understood this. In a revealing question and answer with the *Washington Post* in January 2009, he suggested he had already applied his mind to the flaws and hypocrisies underlying the neo-Cons' promotion of democracy. "It needs to be a central part of our foreign policy. It is who we are. It is one of our best exports, if it is not exported simply down the barrel of a gun," he said. He spoke of the need to build democratic institutions through civil society, and by example. One of the mistakes of the Bush years was to have drawn "equivalence between democracy and elections. Elections aren't democracy, as we understand it. They are one facet of a liberal order, as we understand it. And so in a lot of countries, you know, the first question is, if you go back to Roosevelt's four freedoms, the first question is freedom from want and freedom from fear. If people aren't secure, if people are starving, then elections may or may not address those issues, but they are not a perfect overlay."

Thanks to Bush, the years that followed the failed Iraq war constituted a springtime for autocrats. An America weakened by failed diplomacy and military endeavour, and by a reeling economy, was in no position to lead others into pushing for greater social justice or human rights around the world. It was hamstrung in its dealings with Iraq. It relied on China to support its moves against North Korea. It did nothing to alleviate the suffering of Zimbabweans. More crucially, the US had lost its powers to cajole or coerce the populist authoritarians in Russia, China and elsewhere. They were able to swat away the complaints of the Bush White House with consummate ease.

So did it all boil down to the excesses of Guantánamo and Abu Ghraib or to the fact that weapons of mass destruction were never found in Iraq? These excesses certainly energised Bush's critics. They allowed human rights groups and others to recapture their voice. These failures played a major role in undermining confidence in the US around the world. Ask, however, a different question: what would have happened if the invasion of Iraq had proven a success, in military terms? US forces had, after all, taken Baghdad easily and deposed Saddam easily. It was only once American forces had occupied Iraq that the blunders really began. I ask these points less to revisit issues of the war, more to suggest that the collapse in Bush's personal ratings among the American public was not an inevitable consequence of his administration's pugilistic approach at home and abroad.

Ultimately, what mattered to American voters was not that the administration was unethical or hypocritical, but that it was incompetent – and was seen to be so. They started to read, even if they could not see the pictures of the body bags, of the increasing death toll among servicemen and women. And what had all these sacrifices achieved, they began to ask themselves? These ventures in Iraq and Afghanistan had not made them feel any safer. They had watched as Bush gave jobs, favours and tax cuts to his friends. That crony capitalism – from Halliburton to other beneficiaries of the military escapades – was being exposed as corrupt and inefficient. Then the people watched with anger and embarrassment as the world's most powerful state failed to deliver relief even during natural disasters such as Hurricane Katrina in New Orleans.

As the circumstances changed, as the Bush administration's ability to bully diminished, many influential figures in US politics and the media replaced their quiescence of the 9/11 and Iraq war years with a new and fashionable vehemence. It was one thing to rail against the use of torture and the avarice of bankers in 2008, quite another to have stuck one's head out and done so in 2001. Compare and contrast the muted reaction of government to the scandal of Kenneth Lay and the other Enron executives back at the start of the Bush era with the fury directed at Bernard Madoff for his crooked Ponzi schemes.

Throughout the Bush years, much of America's political elite – Democrats and Republicans alike – had refused to grapple with the broader reasons behind the widespread rejection of their country's world view. Or if it did engage in these questions, it saw in the discontent only anti-Americanism. It failed to appreciate the extent to which the failings within their own system – from electoral turnout to political participation, to corruption, to an increased uniformity in global communication, and latterly and most importantly, the US-driven recession – had accelerated the attractiveness of the alternatives on offer around the world.

The very questions about economic governance and international institutions, about greed and globalisation – questions that had been decreed around the time of 9/11 to be unpatriotic and dangerous – were, once the recession had taken hold, suddenly rendered not just acceptable, but vital. The grand bargain that provided a link between neo-liberal free markets and Western liberal democracy – a link that American policy-makers had consistently made, and proselytised – was unravelling at home and abroad. Even the high priest of deregulation, Alan Greenspan, the former Federal Reserve Chairman, admitted as much to Congress. "To exist, you need an ideology. The question is whether it is accurate or not. And what I'm saying to you is, yes, I found a flaw. I don't know how significant or permanent it is, but I've been very distressed by that fact."

Yet, for all the manufactured fury that followed, had the Bush regime not simply reflected the priorities of the moment – the supremacy of wealth creation over everything else? America's post-9/11 pact had been voluntarily entered into, and, for several years at least, overwhelmingly popular.

On the eve of Obama's inauguration, Freedom House, an NGO that monitors the condition of democracy around the world, produced a report on the state of American liberty. The report expressed "grave concern about attempts to extend executive authority without the usual congressional and judicial review, extraordinary renditions, mistreatment of those in US custody, and warrantless wiretaps in contravention of the requirements of US law". However, America's approach to civil liberties must, it said, be assessed at least in part within the context of its history in other times of war. Previous excesses had always been addressed and resolved by the "normal workings of the American system", though often after some delay. "A free press and an independent judiciary continue to be linchpins of the American system and are essential to preserving freedom in our society." A process of rethinking and adjustment had already begun. "This is the larger, more important reality that gives Freedom House confidence in the democratic future of the United States. American democracy responds to transgressions and is constantly reinvigorated."

This sanguine conclusion was justified, to a point. America's codified constitution had survived, at least partly intact, after a sustained assault. The election campaign of 2008 rebuilt some confidence in America's democratic credentials at home and abroad. Obama had combined fundraising from major corporations – the usual form of financing, with favours returned – with a remarkable grass-roots campaign. The enfranchisement of millions of African Americans and others who had found themselves previously unregistered was one of the features of the campaign. Millions more voted, people who had not been bothered to do so previously, so great had been their apathy or antipathy.

When it comes to civil liberties, many liberals have assumed that under Obama much of the legislation introduced during the Bush years will be reversed. With his initial steps, the new President did not disappoint. He began by issuing a string of executive orders, among them the closure of the prison at Guantánamo, halting military commission trials, and restricting interrogators to Army Field Manual techniques. This was, in effect, a ban on torture, something Congress had failed to enact early in 2008 when it was considering the Defense Authorization Act. These were hugely symbolic steps. At the same time, he sent out other, less promising signals. Senior members of his administration endorsed continuing the CIA's programme of transferring prisoners to other countries without legal rights, and indefinitely detaining terrorism suspects without trials even if they were arrested far from a war zone. What, some might ask, was the particular moral superiority of Bagram Airbase rather than Guantánamo? Most worryingly, the administration also left the door open to resuming military commission trials, in certain extreme situations. "We are charting a new way forward, taking into account both the security of the American people and the need to obey the rule of law," said the White House counsel, Gregory Craig. "That is a message we would give to the civil liberties people as well as to the Bush people." A similarly downbeat message was given to those who were expecting a shift on concerns such as surveillance and wire-tapping. Obama needed as wide a political constituency as possible for his main task of tackling the economic crisis. He had much to lose and little to gain, therefore, from providing extraneous ammunition for his Republican critics in what he regarded as second order issues.

Then, tentatively but still remarkably, Obama took on the might of the security services and the fury of the many Bush supporters still in the media, first by releasing a series of memos detailing torture techniques approved by the CIA and allowing for the publication of scores of photographs showing abuse of prisoners held by US forces around the world. In so doing, he was making clear that Abu Ghraib had been no aberration, that it had been integral to the actions of the former administration. And yet, only a few weeks later, he apppeared to buckle under the pressure of the military and the security services, saying he would now try to block the release of the offending pictures.

In November 2008, two months before the new President was sworn in, US intelligence chiefs set out the challenges they saw facing the country and the world over the next two decades. The National Intelligence Council said the forthcoming period would be fraught with risk, amid the ever-present dangers of environmental catastrophe, nuclear war and competition over scarce natural resources. America might still retain the dominant role, but it would have to share influence with China and other emerging nations. The hubris of the Iraq war and America's over-reliance on brute force might come to be seen as the final throes of a declining power. The trends set out in the NIC report were, after all, hardly new.

One of the most striking differences between the early Obama administration and Bush is the accent on pragmatism over easy ideology. So, just as he has sought to reach out to Iran, Obama has also avoided antagonising China, aware of its growing power and influence. In her first visit to Beijing as Secretary of State, Hillary Clinton signalled that she was making human rights issues a lower priority. She recognised that both countries were equal partners, and little would be gained by causing undue trouble. In so doing, she was bowing to a shift that had long been taking place, but which the Bush administration had sought to deny: America was no longer in a position to impose democracy at the barrel of a gun.

Therein lies the paradox of the Obama moment. The hopes vested in him are extraordinary. The demands on him are variously to protect the Americans from terrorism, to get Americans back to work and back into prosperity, to save them from environmental collapse and to improve the standing of the United States around the world. Yet he has to do all this just at the time when liberal democracy and free markets – the twin pillars on which the post-1945 settlement rested – have been wrenched apart. Just as it is regaining its taste for liberal values, so is America losing its ability to pass on those values to others.

CONCLUSION: PEOPLE'S PRIORITIES

THIS WAS THE DAY THE WORLD CAME TOGETHER, DECLARED a beaming Gordon Brown. This was the start of a "new world order". Such a grandiloquent claim had been made by Woodrow Wilson with the establishment of the League of Nations at the end of the First World War. It had been decreed again by President George Bush senior in 1990 at the end of the Cold War. So did the London summit of the G20 in April 2009 really mark the closing of a historical chapter, the demise of an economic order that had gone unchallenged for two decades? And what about the political order that had sustained it?

In 1989, with the collapse of Communism and the end of the Cold War, regimes around the world, from China and Russia to South Africa, India and Brazil, concluded that there was no serious ideological alternative to market forces as a means of organising productive activity. In 2009, with the collapse of the global financial order, many seemed to have reached the opposite conclusion – that unbridled free markets had led even the richest and most sophisticated societies to disaster. Many were sceptical about this atmosphere of contrition, speculating that when fortunes improved again, so old habits of greed would resume. But even if one accepted such an admission at face value, would it mark a transformation in the *quality* of democracy, and in the deepening and extending of basic liberty to more people?

These twenty years of globalised wealth creation transformed governments' and people's understanding of freedoms. The pre-eminent freedom had become financial – to earn, to keep one's money and to consume. All the other freedoms were subjugated to that end, with political leaders even extolling shopping as a patriotic duty. This, combined with the internet and other technological advances, created a cultural homogeneity not seen before. The super-rich, the quite rich and the aspiring rich, whether in St Petersburg, Shanghai, São Paulo or South Kensington, inhabited a uniform world of the same designers, the same brands, the same social networking sites and communications tools, the same sports cars and the same holiday destinations. A cultural conformism was born, a herd mentality that provided an easy environment for those in power to operate in.

By the time the great bubble burst, the inequalities of the global economy had become all too apparent. In the US, by 2007 there were one thousand dollar billionaires, compared with thirteen in 1985, owning a staggering $3.5 trillion of wealth. According to *Forbes* magazine, for years the official arbiter of the fortunes of the super-rich, a heady cocktail of global economic growth and soaring asset prices had created 178 new billionaires in just twelve months. "This is the richest year in human history," declared the magazine's editor-in-chief, Steve Forbes. "The best way to create wealth is to have free markets and free people, and more and more of the world is realising it." The richest 1 per cent received 52 per cent of all the benefits of tax cuts under George W. Bush. Yet the median income of American workers had actually decreased in real terms. The most recognised tool for measuring inequality, the Gini coefficient, had increased in virtually every country, with China, India and the US leading the way. In Britain, the top 1 per cent of the population was receiving more of the nation's income than at any time since the 1930s. In 2006, the total amount paid out in bonuses was £21 billion, about a third of the UK's education budget. The income and assets of the top 0.1 per cent of the population became unmeasurable. Trying to put a figure on super-wealth was, as the director of the Institute for Fiscal Studies, Britain's most respected economic think-tank, once told me, like "looking through thick fog". Such were the global flows of cash that the understaffed and demoralised tax authorities could barely cope.

Redistributive democracy had all but collapsed under the weight of unrestricted global transfers of cash. Political parties that professed to care about such as issues, such as New Labour in the UK, all but gave up in this area, confining themselves to palliative mechanisms for those at the bottom of the pile. Across the world, politicians opted out of economic rule-making. It was an area into which they feared to tread. They compensated for this by focusing on the "other", the parts of national life over which they continued to have jurisdiction. The one area where they could be seen to be making a difference was security.

From the early 1980s, politicians and thinkers in East and West – those who might openly identify with the Thatcher–Reagan neo-liberal creed, but many more besides – argued that globalisation and wealth creation could only have a positive political impact. As national economies approached a certain level of per capita income, the growing middle classes would become less submissive, less in awe of authority. They would demand legal and political power, which in turn would provide the basis for democracy. It has not worked out that way.

Instead, with consummate ease, the elites were bought off. They bought into the pact. Those who had only recently acquired wealth were the most susceptible to its inducements, and to the political trade-off that came with it. The most innately conservative forces were those whose parents or grandparents were poor, who had just traded the family motorbike for a family car or had just swapped the flat for a house, who were scared that their gains could disappear at any time. What mattered to those with some money but wanted more, and those who had much but could never have enough, were their private freedoms. They resented the Singapore government telling them who they could sleep with; they disliked the power the Chinese authorities still had to determine foreign travel. The feared the arbitrary use of power by the Kremlin. They wanted more than anything an efficient state that abided by the rule of law. They needed to know that their business contracts would not be torn up retrospectively if someone close to the seat of power did not approve. They resented the sense that their money might not be safe, that their home might be taken away on a whim. They wanted modern infrastructure. They wanted low taxes, and, where possible, no taxes, in the name of encouraging "entrepreneurship". In some countries that constituted legal tax avoidance, encouraged by the indulgent authorities, such as the UK, in others quasi-illegal tax evasion that was ignored by indulgent authorities, such as in Italy. It was fundamentally the same phenomenon.

Other freedoms were regarded as either optional or unnecessary. In each country, people chose which of those freedoms they wished to keep, and which they wished to discard. When it came to national security, the comfortable classes were adamant that the state should assume as many powers as possible to clamp down on any forces that might imperil their way of life. Thus, anyone deemed to be an extremist or a foreigner or member of a minority group who did not appear respectable should face the full weight of the law. They did not begin to wonder whether the economic rules they had set had actually exacerbated social tensions.

One of the consequences of globalisation, with its merging of consumer tastes, was an increasing sense of national and local chauvinism. The lack of social solidarity produced a new atomised form of freedom. Citizens became overwhelmingly privatised in their habits, thoughts and daily practices. They were left free to act as individual players, but they were not encouraged to go beyond that.

This left a gap for charismatic leaders, for populist identity politics to work in harmony with a mindless celebrity culture. Italy and India had much in common in this regard, each seeking to deflect voters' attention away from corroded democratic institutions towards fear of ethnic minorities.

So what in the end is the definition of the modern authoritarianism in which so many acquiesced during this period? Perhaps this: state control that stops short of impeding your freedom to create wealth. The definition of modern democracy might be state control that stops short of impeding your freedom to create wealth, plus certain civil-liberties safeguards – for those who do not step out of the mainstream. The difference, then, between the countries that fall roughly into the "authoritarian" camp, those in the first part of the book, and those who pride themselves on their "democratic" values, may just be one of degree. I have not sought to equate them, but to point out common characteristics. Even in the UK and France, where surveillance is on the rise, most individuals continue to enjoy considerable day-to-day freedoms. In the US, for all the self-censorship in the early Bush years, for all the narrowness of the mainstream political debate, critical media self-evidently do not face anything like the sanctions of their counterparts in Singapore, Russia or China.

All these various countries have, over the past two decades, had much more in common than they would like to admit. What happened was the narrowing of the gap between democracies and autocracies. They each began to adopt manifestations of the other, each drawing the line in their own way between private and public freedoms. With free expression in the West increasingly regarded as a problem to be managed rather than a fundamental right, with the policing of demonstrations increasingly heavy-handed, with more and more people deemed by the state to be necessary to watch, the penalties on those "causing trouble" were not so far apart any more.

What these different systems shared was the complicity of sections of the population that mattered. As was pointed out in the introduction, the pact does not apply to out and out dictatorial regimes. In places such as Zimbabwe and Burma, of course, there are individuals and groups around the leader who stand to benefit, and therefore do the state's bidding. One of the achievements of the past twenty years has been the reduction in the number of states that operate in this way. This has been an admirable achievement, which, as Freedom House and other groups have shown, reached a peak around the turn of the millennium.

It is one thing to rid a country of tyranny, quite another to allow a strong and equitable democracy to grow, particularly in conditions of instability. Among the many strong pieces of work in this area was the final report in 2006 of the Princeton Project, a non-partisan group looking at the challenges posed to the United States in the post-Communist world. It outlined what it called the "deeper preconditions for successful liberal democracy – preconditions that extend far beyond the simple holding of elections". It added: "Labelling countries as democracies or non-democracies, much less as good or evil, also needlessly complicates our relations with many nations and often undermines the very goals we seek to achieve." Such a point of view, recognising an uneasy and precarious middle ground, was naturally targeting the simplistic world view of the neo-Conservatives and their trigger-happy notions of democracy promotion.

Yet these analyses continued to look upon others' democracy from a position of superiority. Even if expressed with sensitivity, they still took as a given the success of the Western economic and political model. They do not acknowledge the extent to which democracy within the West has been undermined not just by the double standards of Western foreign policy, but by the corrosion of its domestic political institutions.

Chris Patten, a passionate advocate of the spread of democracy, is disdainful of the claims made by many of the former Communist states. He points to terms such as "managed democracy" or "sovereign democracy", so beloved of the Russians and Chinese, noting: "It is a good rule of thumb to assume that whenever the word democracy is preceded, as a definition of a form of government, by some descriptive prefix, then one thing it is not is democratic." He is surely right, but does that mean that, in the West, societies have achieved the dream of democracy without prefix? I do not think so. How about "controlled democracy"? That could apply to the UK, France or many European states. Italy would surely qualify for the term "corrupt democracy". As for the US, a number of unflattering prefixes could be applied.

In all of these states, except for China, to a greater or lesser degree voters endorsed the pact that was being offered to them. In Singapore and Russia, those elections might be gerrymandered, but it is hard to deny that the leaders enjoyed high levels of popularity. In India election day is a remarkable feat of freedom, and yet what happens in the intervening four years is the problem. In the US, the election result of 2000 might have been a travesty, but, even after four years of considerably curtailed freedom, in 2004 enough Americans endorsed the trade-off to give Bush another term. So great is the disdain for mainstream politics in the UK, so consistently low is the turnout, that many wonder who their members of parliament actually represent. In many of these countries, the ballot box provides only a limited choice of outcomes. Still, according to the rules, all these countries have passed the constitutional test.

So what does all this say about us, the people? One argument would be that perhaps people require less freedom than they would like to believe. As long as the state looks after them, keeps them safe, and allows them to lead their personal lives as they wish, perhaps that is a pact that a sufficient number of people are comfortable with. How many fall into the category of troublemakers? What percentage of the population consists of oppositionist politicians, activists for non-governmental organisations, defence lawyers for potential subversives, dissidents or investigative journalists? How many people take part in marches, attend rallies or participate in any of the world social forums? Participatory democracy has all but disappeared. And even where it has occasionally broken through into the mass consciousness, such as the huge anti-war march in London in 2003 on the eve of the Iraq conflict, it made no difference. It was a supine parliament that determined the outcome, reinforcing a sense of fatalism in people's minds. The political pact had been redefined in the narrowest sense. Do your duty every four or five years by endorsing representative democracy at the ballot box. Then leave the victor the spoils, the right to determine your liberty and your security for you, and do not seek to intervene.

Economic growth, rather than being a force for democratic involvement, reinforced the confidence of business and political elites. They thrived because they reinterpreted the basic tenets of democracy to suit their needs. These neo-liberal advocates became consumed by their own intellectual overshoot and hubris, redefining democracy and liberty through notions such as privatisation, profit maximisation, disdain for the needs of civil society and social justice, and for the dangers facing the environment. In so doing, they actually made it easier for authoritarians to flourish.

The tragedy of the past twenty years is that the allure of globalised wealth served as a drug, not just for the super-rich, and as much in the West as in the East. When I used the expression "anaesthetic for the brain" about Singapore, I could equally have applied it to any country, irrespective of its notional political system.

Now that the economic recession has met democratic recession, what is the future for freedom? The worst excesses of the globalised era are likely to come to an end. The banks will be more regulated; capital flows will be monitored a little; international institutions will be encouraged to pay more attention to the twin needs of poverty alleviation and the environment. The G20 summit provided *de facto* recognition of the new leading role being played by China in particular, along with India, Brazil and others in determining the future financial architecture. As Luiz Inácio Lula da Silva, the

Brazilian President and former shoeshine boy, declared: "This is a crisis caused and encouraged by the irrational behaviour of white people with blue eyes who before the crisis appeared to know everything, but are now showing that they know nothing."

But will a new generation of world leaders produce something different and more inspiring, a post-crash version of freedom that actually inspires and addresses the many iniquities around the world? People's priorities reflect the socio-economic conditions of their time. So although it may have been the bankers and hedge fund managers who caused the immediate mess, the bigger culprits were we, the people, particularly in the West, for allowing democracy to mutate into something it should never have become – a vehicle to deliver consumption.

That was the pact, a pernicious one, an era of globalised wealth that fed on technological advance and that ancient human failing – greed. Around the world, a critical mass of people vested in their leaders almost unlimited powers to determine questions of liberty. In return they were bought off by a temporary blanket of security and what turned out to be an illusory prosperity.

POSTSCRIPT: OPPORTUNITY MISSED

A YEAR HAS PASSED SINCE I WROTE THE CONCLUSION to the book. More than a year has passed since governments around the world bailed out their banks. In so doing, they saved their economies from falling into an abyss. A repeat of the Great Depression was averted. And yet, alarmingly, few lessons have been learnt.

As I toured the globe, travelling from country to country discussing the book, the financial crash cast an unyielding spotlight. From Brussels to Mumbai one question predominated: would anything change? As a businessman in Singapore put it: "Are we going through one of those natural cyclical downturns, or is something far more important, something epoch-making taking place?" Had we, he wanted to know, been living through a moment as significant as the fall of the Berlin Wall? Had the era of glut that began in 1989 just come to an end?

This question had been nagging me in the final weeks of completing the hardback version of *Freedom for Sale* in spring 2009. I wondered whether I should use the past or present tense to describe the pact, to show how willing we had all become to trade our freedoms in return for the promise of security and prosperity. Had the pact demarcated a specific era which began in 1989 with the collapse of a competing ideology, Communism, and the spread of globalised capital and information flows, and ended with the demise of Lehman Brothers in 2008? Or was the pact still being entered into?

In the conclusion to the last edition, I asked whether a new generation of world leaders might produce something more inspiring, a post-crash version of freedom that addresses the many iniquities around the world. Sadly, the answer is that they have not. Worse still, having been presented with an extraordinary opportunity to change their societies, and to inculcate the need for that change, they have fought shy of doing so.

President Obama could have wrung from the banks an entirely new way of operating; he could have begun the task of rebalancing society. To give him credit, he did use sharp rhetoric about a culture of greed. He signalled his discontent with a system that had rewarded recklessness. But he did not act decisively. During his difficult first year, the incoming President was still finding his feet. Along with the many urgent tasks facing the incumbent, he opted to invest his energies in health care reform. This was no mean task, indeed it was a challenge that had proved beyond Bill Clinton in the early to mid 1990s. But while Main Street continued to suffer from the recession and from the banks' refusal to extend credit to small and medium-sized businesses, Wall Street quickly prospered again. Shares recovered much of their value; indeed 2009 was one of the best years on record for global equities. The big banks began to pay huge bonuses again to their top employees, as if nothing had ever happened.

By the start of 2010, as his poll ratings plunged, Obama appeared to signal a change of heart. He announced plans to limit the size of the major banks, preventing them from engaging in proprietary trading or investing in hedge funds or private equity funds. Inevitably his proposals invoked the ire of the financial-services sector. The longer-term concern, raised by the likes of George Soros, the global investment billionaire and philanthropist, was whether the reforms would bite. Soros suggested that, even if the measures made

it through Congress relatively unscathed, the banks would find ways
of getting round them.

It seemed that it was only in adversity that Obama was acquir-
ing the courage to contemplate radical action. The loss to the
Republicans of the state of Massachusetts following the death
of the veteran liberal senator, Edward Kennedy, deprived the
Democrats of their "super-majority". With the American Right
rediscovering its strength and showing no contrition from the Bush
years, Obama was facing the classic dilemmas of centre-left leaders.
Would he continue to trim in the search for consensus? Or would
he use what time he had available to him to change the socio-economic priorities of the nation? Was his goal simply to deal with the
effects of the financial crash, to bring down unemployment and
restore the US to steady levels of growth? Or was it to use the crash to
rebalance the equation of liberty and prosperity? Several of Obama's
promises relating to his determination to tackle the civil-liberties
abuses of the Bush era were put on hold. The most notable of these
was his pledge to close down the Guantánamo Bay prison. An attempt
by a Nigerian man, trained in Yemen, to blow up an airliner over
Detroit made that task politically all the more difficult for the President
when it was alleged that two of the bombing plotters were former
detainees at the detention facility.

In Britain, a struggling Labour government was not even asking
itself these questions. Gordon Brown's job was survival and for that he
needed a financial services industry upon which he had based his
entire economic strategy. Even though the state had bought a majority stake in several major banks in order to keep them afloat, ministers
did not see it as their business to change the behaviour of the people
in charge of those institutions.

In May 2009, the Treasury commissioned a report entitled "UK
financial services – the future". The report was largely uncritical, looking at ways merely of improving the practice of a sector that the
authors, many of them major names in the banking world, described
as a "centre of excellence working in partnership with the world".

Shortly after the report was published I wrote in the *Guardian*: "It seems hard to imagine that these are the same people who through arguably criminal activity brought this country, indeed the world, to the brink of disaster." I added: "What is most alarming is the continued refusal of ministers to draw the bigger conclusions, to understand the behaviour patterns underlying the bankers' actions."

The case of Sir Fred Goodwin, the former chief executive of the Royal Bank of Scotland, became the most potent symbol of the malaise. When Lord Myners, the government minister responsible for the City, negotiated the bail-out of RBS, he apparently forgot to look into the pension provision of Goodwin and other senior figures. "Fred the Shred" may have become a national hate figure, but what have been the consequences? We were told to be grateful that he had voluntarily decided to forego a small portion of his lucre. Other less publicised cases of greed and poor business practice were even more offensive.

"Britain – the Britain of New Labour – has become the world leader in indulging the super-rich and the very-rich," I wrote. "Forget for one moment issues of natural justice and social harmony: has this culture of greed produced better performance? Excessive wealth has not produced an incentive to improve the nation's lot." Brown's modern-day mantra of trickle-down economics plus palliative care for the disadvantaged, inspired by the former Chairman of the Federal Reserve Bank, Alan Greenspan, had not produced the desired effect.

Towards the end of 2009 the rhetoric among government ministers began to change. Brown saw political mileage in reverting to Labour's more traditional stance of hostility towards the wealthy. The object of the Prime Minister's ire was not, however, the bankers. His attack was party political and directed at the Conservative leader, David Cameron, and others who had, in his eyes, led a privileged life. Even if he had wanted to attack the irresponsibility of the financial whizz-kids, he knew he could not. He had been consistent in championing their buccaneering spirit. "I would like to pay tribute to the contribution you and your company make to the prosperity of Britain," Brown had declared while opening Lehmans' headquarters in London's Canary Wharf in 2004. "During its 150-year history, Lehman Brothers has always been an innovator, financing new ideas and inventions before many others even began to realise their potential."

Brown's new-found concern for the behaviour of bankers was enough to cause some of them to temper their ways – briefly. A number of bonuses due to be paid at the end of 2009 were held back; the 100 or so UK-based partners of the highly profitable Goldman Sachs agreed to limit their bonuses at the end of that year to a mere £1 million each. At other banks, partners and traders ensured that their bonuses were transferred into stocks or other devices recommended by accountants to keep the headline figures out of the public eye – until the coast was clear. For the British government the issue appeared to be confined to the embarrassment caused by these payments. Beyond that, there was little appetite for major reform. The Obama approach was deemed too radical by ministers who fell back on two trusted excuses: they did not want to make London "uncompetitive" in the global market; and they insisted that effective action could be secured only through international consensus.

Towards the end of January 2010 all eyes were on Tony Blair's appearance before the inquiry into the Iraq war led by Sir John Chilcot. Months of industrious but also hesitant probing by the committee had reopened old wounds about Blair's Manichaean zeal and fawning closeness to the Bush administration that had led to his Iraqi misadventure. Blair's appearance reminded voters of his easy rhetoric, his faulty judgement and his ability to create his own truths. Media coverage of the former Prime Minister's brief return to the limelight was intense. Yet these hearings overshadowed another news story that week that reflected an equally powerful failing. A report commissioned by the government produced a devastatingly disappointing audit on its single most important mission – Blair's stated promise back in 1997 to alleviate the plight of Britain's poorest. "Britain is an unequal country, more so than many other industrialised countries and more so than it was a generation ago," declared the National Equality Panel. The "large inequality growth of the Eighties has not been reversed," it said, in spite of all the various schemes to alleviate the plight of the poor, particularly those with young children. The study said the members of the richest 10 per cent of households will have accrued wealth of £2.2 million by the time they reach retirement; for the bottom 10 per cent that figure is less than £8,000. Ministers expressed regret. They said the report reaffirmed the need for action. Their responses showed they had not learnt any lessons; their instinct was to look at the effects of inequality, of excessive greed, not the cause.

Any hopes that the economic crisis might lead to more imaginative thinking about the state of society failed to materialise. A window of opportunity to create a more socially inclusive society, to appeal beyond the lowest common denominator of consumerism, seemed to have closed. That, at least, was the only conclusion that could be drawn from the authoritative annual barometer of British mores. The latest edition of the British Social Attitudes Survey, published in January 2010, suggested that the public was tiring of the issue of redistribution. In 1994, 51 per cent of respondents had agreed with the proposition that the government should use the tax system to redistribute wealth from the rich to the poor. By 2010 that figure had fallen to 38 per cent. Much of this shift could be attributed to long-term global trends. Yet there was also a political explanation. The wealthy and very wealthy had not been touched and had never had it so good. The Labour government had redistributed some wealth, but only from middle earners to the poor. Even then it sought to conceal its actions. Indeed one could go further and say that Labour's approach of limited redistribution by stealth had set back the cause of a fairer society. By taking money out of the pockets of the moderately well-off to help the poor, while leaving the super-rich better off than ever, the government had increased resentment. Ministers were too frightened to make the case for greater equality publicly and even when they did so, by excluding the people who mattered (the very rich) they rendered these notions of equality laughable.

Governments can either seek to nudge societies to change or to follow focus groups. Apart from one or two areas around social liberalism (such as gay civil partnerships), New Labour had seen its job as being to reflect rather than guide opinion in all areas of policy, particularly its approach to economics and civil liberties. As the Labour government lived out its last months, it hinted from time to time at an understanding that the incursions on individual liberties had gone too far. Orders were enacted to local authorities to spy on "antisocial" citizens less frequently; police were instructed to behave differently at political demonstrations after the violence in London during the G20 protests in March 2009. Ministers signalled that they were prepared to look again at English libel law after a national campaign led by free expression organisations. But overall the equation remained the same. Labour saw civil liberties as an optional extra or an inconvenience, not as a core element of any enlightened centre-left value system.

In a piece for the *Independent* in September 2008 I suggested a link between its authoritarian zeal and its economic timidity. "A party that should have intervened for social justice and greater equality instead allowed the markets to let rip," I wrote. "Having raised the white flag to the bankers, ministers instead sought to exert their power elsewhere, at the level of the citizen, seeking ever more ingenious ways of watching us, listening to us and telling us how to lead our lives. I am no Freudian psychoanalyst, but I can find no better example of displacement theory in modern politics."

Voters' response to the financial crisis was a mixture of traditional British docility and also a new-found fury. Yet that anger was directed not at the banking fraternity but squarely at politicians. The public was both appalled and mesmerised by newspaper revelations that began in the *Daily Telegraph* in May 2009 about the extent to which MPs had for years been fiddling their expenses. Some of the claims for items such as fictitious mortgages were plain criminal; others, such as assuming the taxpayer should be responsible for honourable members' floating duck islands and moats, were as quaint as they were arrogant. The scandal led to a number of parliamentarians being forced to repay their ill-gotten gains. Some were forced to announce they would stand down at the general elections. Others did so voluntarily. For the first time in a long time, the public appeared genuinely furious with the behaviour of their politicians. But how would that anger manifest itself? It was certainly not on the streets. Perhaps, I wrote in August 2009, "the weak response of ministers and regulators reflects an unhappy reality that most Britons do not seem to care. The anger predicted six months ago has failed to materialise. At the last count, one of Goodwin's windows has been smashed at his Edinburgh home, and one window at the RBS headquarters in London was smashed during the G20 demonstrations. Such has been the scale of 'people power'. Britons have long displayed a curious deference to people who are paid far beyond their worth."

Yet this sense of resignation, even equanimity, was not confined to one country. With the exception of Greece, where violence flared in December 2009, the overriding priority was to find the means of emerging from recession as quickly as possible. Germany and France led the way, quietening those voices who early on during the crisis talked of the need for systemic change. The penchant for French students, trade unionists and other protesters to take to the streets was curiously unindulged during the banking crisis. At the 2009 European elections, parties of the centre-left, whether in government or opposition, fared almost universally badly. Amid low turnouts, those who bothered to vote tended to opt for the security of Centre-Right parties and their message of debt reduction and public spending cuts. Parties that might have benefited from the excessive greed and irresponsible behaviour of the financial services industry instead suffered from a lack of either analysis – or candid discussion – of the roots of the malaise.

Italy's political pantomime reached its lowest point in December 2009 with a bizarre violent assault on Silvio Berlusconi. At the end of a political rally, the Prime Minister was struck in the face when a

42-year-old electronics engineer with a history of psychological problems hurled a heavy souvenir statuette of Milan cathedral at him.
Berlusconi's nose and two of his teeth were broken. Television pictures of him being bundled into a car and then re-emerging covered
with blood led to a wave of sympathy and soul-searching about a "climate of hate" that had overcome Italians. It also led to various
conspiracy theories, with bloggers wondering – improbably, even for
Berlusconi – whether the extent of some of the injuries might have
been exaggerated for the cameras. The attack reversed months of
opinion poll declines which had followed a decision by the
Constitutional Court in Rome to strip him of his immunity from
prosecution. The decision was never likely to be any more than a
pyrrhic victory for Berlusconi's detractors. Denouncing the judges as
"leftists", the Prime Minister had made it clear that he would fight to
ensure that he would not appear in court. In any case, the statute of
limitations would ensure that enough time would elapse for the various cases to be dropped.

Italy provided an extreme example of a crisis in the quality of
democracy taking place simultaneously with economic disorien-
tation. The financial collapse of Dubai in November 2009
demonstrated economic mismanagement taking place simultaneously with an absence of democracy. It showed in acute, often
colourful detail the folly of governments that had leveraged exces-
sively and were left entirely exposed when the going got tough.

Undeterred by the flight of capital and the collapse in property
prices, the emirate continued to put on a brave and brash face with
the official opening of Burj Dubai. The tallest building on earth was
inaugurated in January 2010 with the now-familiar display of fireworks, B-list celebrities and vulgar wealth. The sheikhs of Abu
Dhabi, the neighbouring and richer emirate, which had to bail out
Dubai to the tune of £10 billion, quietly expressed concern that the
apportioning of £1 billion for a vanity high rise tower suggested
"incoherent planning" of its economic growth. But the exposure of
Dubai's flawed model was regarded as the repudiation of an eco-

nomic model rather than a political one. The issue in question was not the trade-off, not the pact itself, but the way it had been applied through excessive borrowing and spending.

That same quest for instant wealth, at the expense of public freedoms, continued unabated elsewhere. In Russia, the murder of yet more reporters and activists, chronicled by the Committee to Protect Journalists in its report in September 2009, suggested that business was continuing as usual. The death of the most prominent human rights figure in Chechnya, Natalia Estemirova, was the most harrowing in this sorry toll. Her bullet-ridden body was found in a ditch in the neighbouring region of Ingushetia. President Dmitry Medvedev responded to the international chorus of indignation by demanding an investigation. Nothing came of it, though. Whether the murder was the sole responsibility of local warlords or whether in fact the authorities in Moscow had connived in it seemed a mere point of detail. All those working for or investigating issues of human rights were by definition turning themselves into targets. Human Rights Watch, in its report at the end of 2009, said Estemirova's murder and those of others "marked a severe deterioration in the human rights climate", which it said "contrasted sharply with Medvedev's more positive rhetoric recognising the importance of civil society".

Medvedev established his own commission on human rights; he spoke frequently of the need to re-establish the "rule of law" in Russia. Yet, particularly in the more distant regions, the established practices continued unchallenged. One case that caught the popular imagination was that of Alexei Dymovsky, a former police major in the Black Sea port city of Novorossisk, who became a household name when he posted a videotaped open letter to the Kremlin accusing his bosses of corruption and abuse of office. He complained of inhuman working conditions, indifference to civil rights, widespread graft, and routine abuse of authority within his police department. The video was hugely popular on YouTube, achieving more than a million hits, and it inspired dozens of other police officers around Russia to come forward with similar allegations. Dymovsky was then arrested and charged with corruption and abuse of office.

As before, the nexus between the Kremlin and the oligarchs remained the key. Yet over this period the balance shifted. The political leadership was considerably strengthened when several of the country's richest industrialists and bankers were forced to go, cap in hand, and beg for a bail-out. This was granted, in return for yet more political servility. As before, it was Vladimir Putin, biding his time as Prime Minister, who held the economic and political power and controlled all the major media. His return to the presidency seemed a foregone conclusion at the next available opportunity, the elections in 2012. In any case, the broader dynamics of society had not changed. Most Russians, particularly those who had emerged unscathed from a year or two of economic retrenchment, shrugged their shoulders at what "troublemakers" were up to. Predictions by opposition forces at home and abroad that Russia's economic crisis would lead to widespread social unrest proved unfounded. Anti-government demonstrations continued, but these were small-scale and isolated. Some were allowed to proceed; more often than not they were broken up. European and American politicians went through the motions of complaining, such as when police detained Lyudmila Alexeyeva, the 82-year-old head of the Moscow Helsinki Group and one of the 2009 recipients of the European Union's top human rights award, the Sakharov prize, who had dressed as the Snow Maiden at one rally.

The most important developments during this period took place inside China, regarding the country's relations with the rest of the world, particularly the United States. Whereas China began 2009 in some jeopardy, wondering whether it would hit its vital growth targets, and worrying about social unrest that might accompany the closure of factories, particularly in the south, it ended the year remarkably confident. The leadership was ever more convinced that its authoritarian capitalist model had emerged from the financial crisis in better health than the old-fashioned democratic alternative. The Chinese Communist Party set itself a target of 8 per cent growth during the worst year of the recession. It achieved it comfortably thanks largely to a huge and deliberate diversion of spending towards domestic infrastructure projects to compensate for the sudden and deep cut in demand from global markets for Chinese exports. The robust performance did not happen by chance – it was facilitated by the state's massive intervention in the economy (£400 billion in stimulus money) and its "encouragement" to companies and consumers to keep on investing and spending. China's economy was poised to overtake Japan's as the world's second largest. The trajectory was clear. Even though China had a long way to catch up with the United States, even though some economic experts (invariably the same experts who had claimed China was heading for an economic and social fall in 2009) suggested that its stimulus package was unsustainable, it had emerged from the crisis far more robustly than the US.

The more robust was China's economy, the more robust the leadership became about its model for development. The official media suggested that the economic "miracle" of 2009 had come about thanks only to the ability of China's leaders to make quick decisions, unencumbered by the fetters of Western-style democratic accountability.

China became ever more defiant in the face of Western criticism over its treatment of dissent. The crackdown that had preceded the 2008 Olympics was not loosened in any way, particularly censorship of the Internet. Matters came to a head when Google took the extraordinarily risky commercial decision to threaten to withdraw from China after discovering what it said was a "highly sophisticated and targeted attack on our corporate infrastructure originating from China". The response from the Chinese government was a typical combination of bewilderment and expressions of hurt and defiance. The most damaging allegation was that Chinese hackers, presumably working for the state, had infiltrated the Google mail accounts of human rights activists. When Hillary Clinton, the Secretary of State, demanded an explanation, observing that the "ability to operate with confidence in cyberspace is critical in a modern society and economy", she was given short shrift. The reality, as had long been the norm in Russia, China and other authoritarian states, was that for every country or corporation that took a stand on human rights, there were more waiting in the wings to pick up the abandoned contracts.

The economic crisis enshrined the shift in power that had been hinted at for some time. The two G20 summits in 2009, in London and Pittsburgh, established that forum as the key coordinating body for the world's major economies, and China's leading role in it. Policy makers both in Washington and in Asian capitals began talking rather of a G2, consisting of the US and China. The obdurate position of the Chinese leadership at the Copenhagen climate change summit provided an early taste of the new reality. Chinese negotiators ensured that no substantial commitments were made on the environment that would stifle the dash to growth of China and other developing powers.

The Obama administration had based its policy towards China on a long-established set of assumptions, which had influenced both Bill Clinton and George W. Bush. Both believed that unrestricted global flows of capital, trade and information would make political change in China irresistible. On a visit to China in 1998, Clinton proclaimed: "In this global information age, when economic success is built on ideas, personal freedom is essential to the greatness of any nation." The following year, Bush declared almost identically: "Economic freedom creates habits of liberty. And habits of liberty create expectations of democracy. Trade freely with the Chinese and time is on our side."

China's success reinforced the argument that free markets (whether "managed" by the state or not) and free societies did not have to go hand in hand. The thinking that had been prevalent from the late 1980s – that an ever-expanding middle class created an unstoppable surge towards political freedom – had been categorically debunked.

*

From Oslo to Singapore, via Bristol and Jaipur, I spent the autumn of 2009 and winter of 2010 setting out my arguments about the trade-off between freedom on the one side and prosperity and security on the other. The book produced strong coverage and no little controversy. Some detractors sought to traduce my message, suggesting that this was an "anti-capitalist" tract or even that I was an apologist for dictatorships. Such voices were mercifully few and far between.

My audiences varied considerably. In Brussels, I was reminded of the depth of conviction about a more collectivist model, seeing the relationship between state and individual a little more benignly than their Anglo-Saxon equivalents. In the Nordic countries, various questioners suggested my analysis of Singapore might apply, albeit in very different circumstances, to what they regarded as a stifling, state-dominated politics in their own countries.

Some of the fiercest arguments, in public forums and in the opinion pages of national newspapers, came in India. Several interlocutors complained that their democracy had stood the test robustly, citing the elections in May 2009 that had seen a strong return to power for the Congress Party. This, they said, had set back the more authoritarian-minded aspirations of the BJP. They were right in both celebrating the result and the manner in which the campaign was conducted. Once again, India had shown itself in its best light during elections. What mattered, however, was what took place between. Tarun Tejpal, whose *Tehelka* magazine continues to lead the way in investigative reporting in India, reminded one audience that extra-judicial killings remain rampant in India and that so much of what takes place beyond Delhi and Mumbai, particularly in rural areas, is rarely scrutinised by a media obsessed with Bollywood and cricket and by a political and business elite preoccupied by its own well-being. He reminded them of the flight of India's middle class away from a broader responsibility to wider society, seeking self-fulfilment almost exclusively through atomised material wealth.

Whatever the cultural specificities of different audiences, they shared some common characteristics. They were keen to engage with my belief in the essential difference between private and public freedoms and how the former had taken precedence over the latter. They were eager also to explore my argument that the priorities of voters in established democracies are not as different to those of citizens in authoritarian states as they might like to believe.

The most sensitive destination was Singapore, the model for the pact. The city state has a history of "dealing with" its critics. Given that I had been denounced several times by the government, I was surprised and intrigued to receive an invitation to conduct a seminar on the themes of the book by the National University. The event itself was conducted robustly but fairly. This was followed by a one-page feature on the book in the government-controlled *Straits Times*, which dealt with the subject matter entirely properly. It even advised readers where the book was on sale. Local bloggers offered different views about this apparent openness. One suggested that I had allowed myself to become "the perfect straw man", pointing out that my visit had coincided with the ejection from the country of a foreign journalist who had not toed the line. The blogger said the Singapore government would use my example to counter accusations of authoritarianism. He might be right, but few bother to test where the "out of bounds markers" lie, as the Singaporeans like to call them. Just occasionally they are shifted in the right direction, if only for a while.

I visited Singapore just a few days after one of the big set-piece occasions of 2009 when world leaders past and present had converged on Berlin in November to mark the 20th anniversary of the fall of the wall. Although the experiences of the intervening years varied considerably, the peoples in the countries of the former Soviet bloc had much reason to celebrate the demise of dictatorships that had deprived them of their essential freedoms. I had been based in Berlin at the time of the pro-democracy movements and on the night the wall came down.

New democratic systems were enshrined, but over the years what had become of the *quality* of these democracies? And which freedoms had been most nurtured and enjoyed? Invariably these were the private freedoms of individual lifestyles and the right to earn and spend money. The public freedoms that had been fought so hard for – the right to assemble, to a free press, to be active in the political realm – were, in country after country, taken for granted. In some they were taken as irrelevant – or even harmful – to the stronger magnet of conspicuous consumption. The blame for this lies less in the people in newly emerging democracies: after all, for people who have had every aspect of their lives determined by the state, any freedoms are better than none. The real culprits were those of us in countries long regarded as models of democratic development, for giving away old freedoms with such blithe indifference.

Once the markets crashed, people looked around and realised how little they had to fall back on. Yet what is even more dispiriting is that the events of late 2008 and early 2009 could have been used as a trigger, an incentive to recast societies away from worshipping at the altar of consumer greed. The old democracies could have started the process of reviving enthusiasm for the public realm. Again, they chose not to. In so doing, they handed the initiative to countries who quite openly extol private freedoms as the greater good. The conclusions that I had come to at the start of 2009, when the economic crisis was still in its early phase, were reinforced by the developments that followed. Important opportunities were missed in 1989, not just to spread democracy, but to improve it. Twenty years on, the traumas of an economic collapse provided another chance for peoples and governments to reassess their priorities, to look afresh at the balance between wealth-creation, security and liberty, to realign newly won private freedoms with corroding public freedoms. Sadly, in so many places, that opportunity was once more squandered.

John Kampfner, June 2010

BIBLIOGRAPHY

Books and a selection of essays

Singapore

Enright, D.J., *Memoirs of a Mendicant Professor* (Manchester: Carcanet Press, 1990)

Lee, Kuan Yew, *The Singapore Story* (Singapore: Prentice Hall, 1998)

——, *From Third World To First* (London: HarperCollins, 2000)

Neo, Boon Siong, and Chen, Geraldine, *Dynamic Governance* (Singapore, World Scientific, 2007)

Sen, Amartya, *Development as Freedom* (Oxford: Oxford University Press, 1999)

Chua, Beng Huat, '"Asian Values Discourse" and the Resurrection of the Social', *Positions*, 1999

Gordon, Uri, 'Machiavelli's Tiger', Department of Political Science, Tel Aviv University, 2000

Verweij, Marco, and Pelizzo, Riccardo, 'Singapore: Does Authoritarianism Pay?' *Journal of Democracy*, 2009

China

Aiyar, Pallavi, *An Experience of China* (New Delhi: Fourth Estate, 2008)

Alden, Chris, *China in Africa* (London: Zed Books, 2007)

Becker, Jasper, *The Chinese* (London: John Murray, 2003)

Brady, Anne-Marie, *Marketing Dictatorship* (Lanham, MD: Rowman & Littlefield, 2007)

Doctoroff, Tom, *Billions, Selling to the New Chinese Consumer* (New York: Palgrave, 2005)

Fenby, Jonathan, *The Penguin History of Modern China* (London: Allen Lane, 2008)

Hutton, Will, *The Writing on the Wall* (London: Little, Brown, 2007)

Kurlantzick, Joshua, *Charm Offensive* (New Haven: Yale University Press, 2007)

Kynge, James, *China Shakes the World* (London: Phoenix, 2006)

Leonard, Mark, *What Does China Think?* (London: Fourth Estate, 2008)

Mitter, Rana, *Modern China* (Oxford: Oxford University Press, 2008)

Nathan, Andrew, and Chu, Yun-Han (eds), *How East Asians View Democracy* (New York: Columbia University Press, 2008)

Peerenboom, Randall, *China Modernizes* (New York: Oxford University Press, 2008)

Pei, Minxin, *China's Trapped Transition* (Cambridge, Mass.: Harvard University Press, 2006)

Nathan, Andrew, 'Medals and Rights', *New Republic*, July 2008

Russia

Aslund, Anders, *Russia's Capitalist Revolution* (Washington, DC, Peterson Institute, 2007)

Colton, Timothy, *Yeltsin: A Life* (New York: Basic Books, 2008)

Figes, Orlando, *Natasha's Dance* (London: Penguin, 2003)

Goldman, Marshall, *Oilopoly* (Oxford: Oneworld, 2008)

Hoffman, David, *The Oligarchs* (New York: PublicAffairs, 2003)

Jack, Andrew, *Inside Putin's Russia* (London: Granta, 2005)

Korinman, Michael, and Laughland, John (eds), *Russia, a New Cold War?* (Portland: Valentine Mitchell, 2008)

Litvinenko, Alexander, and Felshtinsky, Yuri, *Blowing Up Russia* (London: Gibson Square, 2007)

Lucas, Edward, *The New Cold War* (London: Bloomsbury, 2008)

Politkovskaya, Anna, *Putin's Russia* (London: Harvill Press, 2004)

Shevtsova, Lilia, *Putin's Russia* (Washington, DC: Carnegie Endowment, 2003)

——, *Russia, Lost in Translation* (Washington DC: Carnegie Endowment, 2007)

Trenin, Dmitri, *Getting Russia Right* (Washington DC: Carnegie Endowment, 2007)

Wilson, Andrew, *Virtual Politics* (New Haven, Yale University Press, 2005)

Gambrell, Jamey, 'Putin Strikes Again', *New York Review of Books*, July 2007
Franchetti, Mark, 'How the Oligarchs Lost Billions', *Sunday Times Magazine*, Feb 2009
Karaganov, Sergei, 'The World Crisis: Time for Creation', *Russia in Global Affairs*, October 2008
Lipman, Masha, 'Russia's Free Press Withers Away', *New York Review of Books*, May 2001
Lo, Bobo, 'Russia's Crisis, what it means for regime stability and Moscow's relations with the world', *Centre for European Reform*, February 2009
Lyne, Roderic, 'Reading Russia, Rewiring the West', *Open Democracy*, September 2008
Ostrovsky, Arkady, 'Flirting with Stalin', *Prospect*, September 2008
Remnick, David, 'Echo in the Dark', *New Yorker*, September 2008
Sakwa, Richard, '"New Cold War" or 20 years' crisis?', *International Affairs*, March 2008
Shleinov, Roman, 'Rules of the Game', *Index on Censorship*, May 2007
Soldatov, Andrei, 'How Britain Struggles with the Russian Mafia', *Novaya Gazeta*, June 2008
Whitmore, Brian, 'Inside the Corporation: Russia's Power Elite', Radio Free Europe/Radio Liberty, October 2007

United Arab Emirates

Al Abed, Ibrahim, and Hellyer, Peter (eds), *United Arab Emirates: A New Perspective* (London: Trident Press, 2001)
Davidson, Christopher, *Dubai: the Vulnerability of Success* (London: Hurst, 2008)

Arlidge, John, 'Dubai's Desert Dream', *Sunday Times*, November 2003
Arlidge, John, 'The Party's Over in Dubai', *Sunday Times*, November 2008

India

Das, Gurcharan, *India Unbound* (New Delhi: Penguin, 2002)
Dossani, Rafiq, *India Arriving* (New York: Amacom, 2008)
Guha, Ramachandra, *India After Gandhi* (London: Macmillan, 2007)
Kamdar, Mira, *Planet India* (London: Simon & Schuster, 2007)
Mishra, Pankaj, *Temptations of the West* (London: Picador, 2006)

Roy, Arundhati, *The Shape of the Beast* (New Delhi: Viking, 2008)
Sharma, Kalpana, *Rediscovering Dharavi* (New Delhi: Penguin, 2000)
Varma, Pavan, *The Great Indian Middle Class* (New Delhi: Penguin, 2007)

Das, Gurcharan and others, 'The Rise of India', *Foreign Affairs*, July 2006
Fernandes, Naresh, 'The Big Sellout', *Outlook*, October 2006
Kaplan, Robert, 'India's New Face', *Atlantic*, April 2009
Ninan, T. N., 'Boom and Gloom', *India Seminar*, February 2003

Italy

Foot, John, *Modern Italy* (London: Palgrave Macmillan, 2003)
Ginsborg, Paul, *Berlusconi* (London: Verso Books, 2008)
Jones, Tobias, *The Dark Heart of Italy* (London: Faber & Faber, 2007)
Lane, David, *Berlusconi's Shadow* (London: Penguin, 2005)
Stella, Gian Antonio, and Rizzo, Sergio, *La Casta* (New York: Rizzoli, 2008)

Anderson, Perry, 'An Entire Order Converted into What It Was Intended to End', *London Review of Books*, February 2009

Britain

Campbell, Alastair, *The Blair Years* (London: Arrow Books, 2008)
Davies, Nick, *Flat Earth News* (London: Vintage, 2009)
Gearty, Conor, *Civil Liberties* (Oxford: Oxford University Press, 2007)
Kennedy, Helena, *Just Law* (London: Vintage, 2005)
Lee, Simon, *Best for Britain? The Politics and Legacy of Gordon Brown* (Oxford: Oneworld, 2008)
Malik, Kenan, *Strange Fruit* (Oxford: Oneworld, 2008)
Peston, Robert, *Who Runs Britain?* (London: Hodder & Stoughton, 2008)
Raab, Dominic, *The Assault on Liberty* (London: Fourth Estate, 2009)
Seldon, Anthony, *Blair's Britain 1997–2007* (Cambridge: Cambridge University Press, 2007)

Gearty, Conor, 'The Blair Report', *Index on Censorship*, May 2007
——, 'The Politics of Terror', *Index on Censorship*, August 2008
Lester, Anthony, 'Redefining Terror', *Index on Censorship*, May 2007
Malik, Kenan, 'Out of Bounds', *Index on Censorship*, August 2008
Noorlander, Peter, 'The New Labour Decade', *Index on Censorship*, May 2007

USA

Daalder, Ivo, *America Unbound* (London: John Wiley, 2005)

Fukuyama, Francis, *After the Neocons* (London: Profile Books, 2007)

Lewis, Anthony, *Freedom for the Thought We Hate* (New York: Basic Books, 2007)

Lichtblau, Eric, *The Remaking of American Justice* (New York: Pantheon Books, 2008)

McClellan, Scott, *What Happened* (New York: PublicAffairs, 2008)

Meersheimer, John, and Walt, Stephen, *The Israel Lobby and US Foreign Policy* (London: Allen Lane, 2007)

Nye, Joseph, *The Paradox of American Power* (New York: Oxford University Press, 2003)

O'Harrow, Robert, *No Place To Hide* (London: Penguin, 2006)

Robin, Corey, *Fear: The History of a Political Idea* (New York: Oxford University Press, 2004)

Stelzer, Irwin, *Neoconservatism* (London: Atlantic Books, 2005)

Florida, Richard, 'How the Crash Will Reshape America', *Atlantic*, March 2009

Gaddis, John Lewis, 'Ending Tyranny, American Interest', September 2008

Kirkpatrick, Jeane, 'Dictatorships and Double Standards', *Commentary*, November 1979

Mayer, Jane, 'The Hard Cases', *New Yorker*, February 2009

Robin, Corey, 'Was he? Had he?', *London Review of Books*, October 2006

General

Acemoglu, Daron, Robinson, James, *Economic Origins of Dictatorship and Democracy* (Cambridge: Cambridge University Press, 2006)

Cooper, Robert, *The Breaking of Nations* (London: Atlantic Books, 2007)

Diamond, Larry, *The Spirit of Democracy: The Struggle to Build Free Societies Throughout the World* (London: Times Books, 2008)

Emmott, Bill, *Rivals* (Boston: Houghton Mifflin Harcourt, 2008)

Ferguson, Niall, *The Ascent of Money* (London: Allen Lane, 2008)

Friedman, Thomas, *The World is Flat* (London: Penguin, 2006)

Fukuyama, Francis, *Trust* (New York: Free Press, 1996)

——, *The End of History and the Last Man* (London: Penguin, 2003)

Garton Ash, Timothy, *Free World* (London: Penguin, 2005)

Ginsborg, Paul, *Democracy, Crisis and Renewal* (London: Profile Books, 2008)

Greenspan, Alan, *The Age of Turbulence* (London: Penguin, 2008)

Hardt, Michael, Negri, Antonio, *Empire* (Cambridge, Mass: Harvard University Press, 2000)

Huntingdon, Samuel, *The Clash of Civilisations* (London: Free Press, 2002)

Hurrell, Andrew, *On Global Order* (Oxford: Oxford University Press, 2007)

Kagan, Robert, *Paradise and Power* (London: Atlantic Books, 2003)

——, *The Return of History and the End of Dreams* (London: Atlantic Books, 2008)

Kempf, Hervé, *How the Rich are Destroying the Earth* (Dartington: Green Books, 2008)

Khanna, Tarun, *Billions of Entrepreneurs* (Boston: Harvard Business School Press, 2007)

Klein, Naomi, *The Shock Doctrine* (London: Penguin, 2008)

Krugman, Paul, *The Return of Depression Economics* (London: Penguin, 2008)

Lo, Bobo, *Axis of Convenience* (Baltimore: Brookings Institution Press, 2008)

Mahbubani, Kishore, *Can Asians Think?* (Hanover, NH: Steerforth Press, 2002)

——, *The New Asian Hemisphere* (New York, PublicAffairs, 2008)

Monbiot, George, *The Age of Consent* (London: Harper Perennial, 2004)

Moore, Barrington, *Social Origins of Dictatorship and Democracy* (London: Penguin, 1969)

Munoz, Heraldo, *The Dictator's Shadow* (New York: Basic Books, 2008)

Novak, Michael, *The Spirit of Democratic Capitalism* (London: IEA, 1991)

Patten, Chris, *What Next?* (London: Allen Lane, 2008)

Reich, Robert, *Supercapitalism* (Cambridge: Icon Books, 2008)

Slaughter, Anne-Marie, *A New World Order* (Princeton: Princeton University Press, 2004)

Spengler, Oswald, *The Decline of the West* (Oxford: Oxford University Press, 2007)

Zakaria, Fareed, *The Post-American World and the Rise of the Rest* (London: Allen Lane, 2008)

Carothers, Thomas, 'How Democracies Emerge', *Journal of Democracy*, January 2007

Diamond, Larry, 'The Democratic Rollback', *Foreign Affairs*, January 2008

——, 'How to Save Democracy', *Newsweek*, January 2009

McMahon, Robert, 'The Brave New World of Democracy Promotion', *Foreign Service Journal*, January 2009

Puddington, Arch, 'Freedom in the World 2009', *Freedom House*, January 2009

Welzel, Christian, Inglehart, Ronald, 'The Role of Ordinary People in Democratisation', *Journal of Democracy*, January 2008

ACKNOWLEDGEMENTS

In the course of more than a year's travelling, I have received remarkable assistance from countless people, helping me arrange trips, discuss topics, providing me with interviews and insights and reading versions of the manuscript. If I have omitted anyone by accident, I offer my apologies in advance.

In Singapore, I am grateful to all those at the National University, particularly Kishore Mahbubani, along with Wang Gungwu and Chua Beng Huat. I would like to thank some old friends, including Geh Min, Patrick and Rosa Daniel, Chelvum Raja and Chin Seng Tan. Others have asked to remain anonymous.

In China, my thanks go to Richard Spencer, Arthur Kroeber, Randy Peerenboom, Michael Pettis, Daniel Bell, Benjamin Lim, Louis Kuijs, Chenggen Hu, Kevin Ao, K. T. Mao, Jeanne-Marie Gescher and, particularly, my researcher in Beijing, Jing Wen. In Shenzhen I had the pleasure of meeting Lancel Cui, Wang He Ping and Edward Hoffman. Others are best left unidentified, but I am very grateful to them. In Hong Kong, I am grateful to David Zweig, Joseph Cheng,

Nicholas Bequelin, Geoffrey Crothall and Robin Munro, in Taipei to Dennis Engbarth and Andrew Yang.

In Russia, I am indebted to friends and acquaintances of the past twenty years, too many to mention in these acknowledgements. I wish here to include Art Troitsky, Olga Timyanskaya, Pyotr Kochevrin and Sergei and Lena Zhgun. I would like also to thank Lilia Shevtsova, Andrei Soldatov and Elena Nemirovskaya for their insights. Thanks go to RIA-Novosti for inviting me on several Valdai discussion clubs.

In Dubai and Abu Dhabi, thanks go to Caroline Faraj, Nick Maclean, Mark Lunn, Nic Labuschagne, Ashraf Makkar, Martin Newland, Ayman Safadi, Hasan Al Naboodah, Dr Eckart Woertz, Bob Cowan and Frank Kane.

In India, I was inspired by meetings with Tarun Tejpal, Teesta Setalvad, Barkha Dutt, Swapan Dasgupta, Shobhaa De, Shekhar Kapur, Chiki Sarkar, Kalpana Sharma, Dina Vakil, M. J. Akbar, T. N. Ninan, William Dalrymple, Naresh Fernandes, Mala Singh, Meenakshy Ganguly, Meena Menon, Gautam Mody, Adolf D'Souza, Khozem Merchant, Rashmee Roshan Lall, Ram Reddy and Dilip Cherian. I am grateful to Gautham Subramanyam for helping with logistics.

In Italy, I am indebted to Feruccio de Bortoli, Paolo Flores d'Arcais, Ezio Mauro, Sergio Rizzo, Gherardo Colombo and Michele Polo. Alessandro Speciale provided great help in organisation.

A number of London-based colleagues and friends provided invaluable assistance and insights. These include: Vivienne Lo, Tari Hibbitt, Isabel Hilton, Conor Gearty, Paul Mason, Charles Grant, James Kynge, Ken Macdonald, Chris Patten, Misha Glenny, Christopher Granville, Roderic Lyne, Anthony Brenton, Basharat Peer, Salil Tripathi, Kamila

Shamsie, Christopher Davidson, Alexandra Pringle, Julia Simpson, Rosie Goldsmith and Mukul Devichand. In Oxford, my thanks go to Paul Chaisty, Alex Pravda, Andrew Hurrell, Laurence Whitehead, Rana Mitter, and especially to Graham Hutchings and his colleagues at Oxford Analytica. I am grateful to Ahmad Abdallah, Philip Bobbitt, Fareed Zakaria and Anders Aslund for their time during meetings in the UK. In Paris, my thanks go to Valerie Nataf, Frederic Niel, Yves Charpentier and Violaine de Villemeur, and in Frankfurt to Huw Pill.

Several trips to the US were enhanced by assistance from Eric Foner, Michael Kazin, Francis Fukuyama, Jameel Jaffer, Tom Carothers, Arch Puddington, Corey Robin, Stephen Holmes and Katrina van den Heuvel.

I was extraordinarily fortunate to have a group of friends and experts who as well as helping with trips, were assiduous in reading parts or all of the manuscript in various drafts: Jonathan Steele, John Arlidge, Richard Spencer, Pankaj Mishra, Andrew Stephen, Bobo Lo, Jo Glanville, Jonathan Dimbleby, Naresh Fernandes, David Hoe, Marco d'Eramo, Maxwell Kampfner, Alan Philps, Art Troitsky, Mark Easton and Jonathan Fenby. Two people guided me all the way through the process, providing support and inspiration throughout: my sister, Judith Kampfner, and my wife, Lucy Ash. I am immensely in their debt.

For providing excellent behind-the-scenes work and organising many of the trips, I'm very grateful to my researcher, Dr Milly Getachew. I have been delighted to work for the first time with my US agent, Emma Sweeney, and with Lara Heimert, my editor at Basic Books in New York. It has been a pleasure to work again with my agent Bruce Hunter and with the excellent team at Simon & Schuster in London: Ian Chapman, Managing Director, Hannah Corbett, Publicity Director, and my editor and the Editorial Director for Non-Fiction, Mike Jones.

INDEX